GRAVE TALES
Queensland's Great South West Ipswich to Augathella

By

Helen Goltz & Chris Adams

Atlas Productions

GRAVE TALES – QUEENSLAND'S GREAT SOUTH WEST

Copyright © Helen Goltz and Chris Adams 2019
All rights reserved. No part of this book may be reproduced, stored in a retrieval system, or be transmitted by any form or by any means, electronic, mechanical, photocopying, recording or otherwise, without the prior written permission of the publisher. Helen Goltz and Chris Adams assert their moral rights to be identified as the authors of this book.

First published 2019. Publisher: Atlas Productions, Greenslopes QLD 4102
Web: www.atlasproductions.com.au

National Library of Australia Cataloguing-in-Publication entry: (paperback)
Title: Grave Tales : Queensland's Great South West – Ipswich to Augathella / Helen Goltz ; Chris Adams.
ISBN: 978-0-9941822-1-0 (paperback)

 A catalogue record for this book is available from the National Library of Australia

Authors' note: We have taken great care to be respectful to the people featured in *Grave Tales* – in the telling of their life stories, and to any living descendants. **Please note:** where errors have appeared in quotes and newsclippings, we have left them as they were originally written or intended.

Cover images (please see individual chapters for full source details): Drayton & Toowoomba Cemetery and featuring: Harry Corones (*State Library of Queensland*); Norah Murphy (courtesy of Mike Fitzpatrick); Dr Reginald Whishaw (kindly supplied by Dr Whishaw's grandson, Mr Paul Vellacott); Nurse Elizabeth Kenny (*The Sydney Mail*, retrieved from the *State Library of Queensland*); Victor Denton (kindly provided by the Denton family and descendant, Trish Wearne); Emma Webb, (reproduced with kind permission from the *Local History and Robinson Collections*, Toowoomba City Library); Dan Kelly (*State Library of Queensland*); Len Waters (*Wikimedia Commons*); Ella McGoldrick (*The Bulletin*); and Helen McDonald (*The Courier-Mail*).

Cultural sensitivity note: Please note that this volume includes images of deceased Aboriginal and Torres Strait Islander people. Readers please also note that certain words or expressions reported may be inappropriate and distressing today, but reflect the period in which they were written as quoted.

*"If history were taught in the form of stories,
it would never be forgotten."*

Rudyard Kipling

Contents by cemetery:

Ipswich General Cemetery
- Bridget and Mary Jane Broderick – The *Babies of Walloon*
- Kenneth Cobbin and Walter Williams – The Box Flat mine disaster
- Dan Kelly – Back from the dead, the mystery of outlaw Dan Kelly
- Patrick James McCarthy – The railway widows

Tallegalla Cemetery
- William Drysdale – The Box Flat mine disaster

Laidley Cemetery
- Barbara and James Little – The railway widows

Gatton Cemetery
- Norah, Ellen and Michael Murphy – The Boxing Day murder

Toowoomba and Drayton Cemetery
- Ella McGoldrick – The swansong of Miss Ella McGoldrick
- Dr Reginald Wishshaw – The residents of the asylum
- Isobel Gray – The residents of the asylum
- The Trevethan brothers – Toowoomba terror
- Emma Webb and Helen Tolmie – The medical history makers

Nobby Cemetery
- Victor Denton – The March of the Dungarees
- Elizabeth Kenny – Healing hands, fighting spirit

Goondwindi Cemetery
- Germain 'Winks' McMicking – Once upon a wonder horse – Gunsynd
- Edwin Fletcher and Florence Monro – When Goondiwindi helped Albert Einstein

St George Cemetery
- Len Waters – 'Black Magic'

Roma Monumental Cemetery
- Henrietta Tosi – The utopian experiment: Roma's communes
- Lawrence Tobin – The man who breathed in three centuries

Charleville Cemetery
- Ethel, Ada and Elsie Switzer – The drowning of the Misses Switzer
- Harry Corones – The best in the West
- Margaret Roche – The poisoning of Mrs Roche

Augathella Cemetery
- Edwin Helton – The poisoning of Mrs Roche

Contents by story:

Introduction by **Helen Goltz** 2
The land of lost children: **The *Babies of Walloon*** 7
The Box Flat mine disaster: **Men of the mines** 25
Back from the dead: **The mystery of outlaw, Dan Kelly**...............37
The railway widows: **Barbara Little, Jane McCarthy
and Annie Freese**..59
The Boxing Day murders: **The Murphy siblings**.......................75
The swansong of Miss **Ella McGoldrick**....................................99
The residents of the asylum: **Dr Reginald Whishaw**
and **Isobel Gray** 109
The Toowoomba terror: **The Trevethan brothers** 121
The medical history makers: **Emma Webb and Helen Tolmie**...135
The March of the Dungarees: **Victor Denton**................................ 145
Healing hands, fighting spirit: **Elizabeth Kenny**......................163
Once upon a wonder horse – Gunsynd, the Goondiwindi Grey:
Germain 'Winks' McMicking 179
When Goondiwindi helped Albert Einstein – **Florence
Monro and Edwin Fletcher**..191
'Black Magic': **Len Waters** 207
The utopian experiment: Roma's communes – **Henrietta
Tosi** 225
The man who breathed in three centuries: **Lawrence Tobin** 241
The drowning of the Misses Switzer: **Ethel, Ada and
Elsie Switzer** 253
The best in the West: **Harry Corones** 263
The poisoning of Mrs Roche: **Edwin Helton** 277
Acknowledgements and about the *Grave Tales* team................ 290

Introduction

Forgive this indulgent introduction and trip down memory lane, but there is in most of us—especially as we mature—an intrinsic desire to return to our childhood home and town. It seems that no matter how far and wide we travel, how long ago we left and established elsewhere, when we are asked where we are from, don't we still feel the need to start with that childhood place?

For co-author Chris Adams, although born in Camberwell, Melbourne, he often refers to the small towns of Heywood and Cranbourne where he spent his childhood. For me it is Toowoomba where I spent the first sixteen years of my life immersed in school, sport, and what then felt like a country upbringing. Dad was actively involved in the West Toowoomba Rugby League Club, Mum worked at the TAB, and often on the radio they would cross to Merle (Mum) for the race results. In the early 1970s the family moved to the shiny new Smithfield estate and with the kids in the neighbourhood, I rode my bike around the old Smithfield ghost house. We dared each other to get closer and closer… and in 1975 it became the renowned

Smithfield Restaurant – a fascinating piece of architectural history in its own right and heritage listed.

I did my Grade 10 school placement work experience at *The Chronicle* when Mr Bruce Hinchliffe was the editor (no, not his father, Bert, who was the editor for two decades prior to Bruce – I'm not that old!). It was one of the best weeks of my life – I went out with journalists on stories, found out the truth behind the horoscope columns (no, I will take it to my grave) and even had my photo on the front page. I knew then that I would be a journalist.

Of course, childhood memories are rather blown out of proportion in the grand scheme of what really is important. I remember being afraid of Baillie Henderson, the 'asylum', which features in this book. It was a different time and mental illness was somewhat feared or misunderstood.

Smithfield Homestead after renovation in 1980. Photo courtesy of Aussie~mobs, public domain.

I remember running through the Toowoomba and Drayton cemetery to visit my grandfather's grave, only to be reined in with dire warnings that a headstone might fall on me as one had, killing a small child. I always believed this to be a grandparent's idle threat, but have since found it to be true. The accident was in 1964 and the little four-year-old girl killed was Leah Hart. Today, she is survived by her brother, Mark.[1]

I remember farewelling Sister Saint John and Mrs Rose on their retirement from Our Lady of Lourdes – all of us full of the dew of youth as Sister rang the bell for the last time, and Mrs Rose hugged each one of us as we left on her last day. I never realised the significance for those ladies until later in life.

I remember celebrating very special occasions at Weiss restaurant, but more importantly to a youngster, when the golden arches, McDonald's, first came to town in 1978. Before that, a takeaway was a roast chicken from the PF Chicken Bar. I remember my anger when *Sherbet* came to town – they were big, I was 15 and not allowed to go. A teenage tragedy for someone who planned to marry lead singer, Daryl Braithwaite.

Later, when I was in my twenties and ever so cosmopolitan and worldly, seeking a job at Queensland House in the Strand, London, I got the position because the Agent-General knew my Principal, Sister Rita (Saint Saviour's). He was Tom McVeigh – former National federal member for Groom – small world; it appears I wasn't that far from home after all.

The stories we write about in this book are so familiar to me, the neighbouring towns and the names that came and went in our classroom textbooks or newspapers. As always, we are surprised and amazed at what we discover and what we learn. Who would have thought Alan Alda (actor, Hawkeye from *MASH*) and Sister Kenny had a connection?

Or that young Len Waters, who left school at 13 and had virtually no education, would become Australia's only and celebrated Indigenous fighter pilot; he is buried at St George.

Australia's first appendectomy was performed in the back of a Toowoomba bakery (yes, really) and Queensland's oldest unsolved murder to this day happened to the Murphy siblings in Gatton. In Nobby, a beautiful young man, Victor Denton, went to fight for his country in a time when it was naively believed the job would be done, and the boys would all return home safely. Victor's death shocked the town and the men on the March of the Dungarees visited his memorial and paid their respects.

Ipswich drew some big names – some famous, some infamous including Henry Lawson's tribute to two little drowned girls, and a man claiming to be Dan Kelly, of the Kelly gang. Up Roma way, a man who lived in three centuries finally succumbed to his grave – he was still playing football at 80, and hopeful of getting a game at 100. And Goondiwindi helped Albert Einstein to prove a theory that would change how we viewed the world. That's just a few of the stories.

I love this beautiful piece of the world and hope you enjoy reading the stories as much as we enjoyed digging them up, researching them and bringing them to you with help from our team, Joanne (editor) and Stephanie (researcher).

Thanks for the headstart, Mr Hinchliffe. Regards,

1 Hart, Mark, The story in Mark Hart's own words..., *The Chronicle*, 11th Jan 2014. Retrieved 24 July 2019 from URL: https://www.thechronicle.com.au/news/the-story-in-mark-harts-own-words/2136337/

Smithfield Homestead after renovation in 1980. Photo courtesy of Aussie~mobs (2019). *Historic Smithfield Homestead, Toowoomba, Qld - circa 1980*. Public domain, retrieved 20 August 2019 from URL: https://trove.nla.gov.au/

The land of lost children
'The Babies of Walloon'

Interred: **Bridget Kate Broderick,** 11 June 1883 – 21 March 1891 (aged 8 years).*[1]

Mary Jane Broderick, 9 November 1884 – 21 March 1891 (aged 7 years).*

Location: See notes at the end of the chapter to locate Bridget Kate and Mary Jane's grave.

Cemetery: Ipswich General Cemetery, Cemetery Road, Ipswich QLD 4305.

(*Some sources list the Broderick girls' ages as Bridget Kate, 9 and Mary Jane, 6. The Queensland Register of Births, Marriages and Deaths gives their ages as 8 and 7.)

By the time Henry Lawson wrote his 1891 heart-wrenching poem, *The Babies of Walloon*, the price paid by those who tried to conquer the hostile wilderness of this rugged land was already high. The cost was the lives of hundreds, possibly thousands of settlers' children claimed by chronic disease, epidemics, lack of proper food and sanitation and the very place itself.

Those who came here, many from the crowded slums of England, Ireland and Scotland, had little idea of the natural dangers. Who among them had experienced the ferocity of a rampant bushfire with its roaring flames literally dancing across the tree tops, consuming all in its path; who of them understood the power and treachery of floodwaters, and the beguiling deception of the Australian bush that refused to release those who had wandered off the beaten track?

Tragedy at Walloon

And so it was with the Broderick children who became known, thanks to Lawson, as the *Babies of Walloon*. They were probably victims of their own curiosity and inability to get out of trouble.

The story is not very long but it still strikes a chord with many Australians. It took place on 21 March 1891 in the tiny settlement of Walloon near Ipswich in Queensland. The town, which had a population of only 53 in 1891[2], lies on the Ipswich and Rosewood railway line, the main reason Patrick Broderick and his family lived in Walloon.

Patrick was what is known as a 'lengthman', that is, a person whose job it is to maintain a particular length of road or railway line.[3] He was responsible for a few miles of track either side of Walloon and perhaps even sections in the village itself. He was employed by Queensland Railways and among other things kept weeds down and grass cut on the line verges and in drainage ditches, and kept the line neat and tidy for which he received the princely sum of six to seven shillings a day (approximately $45 per day in 2019 dollars).

On that six or seven 'bob' a day, as he would have put it, Patrick supported his wife and five children, all of whom in all probability went to the local school. But 21 March 1891 was a Saturday, no school, and as was their custom Patrick Broderick and his wife Kate sent two of their children on an errand. Apparently the family had been in the habit of buying butter from a neighbour who lived just a half a kilometre or so from their house and on this Saturday at about four o'clock in the afternoon eight-year-old Bridget Kate and her seven-year-old sister, Mary Jane, were dispatched to fetch their daily supply.

But what the parents did not know was that Abraham Phelps, their butter-providing nearby neighbour, had died and there was no one at his house, the housekeeper having cleaned, locked up the house and departed the day before.[4]

A mystery forever

It's not known whether the girls reached the Phelps' place. What is known though is that when they did not return home for some considerable time, a search for them was begun. Tragically it wasn't long before the dreadful news was conveyed to Patrick Broderick that his two daughters had been found dead in a waterhole that lay between their home and that of their late neighbour.

Sad Drowning Fatality.

TWO YOUNG GIRLS DROWNED AT WALLOON.

A sad mishap occurred at Walloon on Saturday afternoon last, when two young daughters of Mr. Patrick Broderick, a lengthsman on the Southern and Western Railway line, were drowned in a waterhole, near the residence of the late Mr. Abraham Phelps, sen. It appears from the report furnished to Senior Sergeant Brown by Mounted-Constable M'Neill that Bridget Kate and Mary Jane Broderick, aged nine and six years respectively, were, about 4 o'clock, sent to Phelps's (as w........ary), about 500 or 600 yards fro............. place, for some butter, but .... living there then, the h................ on the previous day, c................ departed. The childre................ have been attracted to t................ about 6ft. deep, by s................ growing there, but wh................ is not known. It is .... reaching over for some .... both fell in, or that one .... attempted to rescue her s................ that both were drowned. .... return home, a search was i............ their father and some others ....

How the Queensland Times, Ipswich Herald and General Advertiser reported the sad drownings on 23 March 1891. Inset: poet Henry Lawson in 1915. Source: State Library of New South Wales.

We will never know what happened to Bridget and Mary, but Lawson, in the following extract from his poem, alludes to the possibility of similar circumstances that had taken other children and young people… one gets into trouble and the other tries to help and also becomes a victim. He also talks of the children being attracted by water lilies in water which was almost two metres deep.

"All is dark to us. The angels sing perhaps in Paradise
Of the younger sister's danger, and the elder's sacrifice;
But the facts were hidden from us, when the soft light
from the moon
Glistened on the water-lilies o'er the babies at Walloon."[5]

The *Queensland Times*, the Ipswich newspaper, reported the events that followed: "As there were no suspicious circumstances in connection with the case, Mr G. F. Müller, of Marburg, gave an order for burial, and the remains of the children were interred in the Ipswich cemetery, yesterday afternoon, the funeral being attended by a large number of mourners in vehicles and on horseback. Much sympathy has been expressed for the family in their terrible bereavement in and around Walloon where Mr Broderick is very well known."[6]

But what were the circumstances… and why hadn't the girls noticed the water lilies before, if that was what lured them into danger?

Had they been with other siblings, their sister Annie or brothers Tom and John, when they went to get butter previously or had they travelled by a different path?

Had the waterlilies flowered since the children last

passed that way? There are a million questions that haunt a parent who loses a child so tragically – and pain of the loss is unceasing because they know there will likely never be answers to those questions.

The settlers' lot

And there were many families that suffered. There were many accidents, children in the wrong place at the wrong time. Like the Lindsay boys who were victims of the Erskine River where present-day Lorne stands on Great Ocean Road in Victoria.

William Lindsay was the first settler here. He came to the area in 1849 with his wife and two small boys and found valuable stands of timber. Lindsay built a dwelling for his family on what is now the north side of the swing bridge at the mouth of the river. Tragically in 1850 his two sons, eight-year-old William and Joseph who was four, perished not far from where the family home was situated. There are several stories as to what caused their deaths.

One of them is from a 1940 article in Melbourne's *The Age* newspaper titled 'Lorne's Abiding Charm', where the author writes: "When the timber splitters had possession, there were quicksands at the head of the Erskine River. There one day a forester's wife, named Lindsay saw her two little children swallowed up while they played at the water's edge. The bodies were recovered and buried at the foot of the old coach road." [7]

So, version one – quicksand. But the more accepted and certainly more widely quoted cause of the children's demise was that they were playing by the side of the river mouth and had been building a tunnel in the sand when it collapsed, smothering them both.[8] The third explanation is that on the *waymarking.com* website and on their gravestone, which says the boys were drowned in the Erskine River near where the grave is situated (the full story of the Lindsay boys is in *Grave Tales: Great Ocean Road Country – Geelong to Port Fairy*).

There were no answers for the Lindsay family except that the vulnerability of a child and the helplessness of parents against accident were very much the settlers' lot. And as this toll of young lives grew, the stories of missing children took on almost legendary status and were the subject of poems, stories and even songs.

The poet's lament

Henry Lawson wrote about the 'babies' of Walloon and Banjo Paterson wrote about another lost child:

*"He ought to be home," said the old man, "without there's something amiss.
He only went to the Two-mile — he ought to be back by this.
He would ride the reckless filly, he would have his wilful way;
And, here, he's not back at sundown — and what will his mother say?"*[9]

Poet Banjo Paterson, 1890. Source: State Library of Qld.

This is the first verse from a remarkable poem called *Lost* about a riding accident and a mother's desperate search for her son who was missing in the bush.

'Lost,' the 1886 painting of a child lost in the Australian bush, by Frederick McCubbin. Source: kindly provided by the National Gallery of Victoria.

In 1892 Barcroft Boake took a different angle when he wrote *At Devlin's Siding*. The poem is a wrenching tale of infanticide and events at a country railway station in New South Wales called Devlin's Siding. The name of the place just 10 minutes down the road from Grong Grong, for those who drive the Newell Highway, was changed to Matong in 1900.

In the world of art, Frederick McCubbin captured the spirit of the bush versus the child in his 1886 painting titled, *Lost*, depicting a child dwarfed by nature in the Australian bush.

But a case that fascinated the whole country had a happier climax than those in the writings of Lawson, Paterson and Boake. It was that of the Duff children who went missing in north western Victorian scrubland in August 1864.

The Duff children, 1864. Source: Argus Newspaper, State Library of Victoria.

The children had set off mid-morning to gather heath to make brooms in the bush near where they lived, some 35 kilometres or so west of Horsham, towards Natimuk and Goroke. When the children, Isaac, Jane and Frank—aged nine, seven and nearly four—hadn't returned home by dusk their father rode out to look for them.

As stories of lost children stirred the imagination of increasingly urbanised Australians, it wasn't long before newspapers in Melbourne were syndicating the story around the country. The *Melbourne Herald* reported: "He reached the heath where they were supposed to be – but found them not. He searched for several hours, but, full of apprehensions for their safety, he was compelled to relinquish his search and return home. Early the following morning the alarm was given. All the men on the station turned out... During Saturday and Sunday there were no less than thirty-six men on horseback searching in the most systematic manner." [10]

The riders eventually found the tracks of the children which showed that they had left the heathland in entirely the wrong direction... heading further away from their humble home with every step. For nine days and eight nights in the bitterly cold Victorian mid-winter, the Duff children survived with nothing to eat and only water they found on the ground to keep them going. The newspaper headlines said what many were thinking – *Loss and apprehended death of three children.*[11]

Native trackers were brought in to help in the search and thanks largely to them the kiddies were found alive but the youngest, Frank, and to a certain extent the eldest, Isaac, only made it through because their sister Jane covered them during the worst of the cold nights with her dress, which she took off to protect them.

While the efforts of the trackers were vital in discovering the missing children, over the years the emphasis gradually shifted from their endeavours to the sacrifice of Jane Duff. In fact, when she died in 1932 the Victorian Education Department raised money to erect a memorial stone near where the children were found. On it is the inscription: "In memory of the bush heroine, Jane Duff, who succoured her brothers, Isaac and Frank, when lost in the dense scrub near this spot in 1864. Erected by the school children and citizens of Victoria March 1935."

Victorian education authorities saw fit to include a version of the miracle of the Duff children in school readers in that state from 1930 until the 1960s.[12] The readers were an essential part of the state school primary curriculum. And so the fascination with stories of children missing in the Australian bush continued – and not only in Victoria.

A painting by S.T. Gill (1864) depicting the finding of the Duff children.
Source: State Library of Victoria.

Little Boy Lost

Probably the most remarkable example of the impact of a work of art or performance on the Australian public relating to missing children followed the disappearance of four-year-old Steven Walls in February 1960. He vanished from a farm in the New England Ranges, the area abutting the Queensland border in north western NSW.

The boy was last seen at his father's farm, about 25 kilometres north of Guyra at nine o'clock on a Friday morning. He was with his father in a car rounding up cattle. When his father returned to the vehicle from heading up a couple of strays, young Steven was gone. During the search it was estimated that more than three thousand volunteers on foot combed the one-metre high grass which hid swamps and cavernous trenches, dingoes and deadly snakes, 200 men on horseback as well as five light aircraft also joined the search. After Steven had been missing for three days and two nights police said they didn't believe he could survive a third night in the open, but the search would continue in the morning.[13]

And in the morning— despite the odds—Steven Walls was found alive, cut and bruised but happy, and according to the *Canberra Times*, in better condition than many of the thousands of people who had been searching for him. His discovery made headlines around the country and his first words to the men who found him were "Where's my daddy?" They were words that would echo around the nation for months and they may have for years had it not been for another missing child.

"Where's my daddy – where's my daddy?" became the key line in the lyrics of a song written and recorded by country music entertainer, Johnny Ashcroft, about the search for and rescue of Steven Walls. And Australia's captivation with lost-in-the-bush children came to the fore again. *Little Boy Lost* was a smash hit, topping the charts for longer than the two other hits of that time put together – *Tie me Kangaroo Down Sport* (three weeks) and *The Pub with No Beer* (one week). *Little Boy Lost* held number one spot for six weeks.

But at the peak of the song's success, another tragedy in a very different setting caused Johnny Ashcroft to take humanitarian action that virtually saw the end of *Little Boy Lost*. On 7 July 1960 Sydney schoolboy, eight-year-old Graeme Thorne, disappeared on his way to school at Bellevue Hill. For three weeks Sydney was shocked as the search for Graeme continued. His father, Basil, had won first prize in the Sydney Opera House Lottery and the kidnapper of his son was demanding a ransom (the full story of the Graeme Thorne kidnapping is in *Grave Tales: Sydney Volume 1*).

Johnny Ashcroft was sensitive and compassionate enough to realise what hearing *Little Boy Lost*, which was getting massive radio airplay, must be doing to Graeme's family and friends. In April 2010 Johnny told CNews: "Because I felt my

Above: Singer Johnny Ashcroft.
Source: Wikimedia Commons.

song must cause suffering to the Thorne family every time they heard it, I appealed to the Australian Radio authorities and with the backing of EMI who produced the record, to seek the co-operation of Australian radio stations to remove *Little Boy Lost* from airplay. And every radio station complied."[14]

Little Boy Lost simply disappeared from the airwaves. It still sold copies in the record shops and both English and US versions were recorded but essentially Johnny Ashcroft had nobbled his own hit, probably the only recording artist ever to request that his chart-topping song not be played.

Remember the children

So, what has happened to our fascination with the 'lost child', wandering directionless amid the dangers of the bush – does it still torment the national consciousness? If Lawson. Paterson, Boake and Ashcroft were still writing would they be reflecting the dangers to our children? Would they be portraying us, as author Peter Pierce suggested with the title of his book, *The Country of Lost Children – an Australian Anxiety.*[15]

If you think they wouldn't, consider the children who have disappeared in more recent times: Jane, Anna and Grant Beaumont, disappeared 1966; Joanne Ratcliffe and Kirste Gordon, 1973; Craig Taylor, 1973; Siriyakorn Siriboon, 1973; Azaria Chamberlain, 1980; Helen Karapidis, 1988; Renee Aitkin, 1984; Rahma El-Dennaouli, 2005; and William Tyrell, 2014.

All of these children, aged between 18 months and 13 years old, vanished from their loved ones. At the time of writing, they are all still missing. There have been some coronial inquiries which have offered some explanations and theories about what may have happened to some them but there have been no solutions, no answers, no comfort.

Perhaps the sentiment of Henry Lawson's *The Babies of Walloon* is as applicable to them as it was to the little Broderick girls those many years ago...

> "Speak their names in tones that linger, just as though you held them dear,
> There are eyes to which the mention of those names will bring a tear.
> Little Kate and Bridget, straying in an Autumn afternoon,
> Were attracted by the lilies in the water of Walloon."[16]*

* Note the children in Lawson's poem are identified as Kate and Bridget, not Bridget and Mary.

How to find Bridget and Mary's grave:

Enter Ipswich Cemetery through the Cemetery Road entrance and drive through the entrance shed. Take the second gravel roadway to your right and travel down about 100 metres or until you are in line with the shop on the corner of Thorn Street across the road from the cemetery. The grave was renewed by the Ipswich City Council in 2015 and is hard to miss.

You can also visit the bronze statue of the girls at Henry Lawson Bicentennial Park in Walloon *(pictured below)*.

References:
1 *The Queensland Register of Births, Marriages and Deaths* https://www.familyhistory.bdm.qld.gov.au/
2 The University of Queensland. *Centre for the Government of Queensland*, 2018. Retrieved 18 March 2019. https://queenslandplaces.com.au/walloon
3 *Collins English Dictionary*, 12th Edition 2014, HarperCollins Publishers. Retrieved 18 March 2019. https://www.thefreedictionary.com/lengthmen
4 Sad Drowning Fatality. (1891, March 23). *Queensland Times, Ipswich Herald and General Advertiser* (Qld.1861-1908), p2. Retrieved 18 March 2019, from http://nla.gov.au/nla.news-article123045715
5 1891 'The Babies of Walloon.', *The Dawn* (Sydney, NSW: 1888 - 1905), 1 May, p. 18., viewed 18 Mar 2019, http://nla.gov.au/nla.news-article76423171
6 Sad Drowning Fatality. (1891, March 23). Op.cit.
7 Lorne's Abiding Charm (1940, April 13). *The Age* (Melb, Vic.: 1854-1954), p12. Retrieved 19 March 2019 from URL: http://nla.gov.au/nla.news-article204426308

8 Lorne and the Great Ocean Road. *Lorne Historical Society.* Retrieved 19 March 2019 from: http://www.lornevictoria.com.au/lorne-historical-society/
9 Lost (1926, August 17). *The Horsham Times* (Vic.: 1882 - 1954), p. 6. Retrieved March 29, 2019, from http://nla.gov.au/nla.news-article73013634
10 Loss and Apprehended Death of Three Children. (1864, Aug 27). *The Herald* (Melb, Vic. 1861-1954), p3. Retrieved 19 March 2019 from: http://nla.gov.au/nla.news-article245505503
11 Ibid.
12 State Library of Victoria – *La Trobe Journal.* No 63 Autumn 1999. Jane Duff's heroism. Retrieved 24 March 2019. http://www3.slv.vic.gov.au/latrobejournal/issue/latrobe-63/latrobe-63-050.html
13 3,000 Searchers Fail To Find Lost Small Boy (1960, Feb 8). *The Canberra Times* (ACT: 1926-1995), p.3. Retrieved 24 March 2019 from URL: http://nla.gov.au/nla.news-article105901923
14 CNews. *50th Anniversary of Little Boy Lost.* Retrieved 14 March 2019. Retrieved 21 May 2019 from URL: https://www.johnnyashcroft.com.au/sites/default/files/CNewsApril_011%20aschcroft.pdf
15 Pierce, Peter. *The Country of Lost Children.* June 1999. Published by Cambridge University Press.
16 1891 'The Babies of Walloon', *The Dawn.* Op.cit.

Images:

Sad Drowning Fatality. (1891, March 23). *Queensland Times, Ipswich Herald and General Advertiser* (Qld.: 1861 - 1908), p. 2 (Daily.). Retrieved May 9, 2019, from http://nla.gov.au/nla.news-article123045715

Johnson, William [photographer], Henry Lawson, 1915, Mitchell Library, *State Library of New South Wales.* Call number: P1/959, IE number: IE3281148.

Unidentified (1890). Poet Andrew Barton Paterson, ca. 1890. John Oxley Library, *State Library of Queensland.* Retrieved 9 May 2019 from URL: https://trove.nla.gov.au/version/167817174

McCubbin, Frederick, *Lost,* 1886. Accession Number: 1077-4, *National Gallery of Victoria,* Melbourne, digital record from the NGV Collection Online. Retrieved 9 May 2019 from URL:http://www.ngv.vic.gov.au/explore/collection/work/5975/

Argus. (1940). Duff-Cooper Children Lost for 9 Days in Bush, 1864 [picture]. Argus Newspaper Collection of Photographs, *State Library of Victoria.* Retrieved 9 May 2019 from URL: http://handle.slv.vic.gov.au/10381/107858

Gill, S.T. (1864). The Duff Children [painting], 20 August 1864. *State Library of Victoria,* retrieved 9 May 2019 from: http://handle.slv.vic.gov.au/10381/186015

Johnny-Ashcroft.jpg. (2017, June 12). *Wikimedia Commons, the free media repository.* Retrieved 9 May 2019 from URL: https://commons.wikimedia.org/w/index.php?title=File:Johnny-Ashcroft.jpg&oldid=247533386

The Box Flat mine disaster
The men of the mines

Interred: **William Alexander Drewett** (aged 35)
Andrew Charles Haywood (age unknown)
Robert Lloyd Jones (aged 55)
William Alfred Marshall (aged 50)
John James McNamara (aged 55)
Walter Michael Murphy (aged 50)
Brian Henry Randolph (aged 40)
Brian Rasmussen (aged 40)
Daryl Trevor Reinhardt (aged 32)
Harold Charles Reinhardt (aged 50)
John Dudley Roach (aged 44)
Lenard Arthur Rogers (age unknown)
Maurice John Tait (age unknown)
Mervyn Verrenkamp (aged 30)
Clarence Edwin Wolski* (aged 43)

Location: Entombed in Box Flat Mine, Swanbank Road, Swanbank, QLD 4306.

*Clarence Wolski died in 1974 from injuries he received in the explosion.

A memorial photograph from the Eclipse Colliery Disaster, Ipswich, 1893. The men in the top photo were the recoverers, below are the seven men who perished. Source: State Library of Queensland.

There is plenty of evidence in the history of coal mining in and around the Ipswich area to show that the practice is troubled by danger and despair. As far back as the dreadful flood of 1893 which tore parts of Brisbane apart there has been tragedy on the Ipswich fields. In that deluge, which took out the northern half of the Victoria Bridge in Brisbane city, seven men died in one Ipswich mine calamity alone.

At the Eclipse mine which had been working a major coal seam, the owners were in the throes of leaving the site as their lease had almost expired. On Saturday 4 February 1893, the day the Brisbane River broke its banks, the son of the mine's owner, Thomas Wright, told his father he would recover some of the rails from the works. Despite his father's warning about danger in the mine Tom Wright explained that he would be able to get out faster than the water could rise and took a party of men into the mine on the recovery job.

The work party had taken one load of rails out of the mine and while they were attempting to get another the roof of the tunnel where they were working collapsed under the weight of water that was on top of it. Newspaper reports said the force of the cave-in was so strong that the rush of air it pushed out through the mouth of the tunnel blew pit wagons away like paper.[1] There was no warning and seven miners drowned in the waters that fell from above them. As the town's mine rescue team had not been established yet, volunteers combed the Eclipse mine to find the bodies of their colleagues who had perished.

A special memorial photo was released to remember the men who lost their lives and pay tribute to the party who recovered their bodies. If only it were the last disaster.

Explosions in the deep

The worst disaster in an Ipswich mine would see the terrible Eclipse death toll more than doubled when a massive underground explosion woke much of the city from its slumber in the early hours of Monday 31 July 1972. The explosion was felt more than 10 kilometres away[2] and had such an impact that many thought it was an earthquake.

The dreadful events of the day had their genesis when mine manager, Alex Lawrie, spotted a 'smallish' fire in tunnel No.5 of Box Flat mine at Swanbank. He had reported the fire to Inspector of Mines, Reg Hardie, around 6pm on Sunday evening when he told Hardie the fire was about three to four feet square in area.[3] The next time it was seen by the two men and a group who went to assess the situation a few hours later, it was a raging monster. They returned to the surface at about 10.20pm after miner Pat Farrell advised that there was smoke coming down an intake tunnel and it would be wise to get the men out.[4]

The presence of smoke in the intake indicated to Reg Hardie the presence of re-circulation, a phenomenon that can be lethal in a mine. It exists when mine air passes through the same part or parts of a mine more than once. It can lead to the build up of heat and humidity, of fumes, coal gas and other deadly flammable gases.

Over the next two hours a number of attempts were made to extinguish the fire but with no success. In his evidence at a subsequent inquiry Reg Hardie said: "We actually were in retreat from the fire, rather than advancing on it."[5] Again they returned to the surface at about 12.15am. It was decided now to attempt to control the fire by temporarily sealing off two drives, horizontal passages that were tunnels No.5 and No.7, located about 275 metres below the surface: "A team of men entered the No.7 tunnel with the intention of carrying this decision into effect. A short time afterwards, John Roach, a member of the team, rang the surface and advised that smoke was backing up against the intake in No.7 tunnel, where previously the airflow had been normal. Just after this, the explosion occurred."[6] It was 2.47am.

The miners' stories

Near the entrance to No.5 tunnel, machinist Doug Truloff and three other men had been preparing to seal it off to assist in starving the fire of air. Doug left the other three for a few minutes to gather more material for the job. In the couple of minutes that he was away the mine erupted. In evidence to an initial inquiry in August 1972 Doug said: "I was picked up by the rush of air for a second and knocked to the ground… then I got out into a clear space. Shortly after I got out, I saw a ball of flame come out of No. 7 tunnel mouth and there was a loud explosion". He said he ran back to No. 5 tunnel mouth and saw remains of bodies scattered about." [7]

For some the disaster was closer to home. Mine driver Ray Verrenkamp gave the inquiry the names of those he remembered climbing onto a rake (man-carrying wagons that run on rails) to go underground before the first explosion. One of them was his brother, Mervyn. Ray said he had been near the mouth of No.7 when there had been two enormous explosions. He was injured by the blast and taken for medical help.

And the explosions continued. Acting colliery manager,

Onsite at the Box Flat Extended No. 5 tunnel, Swanbank, in the early hours of 31 July, 1972. Source: Picture Ipswich, Ipswich Libraries. Reproduced with their kind permission.

Ron Hollett, who ticked off the names of the men who went below for the last time, said about 15 minutes later he was sitting in a cabin on the surface when it was demolished by another explosion. Mr Hollett also said that he believed that after an explosion of that size there was no chance of anyone coming out. He said No.7 tunnel had collapsed and smoke was coming out of No.5. There was no way a rescue could have been attempted.

Memories of mates

The day after the tragedy, 1 August 1972, as 150 of their colleagues watched on, the tunnels where the miners were trapped were sealed off by bulldozers. Amid clouds of dust from the work, a burial service was performed by five ministers of religion, the decision having been taken by mining industry officials to abandon any hope of there being survivors. They also said there was imminent danger of more explosions.[8]

Chief Inspector of Mines, Bill Roach, whose nephew was John Roach, one of those killed, made the call.[9] In that initial August inquiry, Ipswich Coroner Mr. K L Hall formally declared the deaths of the 14 men who were entombed in the No.5 shaft. He also found that the three men whose remains were recovered also died as a result of the blast. He indicated that the only reason for the initial inquiry was to establish the facts of the deaths and identify those killed. The explosion and its cause would be matters for another inquiry.[10]

The second inquiry

And they were. When the second inquiry handed down its findings in November 1972 it found that the fire was caused

Aftermath at Box Flat mine, 1972. Reproduced with kind permission from The Australasian Mine Safety Journal: https://www.amsj.com.au/

by a pile of fallen coal spontaneously heating. The heating was assisted by an 11-hour fan stoppage which reduced the air flow through the mine and allowed the coal to reach a point of self-ignition. The fan played another role in the disaster when it was restarted, fanning the flames and causing the blaze to develop into a large fire. Efforts to extinguish or seal the fire didn't work and an explosive mixture of gases generated by the fire and possibly accompanied by water gas (a mixture of carbon monoxide and hydrogen) was ignited. Coal gas was also part of the explosions which spread throughout the mine.

The Australasian Mine Safety Journal says: "Put simply, the timing of the coal's spontaneous heating within the mine could not have been worse – if the fan stoppage had not been in place, the temperatures probably would not have reached the level they did and thus, the fire never would have ignited. Inarguably, the most vital recommendation made by the Inquiry Warden on 7 November, 1972, was that all underground personnel should immediately be withdrawn from the mine once uncontrollable re-circulation of flammable gases is discovered. A mine is perhaps salvageable, but lives, as the families and friends of those killed know so well, are not." [11]

As for whether the correct measures were taken once the Box Flat fire had reached uncontrollable proportions the report said: "It must be observed that it appears that no one questioned the course of conduct proposed, from which it follows that all present were apparently in agreement with the assessment of the position made by the manager, the Inspector of Mines and other members of the team when they conferred from time to time. There were other experienced men present, who were aware that re-circulation was taking place, but it seems that they did not direct their minds to the potential danger of explosion inherent in this condition; rather, it seems that they were more concerned with the danger of being overcome by smoke and gases contained in it… the fact remains that not a single person put forward a contrary proposal at any stage."[12]

Disturbing evidence

But one more thing before we leave this tragic set of events. In evidence at the second inquiry into the Box Flat Explosions a miner by the name of John Henry Sturmer said that he had smelt what miners call 'fire stink', a term they use to describe the paraffin smell of hot coal in a mine. It can also be a sign of fire underground.

Sturmer said he had told the mine manager about the smell which he thought was coming through a crack between tunnels No.5 and No.7 where he had been working. He said he had smelt the "fire stink" for a month before the explosions of 31 July. Apparently, the manager had said it could not possibly come from No.5 tunnel because the tunnels were 80ft (25 metres) apart, and mine officials had put the odour down to chemical smell off a new (machinery) belt.[13] From comments made in the second inquiry, it seems that was the end of the matter as far as officialdom was concerned.

As reported at the Inquiry into the explosion: "With regard to Mr Sturmer's evidence in relation to the previous smelling of 'fire stink' it is somewhat unfortunate that the investigation that followed did not include a sampling and analysis of the atmosphere in that vicinity." [14]

Escape!

If there was one fortunate story from this litany of tragedy then it was that told the day after the explosion in the *Queensland Times*, the local newspaper. It reported that when the last party of miners who went below to try and stifle the flames of the raging fire nearly 300 metres underground were in the rake that would transport them, Inspector of Mines Reg Hardie had one foot onboard when he decided to go back to the mine office to check on the plan of the underground. Other stories say he went to answer a telephone call.[15] But whatever the reason his actions meant he lived to tell the terrible tale of the Box Flat Mine disaster, 31 July 1972.

The Box Flat Colliery ceased operation 15 years later in 1987.

How to pay your respects:

The 14 miners who were the last to go underground at Box Flat are still there, entombed in the now sealed mine complex. A monument out the front of the complex remembers them. Two of the three men whose remains were recovered—Kenneth Cobbin and Walter Williams—are remembered in the Columbarium at Ipswich Cemetery. The third victim, William Drysdale's grave can be found in Tallagella Cemetery. Go to the small rotunda at the top of the cemetery and walk down the zig-zag path and you will find the grave on the right of the path in front of low bushes.

References:
1 The Eclipse Colliery Disaster. (14 Feb 1893). *The Brisbane Courier* (Qld: 1864-1933), p3. Retrieved 1 April 2019 from http://nla.gov.au/nla.news-article3555663
2 17 die in Ipswich colliery horror (1972, Aug 1). *Papua New Guinea Post-Courier*, p 7. Retrieved 2 April 2019 from http://nla.gov.au/nla.news-article250302368
3 *Australasian Mine Safety Journal*. Box Flat burial ground. 30 October 2014. Retrieved 2 April 2019 from https://www.amsj.com.au/box-flat-burial-ground/
4- 6 Mining Inquiry – Box Flat Colliery Report, Findings and Recommendations. 7 Nov 1972. http://www.mineaccidents.com.au/uploads/box-flat(1).pdf
7 Survivor recalls mine explosion (25 Aug 1972). *The Canberra Times* (ACT: 1926-1995), p3. Retrieved 2 April 2019 from http://nla.gov.au/nla.news-article102000965
8 17 die in Ipswich colliery horror (1972, Aug 1). *Papua New Guinea Post-Courier.* Op.cit.
9 Australasian Mine Safety Journal. Box Flat burial ground. Op. cit.
10 Survivor recalls mine explosion (1972, August 25). Op.cit.
11 Australasian Mine Safety Journal. Box Flat burial ground. Op.cit.
12 Mining Inquiry – 7 November 1972. Op.cit.
13 Evidence of mine 'fire stink' (27 Oct 1972). *The Canberra Times* (ACT 1926-1995), p12. Retrieved 4 April 2019 from: http://nla.gov.au/nla.news-article102010785
14 Mining Inquiry – 7 November 1972. Op.cit.
15 Livermore, Don, Account of Box Flat Disaster, prepared for Warden's Court. Retrieved 7 April 2019 from https://www.haenkefoundation.org.au/images/DonLivermore.pdf

Images:
Unidentified. Memorial Photograph from the Eclipse Colliery Disaster, Ipswich, 1893: Collection Ref: 7834, B.Taylor Photographs. *State Library of Queensland*. Retrieved 16 May 2019 from http://hdl.handle.net/10462/deriv/121153

Onsite at the Box Flat Extended No. 5 tunnel, Swanbank, early hours of 31 July, 1972. *Picture Ipswich, Ipswich Libraries.* Reproduced with their kind permission.

The mining aftermath. reproduced with kind permission from *The Australasian Mine Safety Journal*. https://www.amsj.com.au/box-flat-burial-ground/

Back from the dead
The mystery of outlaw Dan Kelly

Interred: **Dan Kelly,** 1 June 1861 – 28 June 1880 or 1 June 1851 - 29 July 1948 (aged 19 or 87 years).

Location: Pauper's grave (see directions at the end of this story).

Cemetery: Ipswich Cemetery, Cemetery and Warwick Roads, Ipswich, QLD 4305
or Greta Cemetery, 1327 Wangaratta-Kilfeera Road, Greta, VIC 3675.

The man who walked into the newspaper office claiming to be Dan Kelly, 1933. Source: State Library of Queensland.

Sunday 13 August 1933 and the front-page headlines of the Brisbane Sunday *Truth* screamed: "When the Kelly Gang rode out – 'I am Dan Kelly' declares aged bushman – thrilling confession of days when hold up terror reigned."[1]

Could Dan Kelly still be alive? "Out of the lurid past he claims to step, heavy-jowled, bullet-headed, the strength of an ox in his stocky frame and the tang of nearly four score of perilous years in his iron-clad philosophy. With a gnarled but steady hand he rakes over the ashes of a shock phase in the history of the colony, more than half a century ago."[2] The man at the centre of the claim had simply walked into the newspaper offices and claimed to be the younger brother of Ned Kelly.

The Truth, 1933, covers the story. Source: National Library of Australia.

*Dan Kelly c1876-1878 age approximately 16 or 17 years.
Photograph by James Bray. Soucre: State Library of Victoria.*

Ned was hanged after being captured at Glenrowan. This man said he had been living under the name James Ryan near Ipswich, but now it was time to tell his story. The journalistic team at the paper didn't miss referring to familiar things that most people remembered about Dan Kelly, his brother Ned and the gang. High up in the story were references to the armour the Kelly gang wore and also to the way Dan was supposed to have died… his charred remains raked out from the smouldering ruins of Jones' Glenrowan Inn in 1880 after he and Steve Hart were consumed in the fire lit by Victoria police to flush the gang out.

Dan Kelly's story

For the next five Sundays, the paper outlined his claims and told his story: "Dan Kelly is now 79 years of age. His full story covers a period of about 69 years, for he remembers very little before the age of 10. His earliest memories, he claims, are of Benalla where the Kelly gang – comprising Ned and Dan, Joe Byrne and Steve Hart originated early in 1878. He was then aged 24, having been born in the year of the Eureka Stockade rebellion."

The paper detailed the murderous rampage which included the killing of three police officers at Stringybark Creek and two major bank robberies, one in Euroa, Victoria and the other over the border in Jerilderie, New South Wales; and of the Glenrowan pub, where the four bushrangers were eventually trapped. The story, told so often, says that Joe Byrne was shot and died almost immediately, Ned Kelly was wounded by police bullets fired at his exposed parts – his hands and legs, and Steve Hart and Dan Kelly died in the flames that consumed the hotel.

Now this man was saying that's not how it happened. He says he managed to escape despite agonising burns and after finding shelter in nearby bush watched as his brother, Ned, was captured and taken away by police. And he certainly did have burns. They were on his back and displayed to anyone who wanted to see them – plus he apparently had the initials DK branded on his buttocks.[3]

Dan Kelly AKA James Ryan probably spent the years between his claimed escape from the Glenrowan fire and his coming-out as Dan Kelly humping his swag around the country, dossing down wherever he could find a dry place for the night and doing odd jobs in exchange for a meal.

But after all the publicity the *Truth* and other papers gave him, he decided his life story was worth paying to hear. In 1934 he set up in Sideshow Alley at the Brisbane Agricultural Show, known locally as 'The Ekka' and charged show-goers to hear his yarns. Many challenged him but none could conclusively disprove his claims to be Dan Kelly.

Sideshow Alley at the 'Ekka' 1933. Source: State Library of Queensland.

Sometime before 1941 he settled at Fairney View, a rural area not far from Ipswich, west of Brisbane. In that year he was charged with having indecently dealt with a girl under the age of 12. He was found not guilty of the charge.[4]

The Ipswich accident

On 29 July 1948 James Ryan/Dan Kelly made the papers again when he was run over and killed by a coal train at Ipswich. It was reported that he had cataracts in his eyes, his night vision was poor and he may have strayed onto the railway line where the train struck him.

Towards the end of 1948 there was an inquiry into his death which dealt more with the issue of who he really was rather than how he died and to that end it was fairly fruitless. All the police could say on the matter was that the old man had never produced anything to substantiate his claim that he was Dan Kelly.[5] Not surprising really, since he had been warned some years ago that he was making a mistake in thinking that he could escape prosecution if he really was Dan Kelly.

The small stone on the grave in the paupers' section of the Ipswich Cemetery says 'James Ryan: Died July 29, 1948'. It is where the man who said he was Dan Kelly was laid to rest. Since 1998 above the grave there is a memorial made up of a shield with the words 'Tell 'em I died game… in Ipswich'. Beside it hangs a replica of part of a Kelly-style suit of armour, complete with two bullet holes in the torso.

So, what do we make of this old bushie whose claims turned established lore on its head?

Formative years

Most Australians are at least vaguely aware of the Kelly gang, they should be – it has been one of the most written about groups of people in Australian history. Brought up in northeastern Victoria in the 1850s, 60s and 70s – its members lived in a time when the poorer Irish immigrants felt they were under the heel of the squattocracy and victims of police persecution. They were by far the best known of Australia's bushrangers. Sometimes, their leader, Edward—or Ned—Kelly has been likened to Robin Hood – taking from the rich and giving to the poor. There are as many who think he and his gang were just thieving murderers.

Ned Kelly in 1880. Source: Wikimedia Commons.

Ned was the eldest male of the Kelly siblings – he had five sisters, Maggie, Catherine (Kate), Mary, Anne and Grace; two half-sisters, Ellen and Alice; two brothers Dan and James; and one half-brother John (Jack). His father died when he was just 12 years old and as was the practice of the day, Ned had to step up to be the leader of the family. About this time the family moved from Avenel to a property between Greta and the town synonymous with the Kelly story, Glenrowan.

When he was 13 years old, Ned Kelly was apprenticed to notorious Victorian bushranger, Harry Power.[6] Power taught Ned the finer arts of bushranging, Ned taught his brother Dan and a couple of locals, Joe Byrne who became Ned's lieutenant, and sometime jockey Steve Hart, a mate of his brother Dan. The gang was distinctive and popularly remembered by the home-made bullet-proof armour they wore.

The Fitzgerald encounter

On 15 April 1878 a police constable by the name of Fitzpatrick tried to arrest Dan Kelly for horse stealing. He turned up at the Kelly property drunk and a fight broke out between him and the family. Fitzpatrick said that Ned's mother, Ellen Kelly, hit him with a shovel and Ned shot him in the wrist, both claims that were vigorously denied, in fact Ned claimed he was 200 miles away from the place when the shooting occurred.

As a result of the incident, three people were imprisoned including Ellen and Ned and it signalled the beginning of life on the run for Ned and Dan Kelly. They were joined by Joe Byrne and Steve Hart and the Kelly gang was born. While they had many supporters and sympathisers the only other person ever mentioned as being a prospective member was a man called Aaron Sperritt, who was a childhood friend of Joe Byrne's and of whom we shall hear more later.

The four men plied the bushranger's trade… they did it too well for their safety and by late June 1880, the northeast of the state was crawling with police scouring the area for the outlaws. Almost daily, replacements and reinforcements were arriving from Melbourne by special trains. Part of the police strategy was to isolate and starve the gang into attempting a suicidal break out. But Ned had a plan of his own, to relieve the pressure by luring a police contingent into a deadly trap.

The trap is set

When they realised the police special train had stopped at the Glenrowan railway station in the early hours of Monday 28 June 1880, Ned Kelly, his brother Dan, Steve Hart and Joe Byrne knew their plan had failed. Just outside Glenrowan—on the Beechworth side to the north—the gang had torn up the railway tracks that would carry the special train transporting indigenous Queensland trackers, police constables and their horses.

The plan was that once through Glenrowan, the train would be derailed on a sweeping bend beside a deep ravine, and the weight of the engine would drag the carriages behind it down into the abyss and kill many – those who survived would have to face murderous firepower from the Kelly gang's guns. The trap was baited with the killing of Aaron Sherritt near Beechworth. Sherritt was to some extent or another involved with the police, probably as an informer – certainly the gang members believed that. On the night of 26 June, he was at home with his pregnant wife and four police constables who were using Sherritt's hut to watch the house next door, that of Joe Byrne's mother.[7]

The Melbourne *Argus* reported: "On Saturday evening the band of outlaws called at the hut of a man named Aaron Sherritt, having with them a German (Sherritt's neighbour) whom they compelled to call on Sherritt to come out. The latter recognising the voice, complied with the request and on his coming out of the door he was instantly shot dead by Joe Byrne, who put one bullet through his head and another through his body."[8]

As soon as news of the Sherritt killing was telegraphed to Melbourne a special train was organised to take police constables and five indigenous trackers to Beechworth to search for the perpetrators… not that there was any doubt who they were after, the four policemen in Sherritt's house had witnessed the whole gruesome affair.

In Ann Jones's Inn

The essence of the Kelly plan was to draw the Beechworth-bound train through the village of Glenrowan to where the trap had been set. But as well as he knew the area, Ned made a basic mistake by presuming the train carrying the police would come from Benalla, the station to the south of Glenrowan, not from Melbourne, 31 hours away. The derailment had been planned for that Saturday night, 26 June… but the train didn't turn up until about 3am on Monday morning 28 June 1880.

Also essential to the plan's success was taking the residents of Glenrowan hostage so there would be no-one to warn the police as the train passed through the village that the tracks ahead had been sabotaged. To that end, while Dan Kelly and Joe Byrne were dealing with Aaron Sherritt, Ned Kelly and Steve Hart had rounded up all the locals, about sixty of them, and held them captive in a local hostelry, Ann Jones' Glenrowan Inn, which was about 200 metres from the railway station.

By the time Dan Kelly and Joe Byrne got to Glenrowan there was a full-blown party happening in the Jones establishment with drinking and dancing and the odd game or two of cards, with most of the 'prisoners' not seeming to be too concerned about their incarceration – after all many were Kelly supporters more than happy to enjoy an ale or two in such illustrious company.

But the wait for the train to pass through Glenrowan had been considerably longer than expected and the gang was severely sleep deprived, not to mention suffering the effects of the revelry that had been going on. But so far their plan was working – Sherritt was dead, the police had reacted and the special train carrying the investigative squad was on its way to Beechworth, which necessitated passing through Glenrowan.

The plot comes unstuck

Maybe it was the effects of having been awake for so long… or maybe Ned Kelly was taken in by a man called Thomas Curnow, the local school teacher, for with no good reason and putting the whole plan and their lives at risk, Ned allowed Curnow and his wife and children to leave the hotel long before the events of the night, as Kelly had planned them, had transpired.

Curnow must have been a brave man to risk the wrath of the Kelly gang because as soon as he was released, he went to his house, which was near the railway line, and managed to stop the police special train by holding a lit match behind a red handkerchief. It is not clear whether he knew that the railway tracks on the other side of Glenrowan had been torn up or whether he was warning the police on the train that they may have been ambushed at Glenrowan station.[9]

Whatever the case, the police were now aware the four outlaws were ensconced in the Glenrowan Inn with most of the town residents and were able to plan their attack on the Kellys. Meanwhile, in the hotel at about 3am on Monday morning, Ned decided all the civilians could leave. He must have given up on the train arriving or again the effects of the last couple of days may have weakened his resolve. As those people were leaving the hotel, the police special pulled into the station. This prompted confusion in the place with gang members putting out fires and lights and struggling to get into their heavy armour. Once into their protective outfits, the four outlaws positioned themselves on the front veranda of the hotel awaiting the arrival of the police.[10]

The upshot of the firefight between the Kelly gang and the police contingent, as we well know, was that Joe Byrne was shot dead in the hotel, the result of a ferocious volley of shots from the police. Steve Hart and Daniel Kelly died while the shoot-out was on or in the fire that police lit to flush out the Kellys. Ned was captured and hanged later that year. Two others, the 10-year-old son of Mrs Jones and a man named Martin Cherry also died, the innocent victims of stray bullets.

The good priest's evidence

Later in the day at about 3pm, when the police set the hotel alight, a Catholic priest, Father Matthew Gibney, who happened to be in the area went to see if he could help. He apparently went to the room at the station

Father Matthew Gibney (Bishop). Source: Wikimedia.

where the wounded Ned Kelly was lying on a stretcher and later told newspaper reporters: "I don't think he is dying. He is penitent, and shows a very good disposition. When I asked him to say 'Lord Jesus have mercy on me,' he said it, and added, ' It's not to-day I began to say that.' I heard his confession, which I shall not be expected to repeat." [12]

Despite advice from police and others Father Gibney decided then to go to the burning hotel to see if he could administer the last rites to more of the outlaw gang. When he entered the hotel, he came across the body of Joe Byrne which was still lying where he had been shot and bodies he believed to be those of Dan Kelly and Steve Hart… but they were already dead and lying side by side.

The burnt remains of the Glenrowan Inn, the scene of the final confrontation, c1880. Source: State Library of Victoria.

In his evidence at the Police Inquiry in 1881, Father Gibney said: "My impression is that they certainly were not killed by the fire—were not suffocated by the heat of the fire. I myself went in there, and stopped there safely, and just when I came into their presence they were very composed looking, both lying at full stretch, side by side, and bags rolled up under their heads, the armour on one side of them off. I concluded they lay in that position to let the police see when they found them that it was not by the police they died; that was my own conclusion.

"Question 12319. You concluded they committed suicide? —Yes, that is my own belief.

"Question 12321. At the time that you entered the little room at the back of the building where the two corpses were lying, had the two men been living, there was sufficient time for them to have escaped with their lives from the fire?—Oh yes, there was if there had been life in either of them."[13]

In Greta Cemetery

The Sydney *Daily Telegraph's* report that was published in *The Queenslander* said: "The charred remains of Dan Kelly and Hart were handed over to their friends, and taken to Mrs. Skillion's place at Greta, and are there now. John Grant, undertaker, of Wangaratta, was employed by their friends to provide coffins of a first-class description, the cost being a matter of no consequence. He arrived with them in a buggy at Glenrowan yesterday afternoon, and they were seen to be high-priced articles. The lid of the one was lettered 'Daniel Kelly, died 28th June, 1880, aged 19 years,' and the other 'Stephen Hart, died 28th June, 1880, aged 21 years.'"

Outside McDonnell's Hotel, 1880. On the buggy are the coffins of Dan Kelly and Steve Hart. Source: State Library of Victoria.

The police apparently attempted to recover the remains and sent a group of 16 policemen to Greta, but they became worried that this would start another fight and they returned to Benalla. Dan Kelly and Steve Hart were buried in unmarked graves at Greta on 30 June 1880. After the graves were filled in, the whole area was ploughed over to keep the site of the graves hidden.

Joe Byrne's body was taken to Benalla and buried in the cemetery there. It is marked with a simple stone.

The question remains

But the question remains, could the two bodies Father Gibney saw laid out in the hotel be identified by him as those of Daniel Kelly and Steve Hart – would he know them?

The priest, who at that time was the Vicar General of Western Australia and would later become the Bishop of Perth, arrived in Western Australia from Ireland before the Kelly gang had reached notoriety. Even if Gibney had passed through Victoria on his way to Perth there is little likelihood he would have been familiar with either Dan Kelly or Hart.

However, there was another person who would have been very familiar with the outlaws, and the Melbourne *Argus* reported on 29 June 1880: "Constable Dwyer, by-the-by, who followed Father Gibney into the hotel, states that he was near enough to the bodies to recognise Dan Kelly."

Father Gibney may not have immediately recognised Dan Kelly or Steve Hart, but Constable Dwyer was quite clear in his evidence about Kelly to the inquiry. "I knew him to be Dan Kelly from the low forehead, and the description of them, and the other must be Steve Hart. Question 9540. Could you swear those were the two men, Hart and Kelly – Yes, I knew the man I saw in that position, with the black hair and sallow complexion, was Dan Kelly."[14]

Father Gibney and Constable Dwyer's evidence makes it hard to believe that the two bodies in the hotel were not those of Dan Kelly and Steve Hart. One curious explanation—and it is a far-fetched one—was published in the *Argus* under the headline "The Kelly Gang – an extraordinary yarn". It tells of a story run in the *London Daily Express* in October 1902 in which that paper's correspondent in South Africa said he met two men in Pretoria who claimed to be Dan Kelly and Steve Hart.

To cut a long story short, they claimed that some of the Glenrowan townspeople held prisoner by the Kelly gang became angry at the police for shooting at them, and Dan

Kelly and Hart gave them their own weapons to shoot back. The pair then high-tailed it out the back of the hotel, into the bush and away. The blackened and burnt bodies pulled out of the hotel ruins by the police, according to the two men in South Africa, were those of the townspeople. Unlikely!

Was he really Dan?

Clearly there are timing problems with the James Ryan/Dan Kelly claims. In the Brisbane *Truth* he says that after he escaped from the burning hotel he went into the bush and watched Ned's last stand and the police taking him away. Ned fell and was captured in the early hours of Monday morning; the Hotel was not set alight until closer to 3pm that afternoon.

In the *Truth* story Ryan/Kelly is said to be 79 years old. That was in 1933… therefore according to those numbers he was born in, as he says, the same year as the Eureka Stockade uprising, 1854. Now we know that Ned was born in 1854, in fact in December, the same month as the beginning of the rebellion. All records show that Dan Kelly was born on 1 June 1861 – so again a major timing mistake.

And there are other errors in his story regarding the shooting of the constable, Fitzgerald and the timing of the shooting of the three constables and the bank robbery at Euroa… but perhaps they are incidents his memory simply got out of order after 50 or more years.

Judge for yourself - compare the images of the boy Dan Kelly – an image taken by photographer James Bray around 1877 when Dan was 16… and a photograph of James Ryan, the man who claimed to be Dan Kelly taken at Toombul in Brisbane, presumably by the Sunday *Truth* in 1933. They are held by the State Library of Queensland.

But despite the debate through the years and the number of 'Dan Kellys' that have turned up… and despite the wishful thinking, whatever the motive – and despite it being a fascinating yarn which has captured the imaginations of many Australians, the evidence strongly suggests that as the inscription on his coffin says, Dan Kelly died when he was 19. He is buried in an unmarked grave somewhere in Greta Cemetery.

Merged by aligning the ears and eyes of the young Dan Kelly (left) with the senior man claiming to be Dan Kelly (right). Source of left and right image: State Library of Queensland. Merged image created by Atlas Productions.

How to find Dan Kelly/ James Ryan in Ipswich Cemetery:

To find the James Ryan grave and Dan Kelly memorial, enter through the Cemetery Road gate and drive through the entrance shed. Travel approximately 50 metres until you come to the second track off to the right. Turn right and drive about 200 metres until you come to a bitumen road and the 'Baptist A' sign. Turn left and travel about 40 metres and you will see the Kelly Shield and armour in a clear area 50 metres away on your right.

References:

1 (1933, August 13). *Truth (Brisbane, Qld. : 1900 - 1954)*, p. 1. Retrieved April 15, 2019 from URL: http://nla.gov.au/nla.news-page21888190

2 Ibid.

3 *The Age*. Coroner cast doubt over Kelly gang remains. 29 Sept 2005. Retrieved 15 April, 2019, from URL: https://www.theage.com.au/national/coroner-casts-doubt-over-kelly-gang-remains-20050929-ge0yma.html

4 Octogenarian Takes Dog Into Court (1941, March 12). *The Courier-Mail (Brisbane, Qld.: 1933 - 1954)*, p. 5. Retrieved April 15, 2019 from URL: http://nla.gov.au/nla.news-article44907992

5 "Dan Kelly" Mystery Not Solved By Inquest (1948, November 7). *Truth (Brisbane, Qld. : 1900 - 1954)*, p. 19. Retrieved April 15, 2019 from URL:http://nla.gov.au/nla.news-article203225412

6 Ian F. McLaren, 'Power, Henry (Harry) (1820–1891)', Australian Dictionary of Biography, National Centre of Biography, *Australian National University*. Retrived 14 April 2019 from URL: http://adb.anu.edu.au/biography/power-henry-harry-4412

7 Revolvy. Aaron Sherritt. Retrieved 9 April 2019. https://www.revolvy.com/page/Aaron-Sherritt

8 Another Kelly Outrage. *The Argus (Melb, Vic.: 1848-1957)* 28 June 1880: P5. Retrieved 9 Apr 2019 from: http://nla.gov.au/nla.news-article5983167

9 The Kelly Gang. (1880, July 10). *The Queenslander (Bris, Qld.: 1866-1939)*, p. 56. Retrieved 12 April 2019 from: http://nla.gov.au/nla.news-article20334078

10 Culture Victoria. Ann Jones Inn. Retrieved 12 April 2019 from URL: https://cv.vic.gov.au/stories/a-diverse-state/the-last-stand-of-the-kelly-Gang-sites-in-glenrowan/ann-jones-glenrowan-inn/

11 Destruction Of The Kelly Gang. (1880, June 29). *The Argus (Melbourne, Vic. : 1848 - 1957)*, p. 6. Retrieved April 14, 2019 from URL: http://nla.gov.au/nla.news-article5975546

12 The Royal Commission on the Police Force of Victoria 1881. Minutes of Evidence P442. Retrieved 13 April 2019 from URL: http://www.ironicon.com.au/the-royal-commission-kelly-outbreak.html

13 The Royal Commission on the Police Force of Victoria 1881. Minutes of Evidence P345. Retrieved 14 April 2019 from URL: http://www.ironicon.com.au/the-royal-commission-kelly-outbreak.html

14 The Kelly Gang. (1902, October 15). *The Argus (Melbourne, Vic. : 1848 - 1957)*, p. 7. Retrieved April 15, 2019 from URL: http://nla.gov.au/nla.news-article9080926

Images:

Queensland Newspapers Pty Ltd. *Dan Kelly, 1933*. Photographic print, 13 August 1933. Negative number: 196308. *State Library of Queensland*, retrieved 7 May 2019 from URL: https://hdl.handle.net/10462/deriv/115170

Truth front page: (1933, August 13). *Truth (Brisbane, Qld.: 1900 1954)*, p1. Retrieved May 7, 2019, from http://nla.gov.au/nla.news-page21888190

Bray, James [photographer] (c1876-1878). Dan Kelly [picture], *State Library of Victoria*. Retrieved 7 May 2019 from URL: http://handle.slv.vic.gov.au/10381/146219

Unidentified, and Queenslander. Another Busy Day in Sideshow Alley, Brisbane Exhibition Grounds, 1933. *State Library of Queensland*, retrieved 7 May 2019 from URL: http://hdl.handle.net/10462/deriv/200853

Ned Kelly in 1880. *Wikimedia Commons, the free media repository.* Retrieved 23 May 2019 from URL: https://commons.wikimedia.org/w/index.php?title=File:Ned_Kelly_in_1880.png&oldid=350416872.

Matthew Gibney (Bishop) [photograph], by Unknown. Source *Catholic Weekly*. Retrieved 7 May 2019 from URL: https://commons.wikimedia.org/w/index.php?curid=1640258

Bray, John [photographer], The burnt remains of the Jones's Hotel, the scene of the final confrontation between Ned Kelly and the Victorian Police, c1880, 5 July. *State Library of Victoria*, retrieved 7 May 2019 from URL: http://handle.slv.vic.gov.au/10381/53102

Burman and Madeley [photographer]. (1880). *McDonnell's Hotel, with Group and Coffins [picture]*. State Library of Victoria, retrieved 7 May 2019 from URL: http://handle.slv.vic.gov.au/10381/132464 SEE

Three images melded: Queensland Newspapers Pty Ltd. *Dan Kelly, 1933* (2005). Photographic print, 13 August 1933. Negative number: 196308. *State Library of Queensland*, retrieved 7 May 2019 from URL: https://hdl.handle.net/10462/deriv/115170   and Queensland Newspapers Pty Ltd. *Dan Kelly, 1933*. Photographic print, 13 August 1933. Negative number: 196308. *State Library of Queensland*, retrieved 7 May 2019 from URL: https://hdl.handle.net/10462/deriv/115133

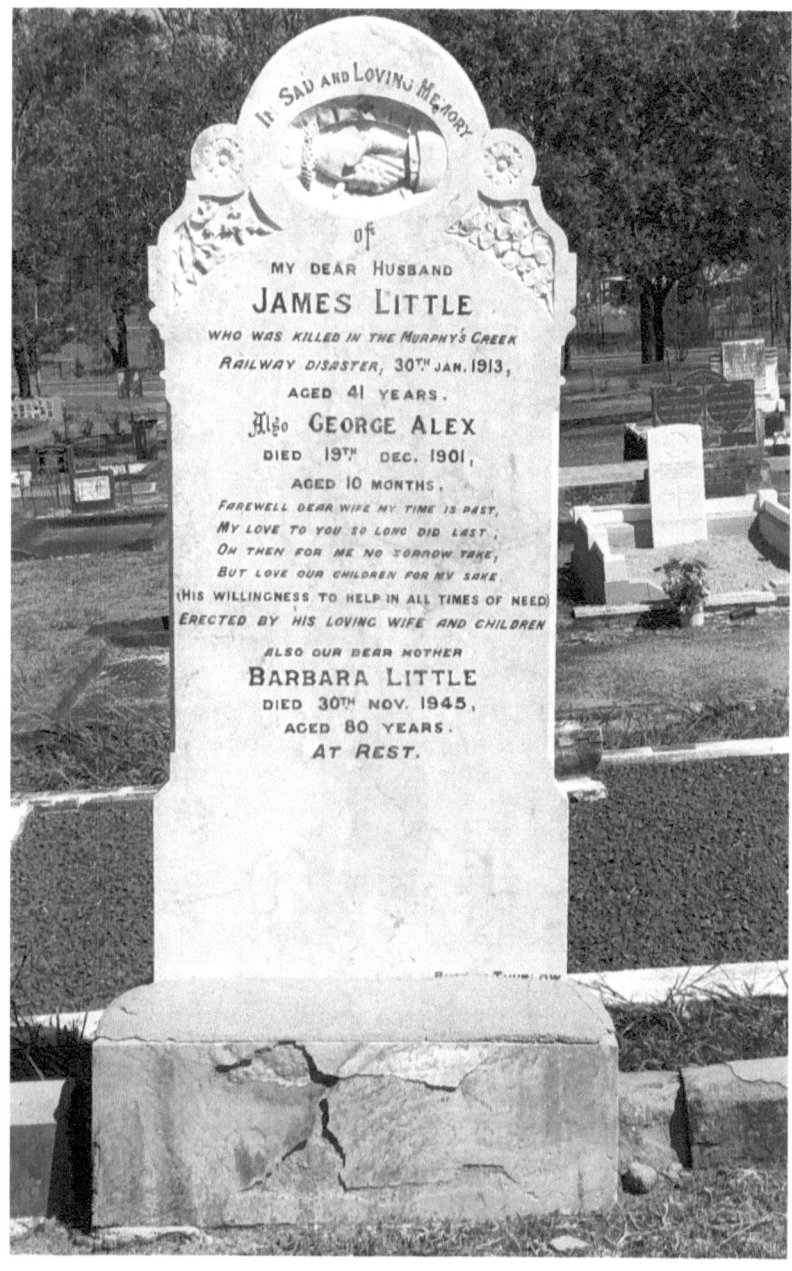

The railway widows
Barbara Little, Jane McCarthy and Annie Freese

Interred:	**Barbara Little**, 23 May 1865 – 30 November 1945 (aged 80).
	James Little, 8 May 1871 – 30 January 1913 (aged 41).
Location:	Section 7, Row 564 (approximately).
Cemetery:	Laidley Cemetery, Southern Street, Laidley, QLD 4341.

Interred:	**Patrick James McCarthy,** 1879 – 30 January 1913 (aged 34).
Location:	Roman Catholic B R12 G20/21 – No headstone but Patrick rests beside the grave of Patrick and William Brennan (headstone) R/C B R12 G18/19.
Cemetery:	Ipswich Cemetery, Cemetery and Warwick Roads, Ipswich, QLD 4305.

They were railway wives – their men worked as lengthsmen, gangers or labourers, and while the men earned their income with the railways, Barbara, Jane and Annie kept the house and home together in neighbouring Laidley and Rosewood.

In the new year of 1913, it was business as usual. On the day before the death of their husbands, Tuesday 29 January, the men got word of a terrible derailment. A livestock train with many hundreds of cattle on board had left Toowoomba for Brisbane and within twenty minutes of its departure, the train derailed near the Murphy's Creek railway station, 18 kilometres from Toowoomba and just over 1.5 kilometres from the station yard limits.[1] Tragically hundreds of the cattle on board were killed as the train came off the rails. Fortunately, the crew were uninjured but the impact had caused significant damage to the train and the track. The line was blocked and it would take hours of work to clear the scene.

The railway department leapt into action sending men and a breakdown train to clear the line. On the relief team was Barbara Little's husband, James, 41. He was a lifetime Laidley resident and the couple had been married seven years. They were raising their family of four children – Robert, 14, William, 13, Nancy, 8, and Margaret, 5, (baby George had passed away). With James at the clearing scene was Jane McCarthy's husband, Patrick, 34, a labourer from Rosewood. Jane and Patrick were the parents of four children – three sons, William, 6, Edward, 2, and Michael,1, and daughter Bridget, 4.

And from the same town of Rosewood, the husband of Annie Freese*, 39-year-old J. Frederick, or Fred, as he was known, joined the men to clear the wreckage. Fred was born in Minden but grew up in the Rosewood area,[2] and at 20 years of age, married Annie. They had been married 18 years and were parents to seven children – Fredericka, 17, David, 15, Daniel, 13, Ida, 11, Norman, 7, Harold, 5, and Elsie Rubina, aged 1.[3]

James, Patrick and Fred joined the workers assigned to prise rolling stock apart, remove the carcasses of dead cattle, carriage frames and shattered timber. The scene was described in *The Daily Standard* at the time: "Shattered wagons, dead cattle, goods smashed into a pulp, fruit, vegetables, wool, hides, and general merchandise lying about all over the place. As a result of the hot sun, the air became quickly nauseating."[4] The clearing continued all day.

The relief crew

The following morning, Wednesday 30 January 1913 a relief crew was sent in – an empty train with workers on board travelling along the same track to the disaster. It's hard to imagine how it happened or why, but the relief train headed towards the workers who were dismantling the wreckage, and suddenly it was upon them without any warning.

On board the relief train were fireman G. Bowtell and guard W. Hall who "glimpsed the wreck through a gap in the trees" at a distance of just over 1900 metres (2077 yards) in a direct line. The train driver reduced his speed to "two or three miles per hour at a point later found to be 200 yards (182 metres) from the breakdown van."[5] The driver, George Thompson, aged 28, had not seen the wreck and continued on and as he was "still thinking he was some distance from the derailment, Thompson released his brakes."

Suddenly the first and only warning that they were close to the breakdown train was heard. In his article, *The battalion of troubles... the Murphy's Creek railway smash of 1913*, author Greg Hallam explains the chaos that followed: "A warning was shouted from about 70 yards (64 metres) from the breakdown van by a workman (Logan) on the line. 'There is a train almost upon us!' A ganger at the site, Millward, also called out to the workers, 'Come out men, you will be all killed!' At the time, most of the workers were at the side of the line preparing to have breakfast.

Thompson threw his locomotive into reverse and applied sand on the rails to help provide adhesion. The engine, however, propelled by 226 tons (230 tonnes) of combined weight behind its tender collided with the rear of the breakdown train. The breakdown locomotive, its tender and the breakdown van had their brakes fully on because they faced 'downgrade', towards Murphy's Creek. The resultant collision drove them forward 3.5 metres (14 feet) to strike an H-class bogie open wagon, which was being re-railed. Six men of the rescue gang who had been working on the 'H' wagon were crushed beneath the wreckage."[6]

Men working on the track were able to leap clear, but twelve men were working on the side where a steep cutting made it impossible to get away. "Indescribable confusion"[7] was how the newspaper reported the scene of the second crash. Train wreckage was piled, forcing it high into the air, four carriages were so tightly jammed "everything battered horribly, and amongst it, were the bodies of the dead and dying"[8] including James, Patrick and Fred who had been at work beneath the wreckage. On impact, they died instantly[9] along with three other men – Charles McGregor and Walter Claydon of Toowoomba, and Alick Matthews of Crow's Nest.

*Above: Clearing the line (1913). Source: State Library of Queensland.
Below: Removing the bodies. Source: Queensland State Archives.*

The disaster had accelerated from one crash to a horrendous accident with human fatalities – the bodies tangled in the wood and steel wreckage. As the men worked to free anyone still alive, Barbara, 48, Jane, 33, and Annie, 42 (approximately), did not know of the accident yet, the children played and life went on as though it were a normal day. But as the doctor on the scene, Dr Freshney, began his task of pronouncing "life to be extinct,"[10] Barbara, Jane and Annie soon received word.

Patrick's body is removed. Source: State Library of Queensland.

The Commissioner "upon learning the extent of the disaster wired to the Traffic Manager at Toowoomba, instructing him to visit the relatives of the men who were killed… and request that the Railway Department be allowed to take charge of the funeral arrangements."[11] Traffic superintendent, Mr Davidson, departed the train at Rosewood to personally deliver the news to Annie about the death of Fred,[12] and to Jane about Patrick's death.[13]

The newspaper reported, "there were very distressful scenes at Toowoomba, Rosewood, and Laidley, where the families of the victims resided, when the news of the fatalities reached those places."[14] The Minister for Railways, Hon. W. T. Paget attended the two Toowoomba funerals and expressed that he was "exceedingly sorry for the widows and children of the unfortunate men killed at their posts."[15] The funerals were respectfully represented by railway and ministerial hierarchy with offers for extra train services if needed to bring the bodies home. But soon, the blame game would begin.

> FUNERAL.—The Friends of Mrs. PATRICK M'CARTHY are respectfully requested to attend the Funeral of her Deceased HUSBAND, who was accidentally killed. The Funeral will move from Deceased's late Residence, at Rosewood, for the Ipswich Cemetery, at 10 a.m. TO-MORROW (SATURDAY).

Patrick's funeral notice, 31 January 1913. Source: *Queensland Times*.

*The bodies arrive at the Toowoomba Railway Station.
Source: Darling Downs Gazette.*

The blame game

Within a month of the accident, a magisterial enquiry was conducted in Toowoomba to determine what happened that fateful day, Wednesday 30 January 1913. The enquiry went on for weeks, blame being bounced back and forward. The train driver, Thompson, survived and it was said by Mr A. D. Graham who was at the inquiry "to represent the interests of the engine drivers and firemen concerned in the accident,"[16] that "it is becoming quite clear that the heads of the department blame Thompson for the accident."[17]

Thompson had been in the employ of the railway for about six years and got his engine driver licence the July previous. On that day, he had been on duty for 18 hours,[18] but he was not new to the route, he had been down the range five or six times.[19] In his own defence, Thompson said he did not know the position of the breakdown van as there were no precautions in place, and if there had been, he could have pulled up in time.[20] The precautions referred to included detonators and flags. The inquest heard if there had been detonators "400 or 500 yards back" from the wrecked train, the second vehicle driven by Thompson could have pulled up in time.[21]

A witness noted Thompson was coming "down very steadily, and had the train perfectly under control." The inquest then heard that the driver checked the speed once "and then witness thought he was picking it up rather quickly. When the impact occurred, witness was thrown back against the gate, and fell out on the right, hand side. Beforehand, he heard the brakes being put on, and that was when the engine seemed suddenly to be gathering speed."[22]

Train driver George Thompson. Source: Truth, 1913.

The chief mechanical engineer, Mr C.F. Pemberton said the driver "should have been more cautious… Thompson knew he was near the scene and should have gone slower."[23] But Pemberton acknowledged the stopping place should have been marked for the driver and that "reasonable precautions were not taken for the protection of the men engaged clearing the debris."[24]

There was also confusion in regards to who was in charge of the men including James, Patrick and Fred, working under the derailed wagons. A witness said all the heads of department were present but there was no protection set up from the train that caused the second accident.[25]

The Guard, J.M. Scanlan, was questioned as to why he didn't protect 'his' train and he advised he received orders from the traffic manager, Mr Lloyd, to help passengers, and that Mr Lloyd didn't enquire what he was doing at the time before making the request.[26] Another witness agreed that it was then the traffic manager's duty to reassign someone to the guard's role [Scanlan] if he removes him for other duty.[27] Chief mechanical engineer Pemberton stressed that guards "were relieved of responsibility of protecting their trains if they were taken away from such work by superior officers, and also that gangers and lengthsmen were not responsible for protecting in this case, which was a case of permanent obstruction."[28] A distinction of little comfort to the bereaved.

Some spoke of hearing the train whistle as it came towards the first derailed train, other witnesses claimed this never happen, while some claimed it happened just as the train impacted.[29] All witnesses agreed there was no sign of alcoholic drink involved.[30]

A Board of Inquiry submitted their findings with the three key points being: "the driver (Thompson) was found to not have approached the scene of the derailment with 'the caution demanded of him'; the Guard of the breakdown train had failed to adequately protect the rear; and a lack of adequate protection through the provision of warning flags, detonators and other signals, and dangerous pilot working were found to have contributed to the fatal collision."[31]

Everyone under questioning seemed to have an opinion on who was responsible but no-one put up their hand to take responsibility.

The result

The enquiry closed 17 March with 56 witnesses having been interviewed.[32] The evidence was then forwarded to the authorities and in May, a most unwelcome result was announced, particularly for Barbara, Jane and Annie. The Attorney-General, Mr O'Sullivan, after wading through the 1129 pages of depositions supplied to him, decided that no further action be taken.[33]

The *Daily Standard* wrote: "And so ends everything in connection with one of the most lamentable happenings in the history of the State… as if nothing had happened to disturb the accustomed tranquillity of every-day life… a deplorable bungle. Not a soul outside official circles knows how it happened or who was to blame."[34]

The only two employees to be penalised were the Acting Traffic Manager, Carmody, for not setting up protection when he arrived at the scene of the serious derailment, and the General Traffic Manager, Lloyd, for not satisfying himself that the protection had been put in place at the Toowoomba end.[35] They were both demoted.

How Barbara, Annie and Jane survived

With no real closure and no responsibility apportioned, the railway widows continued raising their children and living without their husband, friend, children's father and breadwinner.

How they survived with their brood and little income can only be imagined. The probate amounts on their husbands' estates were minuscule – James left 34 pounds for Barbara (approximately $4000 today), Annie and Jane received 10 pounds from Fred and Patrick's probate respectively (the equivalent of $1200 in today's money).[36]

Perhaps they relied on the charity of family and friends and the promise of some financial support from the railway that took away their breadwinner, or perhaps they sought work, like Jane, who took on the role of Gatekeeper/Station Mistress at Lanefield in Ipswich and later Station Mistress in Clayfield, Brisbane.[37]

The three widows issued writs for £2000 each, served against the Commissioner for Railways for their husband's death "from injuries caused by negligence and breach of statutory duty."[38] Jane and Annie succeeded in their claims in December 1913. James' wife, Barbara, had her case adjourned seeking further evidence until early 1914.[39] But one year and three months after the accident, in April 1914, compensation was finally paid to these three widows.

They were granted £1250 (approximately $145,300[40] in today's money), with half of that for their own maintenance and the other half to be divided amongst their children to be kept in trust for their education and maintenance.

What became of…

Barbara Little: James' wife never left their family home after James' death. She remained in Wickham Street, Laidley for the rest of her days, dying in 1945 at the age of 80, and 32 years after James' death at Murphy Creek.[41]

Barbara and James' four children were all alive to farewell their mother. Barbara is buried with James.

Jane McCarthy: as tragic as Patrick's death was for his wife, Jane, Patrick's extended family were no strangers to tragedy. He hailed from Thagoona (Ipswich) where his mother and other family members remained.[42] His mother lost two sons to the railway (including Patrick), her husband to a fire at Walloon, and another son who was a jockey died at Esk.[43] Patrick also had a brother who was a police sergeant in Toowoomba. Every year for the next five years on the anniversary of his death, Jane ran a small advertisement in the newspaper in loving memory of her husband, and then it ceased. Jane worked for the railways for over 25 years and died 9 May 1961, aged 86 (approximately). She is buried in Brisbane's Toowong Cemetery.

Annie Freese, wife of Fred (John Frederick) died in September 1944, 31 years after her husband. With the exception of Fred's accidental and premature death, it seems the longevity gene was in the family with many of her seven children living long lives: Fredericka died aged 81, David aged 83, Daniel, 73, Norman 76, and Harold 80. Annie is buried with Fred, but at the time of publication their graves could not be found. They are likely to be in unmarked graves in Tallegalla Cemetery which was formerly known as Rosewood Cemetery.

None of the three women remarried.

Please note in some news stories, Annie and Fred's surname is spelt as Freise, but the death certificate is Freese.

References:

1 Murphy's Creek Railway Accident, Stories from the Archives, *Queensland State Archives*, 28 September 2016. Retrieved 14 March 2019 from URL: https://blogs.archives.qld.gov.au/2016/09/28/murphys-creek-railway-accident/
2 Railway Smash (1913, January 31). *Queensland Times (Ipswich, Qld.: 1909-1954)*, p.5. Retrieved March 15, 2019, from http://nla.gov.au/nla.news-article113094057
3 The Murphy's Creek Disaster. (1914, April 9). *The Brisbane Courier (Qld.: 1864 - 1933)*, p. 6. Retrieved 14 March 2019 from http://nla.gov.au/nla.news-article19947021
4 At Murphy's Creek. Terrible Railway Disaster. (31 January 1913). *Daily Standard (Bris, Qld. 1912-1936)*, p5 (2nd ed). Retrieved 14 Mar 2019 from http://nla.gov.au/nla.news-article179870717
5 - 6 Hallam, Greg. 'The battalion of troubles...' the Murphy's Creek railway smash of 1913 [online]. *Queensland History Journal*, Vol. 22, No. 3, Nov 2013: 253-263. Retrieved 18 Mar 2019 from URL: https://search-informit-com-au.ezproxy.slq.qld.gov.au/documentSummary;dn=844616509712162;res=IELAPA
7 - 8 At Murphy's Creek. Terrible Railway Disaster. (31 Jan 1913). Op.cit.
9 Double Railway Disaster. (31 Jan 1913). *Daily Mercury (Mackay, Qld.: 1906-1954)*, p4. Retrieved 14 March 2019 from http://nla.gov.au/nla.news-article169618717
10 At Murphy's Creek. Terrible Railway Disaster. (31 Jan 1913). Op.cit.
11 - 12 Double Railway Disaster. (31 Jan 1913). *Daily Mercury*. Op.cit.
13 - 15 Railway Double Disaster. (31 Jan 1913). *The Telegraph (Bris, Qld. 1872-1947)*, p7. Retrieved 14 Mar 2019 from http://nla.gov.au/nla.news-article175913060
16 Murphy's Creek Disaster. (25 Feb 1913). *The Journal (Adelaide, SA: 1912 - 1923)*, p1. Retrieved 18 March 2019 from http://nla.gov.au/nla.news-article200868496
17 Murphy Creek Disaster. (8 March 1913). *The Dalby Herald (Qld 1910-1954)*, p.7. Retrieved 18 March 2019 from http://nla.gov.au/nla.news-article215333530
18 Hallam, Greg. 'The battalion of troubles...' Op.cit.
19 Murphy's Creek Railway Disaster (1913, February 25). *The Northern Miner (Charters Towers, Qld.: 1874 - 1954)*, p. 7. Retrieved March 18, 2019, from http://nla.gov.au/nla.news-article81134723
20 Hallam, Greg. 'The battalion of troubles...' Op.cit.
21 Railway Disaster. (28 Feb 1913). *The Week (Bris, Qld.: 1876 - 1934)*, p. 15. Retrieved March 14, 2019, from http://nla.gov.au/nla.news-article201059138
22 At Murphy's Creek. Terrible Railway Disaster. (31 Jan 1913). Op.cit.
23 - 24 Murphy's Creek Railway Disaster. (28 Feb 1913). *Daily Mercury (Mackay, Qld. 1906-1954)*, p.4. Retrieved 14 Mar 2019 from http://nla.gov.au/nla.news-article169614255
25 Railway Disaster. (27 Feb 1913). *The Telegraph (Bris, Qld.: 1872-1947)*, p7 (2nd Ed). Retrieved 14 March 2019 from http://nla.gov.au/nla.news-article177812468
26 Murphy's Creek Railway Disaster. (13 March 1913). *Daily Mercury (Mackay, Qld. 1906-1954)*, p.5. Retrieved 14 March 2019 from http://nla.gov.au/nla.news-article169627554
27 Murphy's Creek Railway Smash (1913, March 8). *Gympie Times and Mary River Mining Gazette (Qld.: 1868 - 1919)*, p. 5. Retrieved March 14, 2019, from http://nla.gov.au/nla.news-article190692949

28 Railway Disaster. (1 March 1913). *The Telegraph (Bris, Qld. 1872 - 1947)*, p. 2. Retrieved March 14, 2019, from http://nla.gov.au/nla.news-article175439612
29 Murphy's Creek Railway Disaster. (3 March 1913). *Daily Mercury*. Op.cit.
30 Railway Inquiry (5 March 1913). *The Telegraph (Bris, Qld. 1872-1947)*, p.7 (2nd ed). Retrieved 14 March 2019 from http://nla.gov.au/nla.news-article175443126
31 Hallam, Greg. 'The battalion of troubles...' Op.cit.
32 Murphy's Creek Inquiry. (17 Mar 1913). *The Daily Telegraph (Syd, NSW: 1883-1930)*, p15. Retrieved 14 Mar 2019 from http://nla.gov.au/nla.news-article238945541
33 -34 Murphy's Creek Disaster. (10 May 1913). *The Brisbane Courier (Qld. 1864-1933)*, p4. Retrieved 14 March 2019 from http://nla.gov.au/nla.news-article19881940
35 Hallam, Greg. 'The battalion of troubles...' Op.cit.
36 Probates. (11 Nov 1913). *Daily Standard (Bris, Qld. 1912-1936)*, p6 (2nd ed). Retrieved March 15, 2019, from http://nla.gov.au/nla.news-article181069801
37 Raftery, Jane, 1880-1861, *Ancestry.com.au* (https://www.ancestry.com/family-tree/person/tree/160974292/person/102099093732/facts). Accessed May 2019.
38 Notes and News. (4 Dec 1913). *Gympie Times and Mary River Mining Gazette (Qld.: 1868-1919)*, p3. Retrieved 14 March from http://nla.gov.au/nla.news-article189708232
39 Murphy's Creek Accident. (11 Dec 1913). *Queensland Times (Ipswich, Qld.: 1909-1954)*, p6. Retrieved March 14, 2019, from http://nla.gov.au/nla.news-article118661661
40 https://www.thomblake.com.au/secondary/hisdata/calculate.php
41 Obituary (4 Dec 1945). *Queensland Times (Ipswich, Qld: 1909-1954)*, p4. Retrieved March 15, 2019, from http://nla.gov.au/nla.news-article114610723
42 Sensational Railway Smashes. (31 Jan 1913). *The Brisbane Courier (Qld.: 1864-1933)*, p7. Retrieved 15 March 2019 from http://nla.gov.au/nla.news-article19880567
43 Railway Disaster. (31 Jan 1913). *The Telegraph (Bris, Qld. 1872-1947)*, p.2 (2nd ed.). Retrieved 14 March 2019 from http://nla.gov.au/nla.news-article175912765

Images:

Unidentified (1913). Clearing the line at the railway accident at Murphy's Creek, Qld, 1913. *John Oxley Library, State Library of Queensland*. Retrieved 18 March 2019 from: https://trove.nla.gov.au/version/49026401

(1910). Removing some of the bodies - railway accident at Murphy's Creek, 30 January 1913. *Queensland State Archives*, Item ID: 1742408. Retrieved 18 March 2019 from URL: https://trove.nla.gov.au/version/252859684

Removing the body of P. McCarthy: Unidentified (1913). The railway accident at Murphy's Creek, Queensland, 1913. John Oxley Library, *State Library of Queensland*. Retrieved 18 March 2019 from URL: https://trove.nla.gov.au/version/49026401

Funeral notice: Family Notices (31 Jan 1913). *Queensland Times* (Ipswich, Qld. 1909-1954), p4. Retrieved 15 Mar 2019 from http://nla.gov.au/nla.news-article113094014

Scenes at the Recent Railway Accident on the Range (1 Feb 1913. *Darling Downs Gazette* (Qld. 1881-1922), p5. Retrieved 18 Mar 2019 from: http://nla.gov.au/nla.news-article182655396

Driver George Thompson: The Magisterial Inquiry. (2 Mar 1913. *Truth* (Bris, Qld. 1900-1954), p.2. Retrieved 18 Mar 2019 from: http://nla.gov.au/nla.news-article202660376

The Boxing Day murders
The Murphy siblings

Interred: **Norah (Honora) Murphy**, 19 December 1871 – 26 December 1898 (aged 27).

Ellen (Theresa) Murphy, 31 May 1880 – 26 December 1898 (aged 18).

Michael Murphy, 23 January 1870 – 26 December 1898 (aged 28).

Location: Roman Catholic Section, Section R. Norah – Grave 2734, Ellen – Grave 2735 and Michael – Grave 2736.

Cemetery: Gatton Cemetery, Lake Apex Drive, Gatton, QLD 4343.

This beautiful photo of Norah was taken by Poul C. Poulsen who opened a photographic studio in Queen Street, Brisbane in 1885 and is now considered one of Queensland's most important photographers. It is reproduced with the kind permission of Mike Fitzpatrick.

In a paddock on Boxing Day evening 1898, three young people lay still and silent. Beside them, lay their horse. Not a sound, no one passing, just a scene of complete stillness late on a dark, balmy evening in the country. The next morning, they looked like they were sleeping in the sun, except for the ants that could be seen crawling on their bodies. That is how their brother-in-law would describe the scene to police that morning.

The local dance

Twenty-seven-year-old Norah Murphy *(pictured left)* didn't want to go to the dance in Gatton that night. It was Boxing Day and she had enjoyed the day at home with her young nieces while her siblings had gone to the races at Mount Sylvia.

Norah, bright and capable[1], helped run the household; there were ten Murphy children, six still living at home and only one married, but it was a working farm and all hands were on deck for the dairy and crops. As most of the family was home for Christmas, Norah was content to stay home that evening, but Michael, 28, her big brother and the brother she was closest to insisted she needed to get out of the house and that it would be good for her.[2] Amiably she agreed and put on her best wear, the fashion of the day – a black tweed skirt, pale blouse, a black straw sailor hat to match and black high-heeled riding boots.[3]

Despite being at the races all day, Ellen, Norah's clever, happy and fun[4] eighteen-year-old sister, was keen to go to the dance. Ellen's teachers described her as "the most popular and exemplary girl under their charge."[5] She was a keen horse rider, good with her hands and won prizes for her needlework[6], copy book writing[7] and pencil drawings. The prize books that she gained were later held in high esteem by her mother, "as sacred tokens of the dear one gone."[8] Like all eighteen-year-old girls, friends and romances made life exciting. Bill Connolly had been talking to Ellen at the races[9] that day and tonight, the neighbouring Forster brothers might be at the dance,[10] and Simon Laffey who Ellen was "rather taken by… was to play the fiddle for the Gatton dance."[11]

It was a lively area with plenty of young people and there were two dances on that night – one at Mt Sylvia and one at Gatton. The Murphys chose the Gatton dance which was 13 kilometres (8 miles) from their family farm at Blackfellow's Creek. Michael would escort them.

Left: portrait of Ellen, aged 13, provided by her parents to the Toowoomba Chronicle. Right: Michael Murphy, aged 28, and inset photo of Ellen, aged 18. Photos courtesy of the Queensland Police Museum.

Michael was home for Christmas holidays – he worked at Westbrook experimental farm, about 14 kilometres south-west from Toowoomba, where varying farming techniques were trialled.[12] Michael knew many people in the area – he was a "quiet, good-natured man of about 5ft, 10inch tall (178cm) and powerfully built, an expert bushman, and Sergeant in the local corps of Mounted Rifles, of which he was one of the most capable members."[13]. His friends and colleagues said he was popular and "without an enemy."[14]

They were a tight and hard-working family. Mrs Mary Murphy was a strong woman and she insisted her daughters be accompanied by one of their brothers if they wanted to go out, which was appropriate conduct in that era. Of the remaining siblings, brother, Daniel, 21, was a Police Constable stationed in Brisbane;[15] he didn't make it home for Christmas. Patrick, 24, was a labourer at the Gatton Agricultural College and required to live-in during the week. Jeremiah, 20, worked on the farm and served in the Gatton Mounted Infantry.[16]

Polly, now Mrs McNeil, 32, the eldest, was married but living with her parents – Polly had suffered paralysis after childbirth and the family was looking after her and her two children.[17] Her husband, William, 31, was a Protestant to the dismay of the very Catholic Mrs Murphy. He stayed with the Murphy family on weekends. The youngest Murphy members were John, 15, and Catherine (or Katie), 13.[18]

That evening, it was Norah, Ellen and Michael Murphy who headed off to the dance at 8pm. Ellen dressed in a fashion similar to Norah, sporting a white straw hat, a "navy blue skirt, a blue and red cape and heliotrope blouse with black lace-up boots"[19]; Michael wore—notwithstanding the summer heat—a three-piece navy suit.[20]

The Murphy family c.1898. Seated are parents Daniel (Snr) and Mary, with 8 of their 10 children (from left): John, Jeremiah, Patrick, William, Polly, Norah, Ellen and Catherine. Source: State Library of Queensland.

The Murphy's residence at Gatton, 1898. Source: image courtesy of the Queensland Police Museum.

The last journey

After the hour-long drive in the sulky, the three siblings must have been disappointed when they arrived at 9pm to find that the dance was cancelled; they were all dressed up with nowhere to go. Some reports say the promoters were unable to get a musician[21] while others say the dance was cancelled due to lack of numbers attending.[22] The Murphy siblings spent a little time talking with friends and then turned their horse and sulky around and headed for home. About 2.4 kilometres (a mile and a half) from the township, a local sergeant passed them and saw them talking to a man later identified as their brother (Patrick) who was heading home to the Agricultural College.[23] That was the last time they were seen alive; Ellen, Norah and Michael didn't return home that night.

Next morning, initially no-one was too worried. Michael was with the girls and it was presumed the cart might have broken down and they were waiting for help. Brother-in-law William McNeil was at the Murphy household that morning and volunteered to ride out to find Ellen, Norah and Michael while Jeremiah and John finished milking the cows and then continued on to cut chaff.[24]

William had ridden just over three kilometres (two miles) on Tenthill Road when he found the distinct tracks of the Murphy family's sulky – it had a wobbly wheel. He followed the tracks as they veered through sliprails into Moran's paddock[25] and then he saw them – Ellen, Norah and Michael lying motionless in the paddock. At first, he thought they were just sleeping in the sun, but as he got closer, he saw ants crawling over the bodies and that their clothing was disarrayed.[26]

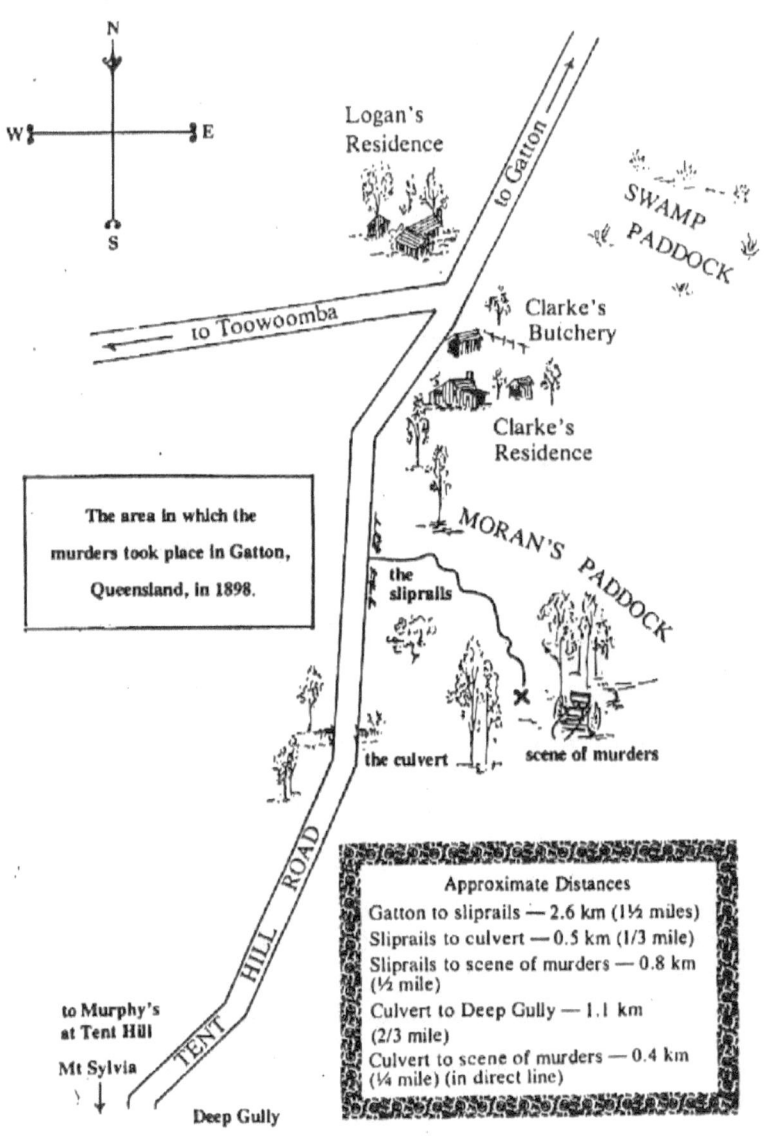

*The area in which the Gatton murders took place.
Image courtesy of the Queensland Police Museum.*

William turned his horse and rode to Gatton to the police station. Unfortunately, prior to alerting Acting-Sergeant William Arrell, he raced into a hotel in Gatton to ask directions to the police station and told the proprietor, Charles Gilbert, about the deaths; soon Gilbert and a number of other men were making their way to the location.[27]

The brutal attack

When Sergeant Arrell and William arrived at the scene, the extent of the Murphy siblings' injuries was evident for all to see. Norah's death was particularly brutal. She was found lying on a rug about 10 metres from her brother and sister with her hands tied behind her by her own handkerchief. She had been raped and was covered in bruises; her body had been excessively scratched all over as though by many frenzied hands.[28] Her clothing was torn revealing her chest and she had a deep cut above the eye that penetrated to the bone, her skull was battered in. The skin was torn from Norah's wrists where tied, her hands had turned blue and were swollen. A harness strap was used around Norah's neck believed to silence her screams and to throttle her,[29] several of her teeth were fractured, and there were fingernail marks upon her thighs.

Ellen and Michael were lying near each other; Ellen was lying on her right side, her clothes drawn up, her knees visible[30] and her hands tied behind her with a handkerchief. Her clothes were not as disarrayed as Norah's but were torn and her underwear stained with blood. On both sisters, semen was present on their clothing and later at the autopsy it would be discovered, internally. The hit to Ellen's head

The crime scene where the Murphy siblings were murdered Photo courtesy of the Queensland Police Museum.

was so brutal that her brain was protruding. Bruises and scratches were found on her body from her struggles to ward off the attacker.[31]

Michael who must have valiantly tried to protect his sisters had been shot and also had a brutal skull fracture.[32] His hands were not tied, but he was lying face down and it appeared he and Ellen had been sitting upright and back-to-back when struck. Nearby lay their horse also shot in the head. The murderer had positioned the bodies of Ellen, Norah and Michael with their feet pointing due west.

The investigation

A crime too severe and a crime scene too daunting no doubt overwhelmed Acting-Sergeant William Arrell, and consequently the police blunders that would follow proved detrimental to the case. After inspecting the crime scene Sergeant Arrell returned to the station to wire the Commissioner for back-up and a tracker.[33] He asked a few of the men to remain with the bodies but failed to secure the crime scene from onlookers. William rode home to his in-laws at the Murphy household to advise them of the tragedy and a shocked Mrs Murphy brought sheets from her home to the scene. With her own hands, she covered each of her children's bodies.

Sergeant Arrell returned to find over forty people traipsing through the murder scene.[34] Later, he claimed that he asked the onlookers to leave the paddock, and they moved back but soon came closer again and he continually had to ask them to leave.[35] The brother of the Murphy siblings, Constable Daniel Murphy was on duty at the Roma Street Station in Brisbane when he received a wire about the murder. He didn't initially believe it and asked for confirmation; it was given and he sought transport to get home.[36]

The investigating officers from Brisbane did not arrive until 48 hours after the discovery of the bodies exposing the crime scene to traffic and the elements. The soil on the paddock was described as soft, the murderer may have left tracks but the traffic that had accessed the site since the murder largely obliterated any tracks or tell-tale marks[37] and made it difficult for the trackers to do their work. Sergeant Arrell did not make notes or take measurements at the crime scene when the bodies were in situ; he made notes later, thinking it not necessary at the time.[38] By the time Inspector Urquhart arrived from Brisbane, Norah, Ellen and Michael's bodies had been moved to Gilbert's Hotel and locked in a bedroom awaiting an autopsy.

Within days every public space bore notices offering a reward of 1000 pounds for information that could lead to the capture and conviction of the Murphys' killer.[39] A party of police officers was dispatched from Brisbane to investigate the affair, along with experienced Indigenous trackers and ambitious sleuths, all with no enlightening results.

The autopsies

Conducting the autopsies, Dr von Lossberg advised that he believed "Norah had been 'ravished' four times, and Ellen twice, or possibly three times." He initially thought Michael had been shot, then not finding the bullet exit wound changed his mind on this point[40] and concluded that the hole in the skull must have been inflicted by the limb of a tree—over a metre long (3.28 feet) and 7.5 centimetres (3 inches) in diameter—that was found at the scene with clotted blood and hair on it.[41] However, due to continued speculation that Michael had been shot, about a week after the funeral the police requested his body be exhumed. It was only then that the bullet was found.

The funeral

On Wednesday 28 December 1898, two days after the Boxing Day murders, the bodies of the Murphy three were taken to the Roman Catholic Church. The funeral was presided over by Father Daniel Walsh and took place at 11am, followed by the burial at the Gatton Cemetery after midday. Flags flew at half-mast and businesses were closed. The newspaper reported "there was hardly a dry eye… the coffins rested on a long platform down the aisle, and were literally covered with wreaths and crosses. Almost the whole township attended the funeral. The cortege included over 300 horsemen and a large number of vehicles."[42]

The funeral on 28 February 1898. Source: Queensland Police Museum.

The Magisterial Inquiry and the suspects

Several false arrests were made in the early days and there was an array of potential suspects; the Magisterial Inquiry in January of 1899 threw many names into the mix including those of the family.

William McNeil (Polly's husband) came under suspicion. At the inquest, John Murphy, brother of Ellen, Norah and Michael and brother-in-law to William, said he went to bed at 10.30pm that night and assumed William was in his room. Inspector Urquhart pushed him on this detail:

Inspector Urquhart: Are you sure?

Witness: I could not be sure; he was supposed to be.

Left: Murphy siblings' brother-in-law William McNeil, 1899. Source: The Queenslander. Right: Inspector Frederic Urquhart. Source: Courtesy of the Queensland Police Museum.

Inspector Urquhart: As a matter of fact you do not know whether McNeil was there or not?

Witness: No: I went to sleep almost immediately… Did not see McNeil early next morning. Saw him later in the day; noticed nothing unusual about him.

Inspector Urquhart also grilled Sergeant Arrell about William McNeil raising the alarm after finding the bodies:

Inspector Urquhart: Did you take any steps to test the accuracy of McNeil's statement?

Witness: No.

Inspector Urquhart: Did you try to find out whether he told you the truth or not?

Witness: No.

Inspector Urquhart: It is difficult to think that you rode all the way to the paddock with McNeil without conversing. Did you not ask him for particulars as to how he found the bodies?

Witness: No.

Inspector Urquhart painted the siblings' brother, Jeremiah, in a bad light questioning him as to why he didn't acquire the assistance of the mounted infantry of which Jeremiah was a member, and go searching the area for the "men who committed the murders… you knew they could not have got far away since the previous night. The fact is you stayed at home and did nothing at all."[43] Was this an inference that Jeremiah suspected a family member, thus failed to act?

A former boyfriend of Polly's—Thomas Joseph Ryan—

was grilled on the stand. He dated Polly for close to eight years but Mrs Murphy disapproved. Thomas sent notes to Polly, delivered by Ellen. Eventually, the correspondence stopped and Polly married William. Inspector Urquhart questioned Thomas Ryan:[44]

Inspector Urquhart: Did you ever say you would have Polly in spite of Mrs Murphy?

Witness: Yes. I did not say "in spite of her." I said when I wanted her I would take her.

Inspector Urquhart: Did you ever say you would be revenged on her because she took Polly away from you?

Witness: No: never. She did not take her away. I did not want to be revenged.

Daniel Murphy Snr., the head of the Murphy family, also came under suspicion for the murders, as did every member of the family capable of committing the atrocity. It didn't help that Daniel Jr. (the police constable based in Brisbane) was heard to say at Roma Street Police Station at the time of hearing of the murder "someone at home has gone out of their mind"[45] alluding to it being a family member that committed the crime. Of course he could have been referring to his district as 'home'.

More serious contenders included:

Richard Burgess – described as "a recently discharged prisoner and bush vagabond"[46] but he had an alibi and witnesses that placed him at least 80 kilometres (50 miles) from Gatton on the night. Given how long it would take to cover that area on a horse, it was sound enough to let him off the hook.[47]

Thomas Day – a new face in town who was working for Gatton butcher, AG Clarke. Police found blood on his clothing but with the limitations of testing in 1898, it could have been animal blood. When the clothing was not removed from him, Thomas Day proceeded to "wash and boil the jumper twice and scrub it with a scrubbing brush. No further action was taken against Day and a few weeks later he left the district."[48] Merv Lilley, in his book *Gatton Man*, claims Thomas Day was a pseudonym used by his father, William Lilley—a violent sadist and sexual pervert—and that he was responsible for the murders.[49]

Joe Quinn – believed to be the culprit by author Stephanie Bennett in her book, *The Gatton Murders*. Michael Murphy was a Special Constable during the shearers' strike and Joe Quinn was on the strike committee. Stephanie believes a confrontation most likely took place between the two men during this time. Quinn was believed to be a shady character, with numerous aliases and was in Gatton at the time of the murders to spend Christmas with his brother. Quinn lived until his nineties, dying in 1945[50] after a life of crime.[51]

There was also much conjecture that the murder was the result of rival families and religious hatred; the age-old Catholic versus Protestant tension.

Human nature

Less than three weeks after the murder, the site of the tragedy had become a tourist attraction. Unbelievably, the reporter from *The Queenslander* wrote: "Today I went out again to the scene of the tragedy. It is marvellous that so many people come such distances to visit the spot. Some come from Toowoomba, others from Ipswich, while farmers, with their wives and children, drive in from Helidon, Forest Hill, Spring Creek, and other centres. Today a party lunched under the shade of a gum tree within a few yards at the actual spot where the bodies were discovered." [52]

Several kilometres away, the Murphy family grieved. Jeremiah Murphy told the very same reporter that "his mother will never recover."[53]

In the end, Inspector Urquhart wrote in his police summary of the Gatton Murders: 'We have failed because from the very outset we had no chance of success."[54] Today very little has changed in the area, but the slaying of Norah, Ellen and Michael remains Queensland's oldest unsolved crime.

What became of…

Inspector Urquhart was not well regarded and a report at the Royal Commission noted that his "vindictive and tyrannical nature" made him unfit to serve as a police officer. He continued on, rising to the rank of Police Commissioner from 1917-1921.[55]

Sergeant Arrell was haunted by the murders, his wife claiming that he "walks around the verandah and the police headquarters for hours at night."[56] He died of senility aged 78 and is buried in Toowong Cemetery.

Father Daniel Walsh, the local Catholic priest came to Australia from County Cork, Ireland, in 1886 and to the Gatton parish in 1887. He remained there until the end of his ministry, 52 years later. He had the solemn task of burying the Murphy siblings and providing comfort to the family. Rumour has it that he heard the confession of the killer but could not act upon it. He died aged 81 on 25 September 1939 and following a Requiem Mass at St. Stephen's Cathedral, Brisbane, his body was returned for a mass in the Gatton Church and he was buried in Gatton Cemetery. Record crowds attended his funeral.[57]

Parents, Daniel and Mary Murphy: Mary Murphy (nee Holland) died 24 years after her three children were murdered, aged 78 in 1922. Daniel Murphy died five years after his wife, Mary, in 1927, aged 84.[58]

The Murphy sons and daughter:

Polly (Mary McNeil nee Murphy) and her husband William McNeill: Polly never regained good health from her partial paralysis and died in July 1904,[59] just six years after the death of her two sisters and brother. She was 38 and was survived by her two children, Beatrice and Daniel,[60] and her husband. Widower, William, received a bravery award in 1917 for saving a child from the sulky of a bolting horse. He died in 1950 aged 80 in Kingaroy.

Daniel Murphy (Jr.) – after the murders, Daniel took a month's leave from his police constable role, then requested another month's leave and thereafter resigned. He worked the farm with his brother William, and in 1905, aged 29, he married Violet Mary Fielding. They had four children. Daniel died in 1959, aged 83.[61]

Patrick Murphy remained with his family and lived on the farm. He died in 1947 aged 73.[62]

Jeremiah (Aloysius) Murphy married in 1915 aged 37 to Beatrice Ann Meehan and became a father and grandfather. He died in August 1952, aged 74. Beatrice died 12 years later.[63]

John Murphy, the youngest son, married Margaret Joyce in 1908 when he was 25 years old, and died on 12 November 1928, aged 45.

William Murphy continued to farm the land at the family home and died in 1953, aged 85, and **Catherine (Katie) Murphy** was the last direct link with the family until her death in 1974 aged 89.[64]

Murphy family descendant, Dennis Coutts, told ABC's *Australian Story* that "the brothers and sisters of those murdered and the next generation would not talk about it. They had to deal with the immediate aftermath of a murder, they'd come to the breakfast table in the morning and there's two or three chairs, vacant. Now the next generation which is James and myself and our cousins, we didn't talk about it either."[65] It is understood relatives still live in the area.

Finding Norah, Ellen and Michael Murphy's grave:

In the tidy graveyard in Gatton, you will find the burial site of Ellen, Norah and Michael. The gravestone was donated by the people of Gatton with funds raised by public subscription.

Enter the cemetery from Lake Apex Drive at the northern end and follow the paved path. Walk in approximately 45 metres and the Murphy's grave is one row in from the path on your left. It is marked by a large cross. Hard to miss.

References:

1 From the Vault – The Gatton Murders, 26 December 1898, *Queensland Police Media*, 15 October, 2013. Retrieved 25 March 2019 from URL: https://mypolice.qld.gov.au/museum/2013/10/15/from-the-vault-the-gatton-murders-26-december-1898/
2 - 3 Bennett, Stephanie, *The Gatton Murders*, Pan Macmillan Australia, 2004.
4 - 5 The Gatton Tragedy. (1899, January 7). *The Queenslander (Brisbane, Qld.: 1866 - 1939)*, p. 23 (Unknown). Retrieved March 27, 2019, from http://nla.gov.au/nla.news-article20854960
6 - 7 Section IX. —School Work. (1894, July 21). *Queensland Times, Ipswich Herald and General Advertiser (Qld: 1861 - 1908)*, p. 6. Retrieved March 25, 2019, from http://nla.gov.au/nla.news-article123758438
8 The Gatton Tragedy. (1899, January 7). *The Queenslander*, p23. Op.cit.
9 - 10 Gatton Tragedy. Magisterial Inquiry. (1899, March 17). *The Week (Brisbane, Qld.: 1876 - 1934)*, p. 12. Retrieved March 28, 2019, from http://nla.gov.au/nla.news-article182867935
11 Bennett, Stephanie, *The Gatton Murders*. Op.cit.
12 Agriculture on the Downs. —VII. (1901, January 2). *The Brisbane Courier (Qld.: 1864 - 1933)*, p. 6. Retrieved March 27, 2019, from http://nla.gov.au/nla.news-article19117702
13 From the Vault – The Gatton Murders. Op.cit.
14 The Gatton Tragedy. (1899, Jan 7). *The Queenslander*, p23.Op.cit.
15 Murder near Gatton. (1898, December 31). *The Queenslander (Brisbane, Qld.: 1866 - 1939)*, p. 1283. Retrieved March 27, 2019, from http://nla.gov.au/nla.news-article20854804
16 General News. (1899, January 14). *The Queenslander (Brisbane, Qld.: 1866 - 1939)*, p. 52. Retrieved March 27, 2019, from http://nla.gov.au/nla.news-article20855162
17 Bennett, Stephanie, *The Gatton Murders*. Op.cit.
18 - 20 Bennett, Stephanie, *The Gatton Murders*. Op.cit.
21 The Gatton Tragedy. (1899, January 7). *The Queenslander*. p.23 Op.cit.
22 Bennett, Stephanie, *The Gatton Murders*. Op.cit. .
23 The Gatton Tragedy. (1899, January 7). *The Queenslander*. p.23 Op.cit.
24 Gatton Tragedy. Magisterial Inquiry. (17 Mar 1899). *The Week* p. 12. Op.cit.
25 From the Vault – The Gatton Murders, 26 December 1898. Op.cit.
26 The First Discovery of the Bodies. (1899, January 6). *Albury Banner and Wodonga Express (NSW: 1881 - 1895)*, p. 4. Retrieved March 30, 2019, from http://nla.gov.au/nla.news-article99731831
27 - 28 Bennett, Stephanie, *The Gatton Murders*. Op.cit.
29 The Gatton Tragedy. (1899, Jan 7). *The Queenslander (Brisbane, Qld.: 1866 - 1939)*, p. 4. Retrieved March 27, 2019, from http://nla.gov.au/nla.news-article20854938
30 Gatton Tragedy. Magisterial Inquiry. (17 Mar 1899). *The Week* p. 13. Op.cit.
31 - 32 The Gatton Tragedy. (1899, January 7). *The Queenslander*, p.4. Op.cit.
33 GATTON TRAGEDY. (1899, March 25). *The Queenslander (Brisbane, Qld.: 1866 - 1939)*, p. 524. Retrieved March 31, 2019, from http://nla.gov.au/nla.news-article20857882

34 Kyriacou, Kate, Cold case murder: Deaths of Michael, Norah and Ellen Murphy still a mystery 120 years on, *The Courier-Mail*, 16 Nov 2018. Retrieved 31 March 2019 from URL: https://bit.ly/2M7AOZH
35 Gatton Tragedy. Magisterial Inquiry. (17 Mar 1899). *The Week* p. 14. Op.cit
36 - 37 The Gatton Tragedy. (1899, January 7). *The Queenslander.* p.23 Op.cit.
38 Gatton Tragedy. Magisterial Inquiry. (17 Mar 1899). *The Week* p. 13. Op.cit.
39 General News. (1899, January 14). *The Queenslander (Brisbane, Qld.: 1866 - 1939)*, p. 52. Retrieved March 27, 2019, from http://nla.gov.au/nla.news-article20855162
40 Bennett, Stephanie, *The Gatton Murders.* Op.cit.
41 The Gatton Tragedy. (1899, January 7). *The Queenslander,* p.4. Op.cit.
42 The Gatton Tragedy. (1899, January 7). *The Queenslander.* p.23 Op.cit.
43 Gatton Tragedy. Magisterial Inquiry. (17 Mar 1899). *The Week* p. 12. Op.cit.
44 Gatton Tragedy. Magisterial Inquiry. (17 Mar 1899). *The Week* p. 13. Op.cit.
45 The True History of the Hideous Gatton Murders. (1926, June 27). *Truth (Brisbane, Qld.: 1900 - 1954)*, p. 23. Retrieved March 30, 2019, from http://nla.gov.au/nla.news-article199287088
46 From the Vault – The Gatton Murders. Op.cit.
47 The True History of the Hideous Gatton Murders. *Truth*, p. 23. Op.cit.
48 From the Vault – The Gatton Murders. Op.cit.
49 Lilley, Merv, *Gatton Man,* McPhee Gribble, 1994.
50 When Blood Runs Cold, Australian Story, *ABC,* 17 June 2013. Retrieved 28 March 2019 from: https://www.abc.net.au/austory/when-blood-runs-cold/9169984
51 When Blood Runs Cold, Australian Story, *ABC.* Op.cit.
52 General News. (1899, January 14). *The Queenslander (Brisbane, Qld.: 1866 - 1939)*, p. 52. Retrieved March 27, 2019, from http://nla.gov.au/nla.news-article20855162
53 General News. (1899, January 14). *The Queenslander,* p. 52. Op.cit.
54 From the Vault – The Gatton Murders. Op.cit.
55 - 56 Bennett, Stephanie, *The Gatton Murders.* Op.cit.
57 52 Years at Gatton. (1939, Sept 28). *Queensland Times (Ipswich, Qld.: 1909-1954)*, p6. Retrieved 1 April 2019 from http://nla.gov.au/nla.news-article114183405
58 A Lockyer Pioneer (1927, June 8). *The Telegraph (Brisbane, Qld.: 1872 - 1947)*, p. 3. Retrieved March 30, 2019, from http://nla.gov.au/nla.news-article180100885
59 General News. (1904, July 18). *The North Queensland Register (Townsville, Qld.: 1892 - 1905)*, p. 4. Retrieved March 31, 2019, from http://nla.gov.au/nla.news-article85566435
60 The Players, The Gatton Murders, retrieved 31 March 2019 from URL: http://www.gattonmurders.com/theplayers.pdf
61 - 63 Family history research service, *Queensland Government*, retrieved from URL: https://www.familyhistory.bdm.qld.gov.au/
64 The Players, The Gatton Murders, Op.cit.
65 When Blood Runs Cold, Australian Story, *ABC.* Op.cit.

Images:

Poulsen, Poul C. [photographer], Norah Murphy studio image, published courtesy of Mike Fitzpatrick. Retrieved 29 March 2019 from Flickr at URL: https://www.flickr.com/photos/piedmont_fossil/39989131971

Newspaper portrait of Ellen, aged 13, provided by her parents to the *Toowoomba Chronicle*: MURDER. (1898, December 31). Toowoomba Chronicle and Darling Downs General Advertiser (Qld.: 1875 - 1902), p. 3. Retrieved March 29, 2019, from http://nla.gov.au/nla.news-article218990866

Portrait of Ellen Murphy aged 18. Image No. PM0758 courtesy of the Qld Police Museum. Retrieved 29 March 2019 from: https://mypolice.qld.gov.au/museum/2013/10/15/from-the-vault-the-gatton-murders-26-december-1898/

Michael Murphy, aged 29. Image No. PM0759 courtesy of the Queensland Police Museum. Retrieved 29 March 2019 from: https://mypolice.qld.gov.au/museum/2013/10/15/from-the-vault-the-gatton-murders-26-december-1898/

Unidentified (1898). Murphy family from Gatton, ca. 1898. John Oxley Library, State Library of Queensland. Retrieved 29 March 2019 from URL: https://trove.nla.gov.au/version/47910283

The Murphy's residence, Gatton, 1898. Image No. PM0757, Queensland Police Museum. Retrieved 29 March 2019 from URL: https://ehive.com/collections/3606/objects/553807/the-gatton-murders

The area in which the Gatton murders took place. Image No. PM1027 Courtesy of the Queensland Police Museum. Retrieved 29 March 2019 from URL: https://mypolice.qld.gov.au/museum/2013/10/15/from-the-vault-the-gatton-murders-26-december-1898/

The funeral, 28 February 1898. Image No. PM0761 Courtesy of the Queensland Police Museum. Retrieved 29 March 2019 from URL: https://mypolice.qld.gov.au/museum/2013/10/15/from-the-vault-the-gatton-murders-26-december-1898/

Brother-in-law William McNeil: The Gatton Tragedy. (1899, January 7). *The Queenslander (Brisbane, Qld.: 1866 - 1939)*, p. 23 (Unknown). Retrieved March 27, 2019, from http://nla.gov.au/nla.news-article20854960

Inspector Frederic Urquhart. Image No. PM0785, courtesy of the Queensland Police Museum. Retrieved 29 March 2019 from: https://mypolice.qld.gov.au/museum/2013/10/15/from-the-vault-the-gatton-murders-26-december-1898/

The swansong of Miss Ella McGoldrick

Interred: **Ella McGoldrick**, 1886– 26 November 1916 (aged 30).*

Location: Roman Catholic, OLD1-005-0003.

Cemetery: Drayton and Toowoomba Cemetery, Anzac Avenue and South Street, Toowoomba, QLD 4350.

(*Some sources list Ella's age at death as 26 but Ella's birth and death certificate list Ella's age as 30 years of age).[1]

Soprano, Ella McGoldrick, 1916. Source: The Bulletin.

It was a Sunday morning, just after 10am on 26 November 1916, a delightful day, and a day off for a group of young friends who ventured to Manly, NSW, for a picnic at Queenscliff headland. The party of four included brother and sister, Mr Pritchard and Miss Rita Pritchard, Mr George Mitchell and Toowoomba's own, Miss Ella McGoldrick, aged 26.

After finishing lunch on this warm November Sunday, the four young people sought to get out of the wind. Rita and her brother ventured down the road to find a more sheltered spot. George recalled that after a time Ella said: "I will look and see whether I can see them."[2] He recalls that Ella "stepped on to a ledge to look below"[3] and as she went to step down beside him, he took her hand to assist. But in "stepping down she caught her heel in a crag" and lost her balance.

George grabbed hold of Ella but the weight was too great for him to hold.[4] She fell backwards to the rocks below – a distance of nearly 60 feet [18 metres]. Other witnesses confirmed that it seemed like Ella "sprang towards Mr Mitchell, and landed on the ledge, but the momentum caused her to overbalance."[5]

Her distraught friends ran to assist her, and George on reaching her, held her hand. A doctor was summoned and Ella was conscious for a brief time, telling George "I feel sick" and struggling to rise before becoming unconscious.[6] On his arrival, Dr George Barron of Manly found "that Miss McGoldrick had sustained a serious wound in the base of the skull. There was no hope of her recovery, and she passed away shortly afterwards in the presence of the little party."[7] The coroner held an inquiry in Sydney a few weeks after Ella's passing, declaring her death accidental.[8]

The sheer Queenscliff cliffs and headland, 1920. Source: Northern beaches Council Library Local Studies.

A life of potential

The McGoldrick name was well known to many residents of Toowoomba; Ella was celebrated as a talented, full of life young star of the music scene. With her powerful soprano voice, she had many sold-out performances and had completely filled the Toowoomba Town Hall at one performance.[9] Ella's brother, the Reverend Father William Stuart McGoldrick of St. Stephen's Cathedral,[10] was also known and respected in the Catholic community. Ella had two other brothers, Harry and Joseph, and a married sister, Mrs (Charles) Moore.[11] The family originally heralded from Dalby where her father once worked as a saddler and was a proprietor at the Old Royal Hotel.[12]

Ella had moved to Sydney for her profession. Not content with just singing up a storm, her great ambition was to perform in a grand opera, and she worked hard towards achieving her goal. Ella undertook formal training to develop her voice, a voice that the media described as 'rich, powerful, soprano'.[13] It was exciting times for Ella as she resided in Cremorne[14] in Sydney, making new friends, and studying under Signor di Giorgio.[15]

She was said to be "of a sweet and lovable nature, and was ever ready to use her talent for patriotic purposes",[16] as the First World War was underway and the Government was working hard at encouraging young men to sign up, after the devasting and brutal reality of our Gallipoli campaign. A concert in July of that year was a fundraiser to build homes for returned soldiers.[17]

HIS MAJESTY'S THEATRE.

MONDAY, OCTOBER 2.

MISS ELLA McGOLDRICK,

Assisted by

Signor V. DE GIORGIO, and other Sydney Artists, will give a Vocal Recital.

PRICES : 4/ (Reserved), 3/, 2/, and 1/.

A performance notice two months before Ella's death. Source: Brisbane Courier.

Coming home

The day that started so happily ended in tragedy so quickly and the shocking news was relayed to Ella's parents of Neil Street,[18] family, friends and colleagues, and the Toowoomba community. Ella's body was brought home on the mail train from Sydney to Harristown and escorted by the two gentlemen who were with her at the picnic in the last hours of her life – Mr Pritchard and Mr George Mitchell.[19]

Ella's brother, Harry, joined the train at Wallangarra (just over two hours south of Toowoomba)[20] and family friend, Reverend Father Cashman was also on board for Ella's last journey. At the station, many people had gathered to pay their respects and floral tributes were abundant. Ella's brother, Reverend Father McGoldrick, was present at the funeral but did not conduct the service.[21]

Ella's brother, Reverend Father McGoldrick. Source: Darling Downs Gazette, 1911.

The newspaper of the day described Ella's passing as a: "tragic occurrence which robbed Queensland of the most promising soprano the State has ever produced."[22] Only one month prior to her death, Ella had returned home and performed a concert in Brisbane and Toowoomba. The newspaper reviewed it in glowing terms:

"In these days, when there is so much to perplex and harass it was a welcome relief to enter the serene atmosphere of Her Majesty's Theatre last night, and enjoy the recital provided by Miss Ella McGoldrick and her talented company.... Her voice is of... sweet velvety texture, and it was evident, that she had paid considerable attention to the art of expression, which enabled her to translate the varying sentiments and emotions of her songs in Italian and English."[23]

And the public agreed on the loss of their shining star. Her coffin overflowed with flowers and her family erected a significant monument at her gravesite. The newspaper reported: "This untimely death of one so promising in her profession, and so well-known and loved in a large circle in Toowoomba, has cast a gloom over the whole town."[24]

How to find Ella's grave in Roman Catholic section OLD1-005-0003, Drayton and Toowoomba Cemetery:

Enter through the Anzac Avenue gate and turn left once inside the cemetery. At Fifth Avenue, turn right. Ella's grave is almost immediately on your right, behind a large mausoleum for a young boy, Roy Coorey.

Floral tributes overflow on Ella's grave. Source: The Queenslander.

References:

1 Family Notices (1916, December 9). *Independent* (Footscray, Vic.: 1883 - 1922), p. 2. Retrieved May 15, 2019, from http://nla.gov.au/nla.news-article74255760

2 Miss McGoldrick's Death. (1916, December 11). *Warwick Examiner and Times (Qld.: 1867 - 1919)*, p. 5. Retrieved May 15, 2019, from http://nla.gov.au/nla.news-article82805954

3 - 4 Ibid

5 Late Miss Ella McGoldrick. (1916, November 29). *Daily Standard (Brisbane, Qld.: 1912 - 1936)*, p. 6 (second edition). Retrieved May 13, 2019, from http://nla.gov.au/nla.news-article181090449

6 Miss McGoldrick's Death. (11 Dec 1916). *Warwick Examiner and Times.* Op. cit.

7 Late Miss Ella McGoldrick. (1916, November 29). *Daily Standard (Brisbane, Qld.: 1912 - 1936)*, p. 6 (2nd ed). Retrieved May 13, 2019, from http://nla.gov.au/nla.news-article181090449

8 Miss McGoldrick's Death. (11 Dec 1916). *Warwick Examiner and Times.* Op. cit.

9 - 10 The Week in Brisbane (1914, March 12). *The Catholic Press (Sydney, NSW: 1895 - 1942)*, p. 28. Retrieved May 13, 2019, from http://nla.gov.au/nla.news-article104989710

11 Miss Ella McGoldrick. (1916, November 27). *Darling Downs Gazette (Qld.: 1881 - 1922)*, p. 4. Retrieved May 14, 2019, from http://nla.gov.au/nla.news-article183262621

12 Personal. (1916, Nov 29). *The Dalby Herald (Qld: 1910-1954)*, p.3. Retrieved 14 May 2019 from http://nla.gov.au/nla.news-article215124789

13 The Week in Brisbane (1914, March 12). *The Catholic Press* p.28. Op.cit.

14 A Singer Killed. (28 Nov 1916). *The Advertiser (Adelaide, SA: 1889-1931)*, p. 9. Retrieved 13 May 2019 from http://nla.gov.au/nla.news-article5538962

15 Miss Ella McGoldrick. (27 Nov 1916). *Darling Downs Gazette*, p.4. Op.cit.

16 Red Cross Notes (1916, December 3). *Sunday Times (Sydney, NSW: 1895 - 1930)*, p. 27. Retrieved May 13, 2019, from http://nla.gov.au/nla.news-article121344642

17 Homes for Soldiers' Recital. (1916, July 24). *The Sydney Morning Herald (NSW: 1842 - 1954)*, p. 4. Retrieved May 14, 2019, from http://nla.gov.au/nla.news-article15702974

18 Miss Ella McGoldrick. (27 Nov 1916). *Darling Downs Gazette*, p.4. Op.cit.

19 Late Miss Ella McGoldrick. (29 Nov 1916). *Daily Standard (Brisbane, Qld. 1912-1936)*, p.6 (2nd ed). Retrieved 13 May 2019 from URL: http://nla.gov.au/nla.news-article181090449

20-22 Ibid.

23 A Toowoomba Songstress, (1916, October 4). *Darling Downs Gazette (Qld.: 1881 - 1922)*, p. 6. Retrieved May 14, 2019, from http://nla.gov.au/nla.news-article183259975

24 Sad Death of a Queensland Singer Miss Ella McGoldrick. (1916, December 2). *The Western Champion and General Advertiser for the Central-Western Districts (Barcaldine, Qld.: 1892 - 1922)*, p. 6. Retrieved May 14, 2019, from http://nla.gov.au/nla.news-article77787292

Images:

Ella McGoldrick [image] Vol. 37 No. 1921, p18 (7 Dec 1916). *The Bulletin*. Retrieved May 15, 2019, from http://nla.gov.au/nla.obj-658849362

Queenscliff beach 1920 [photograph], image ID: 60856. Image courtesy of Northern beaches Council Library Local Studies.

Performance notice: Advertising (1916, September 29). *The Brisbane Courier* (Qld.: 1864 - 1933), p. 2. Retrieved May 13, 2019, from http://nla.gov.au/nla.news-article20124923

Reverend Father William McGoldrick: Brilliant Scholar. (1911, December 22). *Darling Downs Gazette* (Qld. : 1881 - 1922), p. 5. Retrieved May 27, 2019, from http://nla.gov.au/nla.news-article180620296

Floral tributes at Ella's funeral: photographer unidentified, *The Queenslander*, p27, Queenslander Pictorial, Supplement to *The Queenslander*, 9 December, 1916. Retrieved 15 May 2019 from URL: http://hdl.handle.net/10462/deriv/315455

Ella McGoldrick [photo *pictured right*]. A Brilliant Songster. (1916, October 7). *Darling Downs Gazette* (Qld. 1881 - 1922), p. 3. Retrieved May 13, 2019, from http://nla.gov.au/nla.news-article183260546

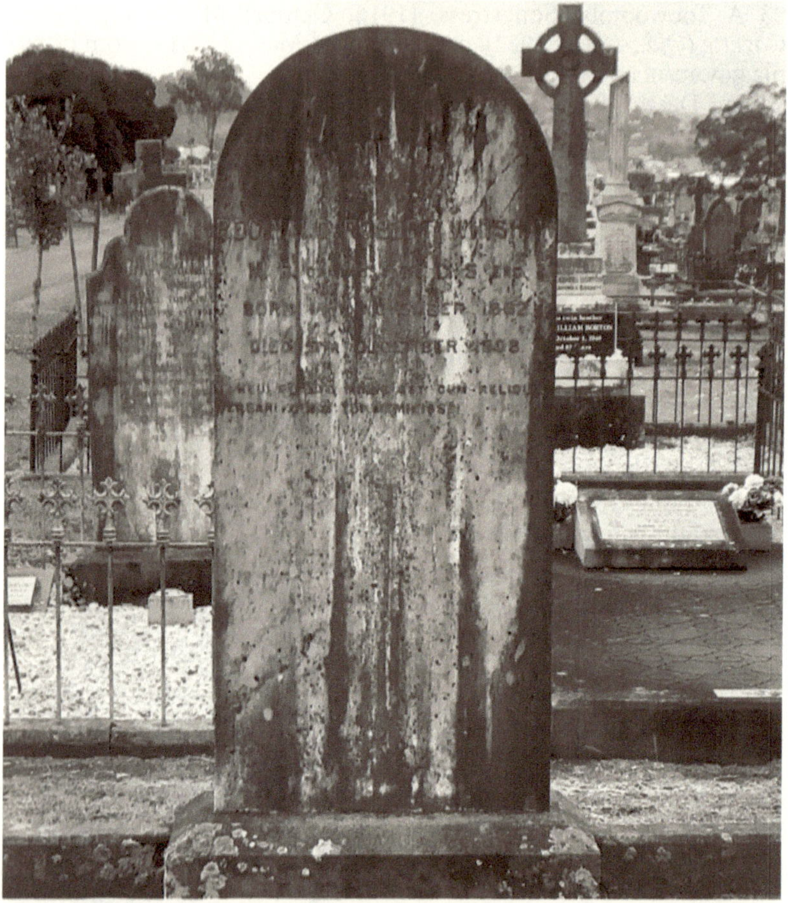

IN LOVING MEMORY OF
THE QUEEN OF EULO
ISOBEL GRAY
NEE ROBERTSON – ISLE OF MAURITIUS
1851 – 7 AUGUST 1929
AGED 78 YEARS
MAY YOU REST IN PEACE
LONG LIVE THE QUEEN

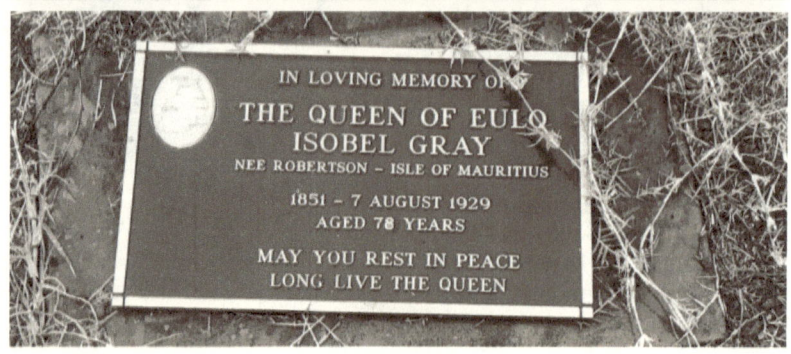

The residents at the asylum
Dr Reginald Whishaw & Isobel Gray

Interred: **Dr Reginald Whishaw,** 14 November 1862 – 8 December 1908 (aged 46).
Location: Section CE 1, Block 3.

Interred: **Isobel Gray** also known as Isabel Richardson, 'Eulo Queen', 1851– 7 August 1929 (aged 78).
Location: PUBLIC 1-048-0072.

Cemetery: Drayton and Toowoomba Cemetery, Corner Anzac Avenue and South Street, Toowoomba, QLD 4350.

Little Helen McDonald was six years old when her family came to live at the Willowburn Mental Asylum in Toowoomba in 1918, or the Lunatic Asylum, as it was known. Her father was Dr James Edward Fancourt McDonald, and up until now, he had been practising in Stanthorpe. But all that was about to change and the asylum was to be the new home for Helen, her two older siblings and her mother. It was an unconventional life to say the least, but not to a six-year-old with little blueprint of what was conventional.

The McDonalds arrived along with their furniture—branded *L.A., T'BA.*, an abbreviation of Lunatic Asylum, Toowoomba—and it was unpacked by capable patients who worked in the carpenter's shop (oddly, their occupation therapy was making coffins). Helen, sharing some of her memories with the Baillie Henderson Mental Health Museum,[1] recalls that she liked the house from day one with its "large vine-covered pergola outside the kitchen… three large bedrooms and one smaller one… a very large dining room and a pleasant drawing room and all the main rooms had good fireplaces… a large porcelain bath and hand basin, and a Malley chip heater which not only gave abundant hot water but heated the whole bathroom!"[2]

Dr James Fancourt McDonald. Kindly supplied by Dr McDonald's grandson, Mr Paul Vellacott. Sourced by Stephanie Johnson.

Dr McDonald, his family, Medical Superintendent Dr Nicol, the carpenters, nurses and orderlies went about their daily duties living and working on the same grounds as the patients.

There may be a fine line between a diagnosis of sanity and insanity, as the Rosenhan experiment of the 1970s illustrated. In this experiment, eight 'sane' people including psychologist, David Rosenhan, went undercover by presenting signs of mental distress and anxiety; they spoke of hallucinations and fears. They were all admitted and remained in the hospital for an average of 19 days. When discharged all eight of the subjects were "diagnosed with signs of schizophrenia (or depression) in remission"[3]. Two notable 'take-outs' from this experiment were that Rosenhan "showed the stigmatising power of psychiatric labels [such as insane] and the inability of psychiatric staff to distinguish normality from supposed abnormality."[4]

In the early 1900s, the Bailie Henderson Lunatic Asylum and other institutions of similar nature were challenged with understanding and treating such disorders. Young Helen's tales of living on the same grounds as the patients, many of whom were actively involved in daily duties, illustrates the understanding even then that as some of the patients were quiet but troubled souls, it was only fitting to show latitude. They were given some freedom and responsibility and it all assisted in their rehabilitation to re-enter the world.

The poet Edgar Allen Poe reflected: "Men have called me mad; but the question is not yet settled, whether madness is or is not the loftiest intelligence – whether much that is glorious – whether all that is profound – does not spring from disease of thought – from moods of mind exalted at the expense of the general intellect."[5] And many of the characters that came and went in Helen's life during her time at the 'Lunatic Asylum' were intellectual and creative people.

Life and latitude

For a young girl, her new surrounds must have been imposing with two-storey structures and dark bricks. The female wards were divided into categories for violent patients, long-term or chronic 'inmates' and those patients soon to be discharged, as all patients were certified, not voluntary.[6] Opposite the women's wards were the men's wards starting at A-Ward for the most violent patients continuing to 'F' ward. There was a church, hospital,

Baillie Henderson – then named Willowburn Hospital for the Insane, 1899. Reprinted with kind permission from the Toowoomba Historical Society and Local History and Robinson Collections, Toowoomba City Library.

nurses' quarters and a hall where dances and recitals were often held for the patients.⁷ And so it was that Helen recalls during her time at the asylum, that after breakfast, patients according to their level of stability went about their business, some "working in the kitchen or the sewing room, the carpenter's shop or the vegetable garden, or the farm."⁸

Asylum friends

Amongst the asylum patients were people that Helen and her family would come to call friends as they interacted with them in the house or garden. Helen remembers: "One whom we all loved was Hannah, an Irishwoman from Kanturk, County Cork… she used to imagine that people were leaning down from the sky to talk to her and she would pause in her sweeping to chat back to them!"⁹ Exposing the young girl to history she would not understand for years to come, Helen remembers how Hannah taught her the Irish alphabet: "I can still remember the lines *'E's for old England who robbed us of bread and F's for the Famine she left us instead'*."¹⁰

Minnie, a young aboriginal woman, took Helen for a walk every afternoon and Helen recalls she "would tell me the native names of all the trees, the birds and the insects. Sometimes we would sit down at a little sandy patch along the creek and with her fingers, she would make in the sand the tracks of a kangaroo, an emu, a dingo, or a duck, and teach me to recognise the footprints of all these creatures."¹¹

There was the tall, graceful Madame Meredith, believed to have once been a dressmaker in Paris, who arrived at the sewing room each morning, and worked away until the day ended. Helen remembers "she always wore a very long dress, and on her head wore a frilled cap, tied with a bow under her chin." She would make the patients' dresses and use the material scraps to make artistic dolls.[12]

There was also Isobel Gray—the 'Queen of Eulo'—a well-known publican in the southwest Queensland area. She earned the name as a result of ejecting an unruly drinker and "dismissing his arguments by roaring: 'I'm the Eulo queen – now get out!'"[13] The name stuck!

Isobel led a colourful life; she was thrice-married, was known to the courts for unlawfully supplying liquor, liked a gamble and trading opals and often entertained lavishly in her bedroom. But as Eulo's importance faded—an opal slump and bypass transport options—Isobel's fortune faded too. By 1926, widowed and living in poverty, she became a resident of the Willowburn Mental Hospital and died there on 7 August 1929[14] aged 78.

But not every patient was manageable and there would always be risk, as Dr Whishaw, who was murdered by a patient would experience. This was a decade earlier than Helen and her family's arrival.

Eulo Queen, Isobel Gray, 1920.
Source: State Library of Queensland.

Death on duty

It was Monday 7 December 1908, when Dr Reginald Whishaw accompanied by William Davis, Acting Chief Attendant, was conducting his usual morning rounds. Patient, Herbert Coulter,[15] sprang "from behind a door, full of delusions"[16] and struck Dr Whishaw a blow to his head with a water hydrant, fracturing his skull.[17] Unbeknown to anyone, Coulter had been hiding in the tailor's shop. When restrained, he nodded towards Dr Whishaw lying on the ground and said: "Leave him alone, he is done."[18] Coulter had only been at the asylum for a few months and "appeared to be a well-educated man."[19]

Dr Whishaw was 46 years old, a husband and a father to four sons from a previous marriage who lived in Hobart[20]. He hovered between life and death for the day, before doctors declared there was no hope of recovery and he succumbed to his injuries. A Magisterial Inquiry began a week after and William Davis, Acting Chief Attendant said the patient, Coulter "was quiet and civil, and well behaved generally, and was, in consequence, allowed a little latitude."[21]

At the time there were over 800 asylum patients and around 70 staff. The inquiry closed after several days. Dr Whishaw was replaced and his large portrait

Dr Reginald Whishaw, 1908. Source: The Brisbane Courier.

joined that of several others hanging on the wall of the Medical Superintendent's office. Who can tell what set off Herbert Coulter that morning. Who can say what caused the patients' minds to close down or to make them retract into themselves. Perhaps it was a safer world there for them to occupy?

Today at Baillie Henderson

Today, the Baillie Henderson Hospital continues its work as a specialist psychiatric hospital offering care to patients with mental disorders.[22] It underwent a number of name changes including Toowoomba Mental Hospital (or Willoburn) from 1940 to 1963; Toowoomba Special Hospital from 1963 to 1968; and in 1968 it was renamed the Baillie Henderson Hospital in honour of Dr John Hector Baillie Henderson. Dr Henderson worked at the hospital for over thirty years and was made a Commander of the British Empire in the Queen's New Year's Honours List 1969 "for his untiring and devoted service to the mentally ill."[23]

What became of...

Dr James Edward Fancourt McDonald: Helen's father died aged 43. The newspaper notice read that Dr McDonald died "at his residence, 15 Curzon St., Toowoomba, on Monday, 3rd May, 1954, suddenly."[24]

Helen McDonald: At 24 years of age, Helen married Geoffrey Vellacott on 12 March 1935 in Toowoomba. They had two sons, Paul and Edward, but eight years after their marriage, tragedy struck and Geoffrey died as a prisoner of war on the Thai-Burma Railway on 19 December 1943, leaving Helen a widow, at 32. Geoffrey is buried in the Kanchanaburi War Cemetery in Thailand.[25]

Post-war, in 1950, Helen, 39, went to study at Cambridge in England and completed a post-graduate qualification from the University of London.[26] She went on to make an enormous contribution to the community as the foundation Vice-President for the War Widows' Guild of Australia.

In 1959, aged 48, Helen inherited from her grandfather, the family home 'Talerddig' in Castlemaine, Victoria.[27] Two years later she became a Councillor in Castlemaine, establishing the area's first social welfare program for the aged. In later years, 'Talerddig' became the hub of many gatherings for the Australian Lancia Register of which son, Paul, remained a lifelong enthusiast.

Vellacott Street in Canberra was named in honour of Helen and her tireless contribution[28] and she also left her mark, authoring several books. Helen died in 2003, aged 91, and was survived by her two sons.

It was a big life with a colourful and unconventional start in the residence of the asylum.

1934, beautiful Helen McDonald.
Source: The Courier-Mail.

How to find Dr Reginald Whishaw's grave in Section CE 1, Block 3 of the Drayton and Toowoomba Cemetery:

Enter through the Anzac Avenue gate and turn right once inside the cemetery. Travel about 80 metres until you come to the first bitumen road off to the left. Turn left and travel down about 20 metres and Dr Wishaw's grave is on the end of the sixth row down on your right.

How to find Isobel Gray's grave in Public Section 1-048-0072 the Drayton and Toowoomba Cemetery:

Continue down the same avenue that Dr Whishaw's grave is in (details above). Travel down about 200 metres until you come to the end of the area marked as Public Section 43-48. Turn left and Isobel's grave is almost immediately on your left by the side of the road.

References:

1 -2 Vellacott, Helen, Some Memories of Willowburn, *Baillie Henderson Mental Health Museum*, 19 July 2010. Retrieved 15 April 2019 from URL: http://bailliemuseum.wikidot.com/willowburnmemories
3 - 4 Jarrett, Christian, Textbook Fail: Rosenhan's classic "On Being Sane In Insane Places" covered without criticism, from *The British Psychological Society Research Digest*, 20 Feb 2017. Retrieved 23 April 2019 from: https://digest.bps.org.uk/2017/02/20/textbook-fail-rosenhans-classic-on-being-sane-in-insane-places-covered-without-criticism/
5 Poe, Edgar Allan, *The Complete Tales and Poems of Edgar Allan Poe*, published 15 Aug 1984 by Doubleday & Company, Inc. (first published 1849), USA.
6 - 12 Vellacott, Helen, Some Memories of Willowburn, *Baillie Henderson Mental Health Museum*, 19 July 2010. Retrived 15 April 2019 from URL: http://bailliemuseum.wikidot.com/willowburnmemories
13 - 14 Shrimpton, James, Outback saga of the Eulo Queen, *Sydney Morning Herald*, 27 Sept 2006. Retrieved 23 April 2019 from: https://www.smh.com.au/lifestyle/outback-saga-of-the-eulo-queen-20060927-gdojlp.html
14 Ibid.

15 An Asylum Sensation (1908, December 16). *The Evening Telegraph (Charters Towers, Qld. : 1901 - 1921)*, p. 4. Retrieved April 15, 2019, from http://nla.gov.au/nla.news-article213986837
16 Vellacott, Helen, Some Memories of Willowburn. Op.cit.
17 Ibid.
18 The Willowburn Sensation. (1908, December 16). *The Brisbane Courier (Qld. : 1864 - 1933)*, p. 5. Retrieved April 15, 2019, from http://nla.gov.au/nla.news-article19554434
19 An Asylum Sensation. (1908, December 16). Op.cit.
20 The Willowburn Sensation. (16 December 1908). Op.cit.
21 Ibid.
22 Baillie Henderson Hospital, Queensland Health, *Queensland Government*. Retrieved 23 April 2019 from URL: https://www.health.qld.gov.au/services/darlingdowns/ddowns-baillie-hosp
23 Thomson, Eileen, Rev., *Baillie Henderson Hospital: A Century of Care 1890 – 1990*, Baillie Henderson Mental Health Museum, 13 July 2010. Retrieved 23 April 2019 from URL: http://bailliemuseum.wikidot.com/the-centenary
24 Family Notices (1954, May 5). *The Courier-Mail* (Brisbane, Qld. : 1933 - 1954), p. 24. Retrieved May 31, 2019, from http://nla.gov.au/nla.news-article50604504
25 Sourced by *Grave Tales'* researcher, Stephanie Johnson from *ancestory.com*
26 - 27 Ibid.
28 Widows' News, Street to be named for war widow, *Australian Government Department of Veterans' Affairs,* Vol 31 No.2 Winter 2015. Retrieved 31 May 2019 by *Grave Tales'* researcher, Stephanie Johnson,
from URL: https://www.dva.gov.au/about-dva/publications/vetaffairs/vol-31-no2-winter-2015/widows-news

Images:

Dr James Fancourt McDonald. Source: Kindly supplied by Dr McDonald's grandson, Mr Paul Vellacott. Sourced by Stephanie Johnson.
Willowburn Hospital for the Insane, Toowoomba (Qld) [picture]: 1899. Reprinted with kind permission from the Toowoomba Historical Society and Local History and Robinson Collections, Toowoomba City Library. Retrieved 8 May 2019 from URL: https://toowoomba.spydus.com/cgi-bin/spydus.exe/ENQ/OPAC/BIBENQ?BRN=482646
Unidentified (1920). Eulo Queen. John Oxley Library, *State Library of Queensland*. Retrieved 23 April 2019 from URL: https://trove.nla.gov.au/version/167824931
Image of Dr Whishaw: Two New Railways. (1908, December 11). *The Brisbane Courier* (Qld. : 1864 - 1933), p. 5. Retrieved June 12, 2019, from http://nla.gov.au/nla.news-article19553587
Announcement of Helen's engagement: Lismore Show (1934, November 28). *The Courier-Mail* (Brisbane, Qld. : 1933 - 1954*)*, p. 22. Retrieved May 24, 2019, from http://nla.gov.au/nla.news-article35648036

IN LOVING MEMORY OF
WALTER MACPHERSON
TREVETHAN
LOVED FATHER OF

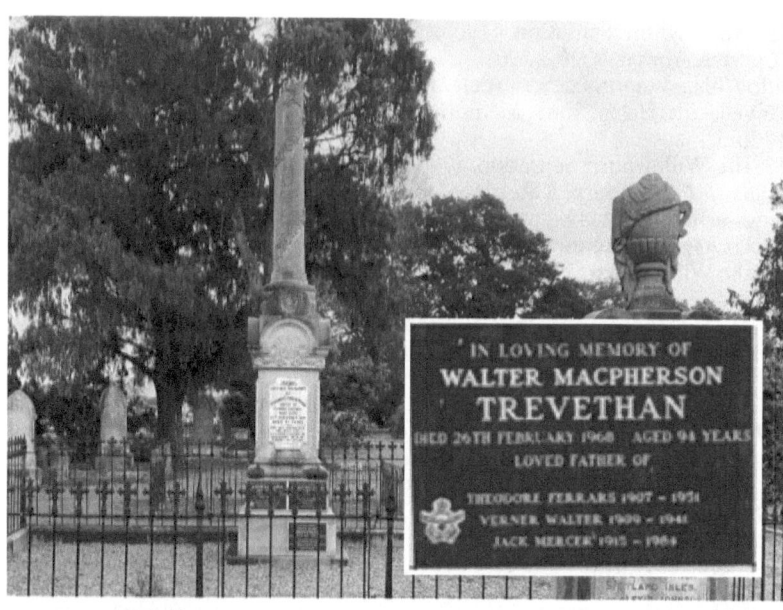

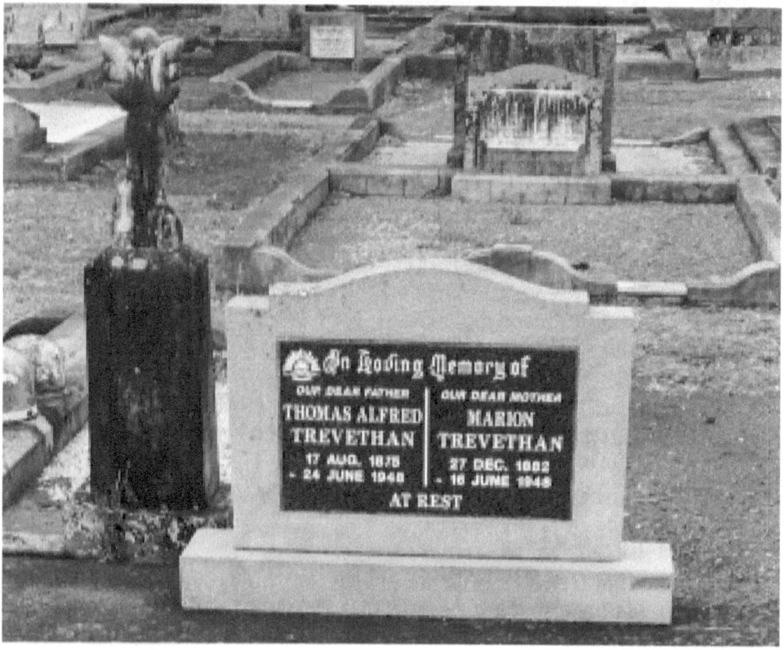
In Loving Memory of
OUR DEAR FATHER
THOMAS ALFRED
TREVETHAN
OUR DEAR MOTHER
MARION
TREVETHAN
AT REST

The Toowoomba terror: the first Queensland-made car
The Trevethan brothers

Interred: **Walter MacPherson Trevethan**, 15 September 1873 – 26 February 1968 (aged 94 years).

Location: BaptCong 1-005-0033.

Interred: **Thomas Alfred Trevethan**, 17 August 1875 – 24 June 1948 (aged 72 years).

Location: PRES 2-008-0013.

Cemetery: Drayton and Toowoomba Cemetery, corner of South Street and Anzac Avenue, Toowoomba, QLD 4350.

Out of the business district, the picturesque streets of Toowoomba around the turn of the 20th century were tree-lined, quiet, relaxed, with nothing to disturb the peaceful pace of life. Ruthven Street even then was the main business area and running parallel to it, Neil Street, which was, unthinkably, to become the place where the device that would spoil the serenity of the town would emerge to frighten children and scare the horses.

Back when the first fleet arrived in what would become known as Australia, the populous of the Great Southern Land increased by 1030 white men and women, 29 sheep, 74 pigs, seven cattle, six rabbits and, vitally, seven horses. And so great was the need for transport and beasts of burden as the nation grew that 100 years later there were 1,501,203 horses in the place.[1] But even by that time, the winds of change were blowing... and not just blowing the smell of the horses' presence through the streets of our

Not a car in sight in Ruthven Street Toowoomba, 1900.
Source: State Library of Queensland.

towns and cities. Just who invented the contraption that would, by the 1920s, put the horse out to pasture is a matter of conjecture but if credit had to go to one person it would almost certainly be Karl Benz in Germany.

The first car?

Many authorities believe the German mechanical engineer created the first true automobile in 1885-86 and some think it may have been even earlier.[2] His vehicle was described as a three-wheeled gasoline automobile powered by an internal combustion engine in which the chassis and engine formed a single unit.[3]

Most of the early cars in Australia were European imports but local inventors were not far behind… the tyranny of distance, as with many things in this far-flung land, being the great motivator. Amongst those with their hands on the wheel and their eyes on the road was a pair of inventors from Toowoomba, brothers Walter and Thomas Trevethan.

Their father, Thomas Trevethan Snr, was a coach builder, and prominent in the town's civic affairs. He was an alderman and in 1888 was elected Mayor of Toowoomba. Both the would-be motorists worked in the coach building business in Neil Street and it was from the family factory that the Toowoomba cars would emerge.

It is widely accepted that in 1897 a man by the name of Harry Tarrant created what was probably the first petrol driven car made in Australia in a tiny workshop in Melbourne. The vehicle was called the 'Tarrant'. Later he and Howard Lewis, who was a bicycle manufacturer, made a second car using a rear-mounted six-horsepower Benz engine.

But the Toowoomba contestants in the race to get on the road weren't far behind. During 1901-02 the brothers built a car to their own design. It was powered by a six-horsepower engine, was a brute to start and had a clutch that had to be worked sideways, across the car. If it looked like a buggy then that was a reflection of what the company produced. It was only natural that this 'horseless carriage' would be out of a similar mould.

*The Toowoomba terror! The Trevethan's car after completion, 1902.
Source: State Library of Queensland.*

Much ado about the Trevethans

The endeavour did, however, cause great excitement in the town as the *Toowoomba Chronical* reported in 1902: "There is at present in the course of construction at Mr T Trevethan's workshop in Neil Street a motor car. Perhaps some may hardly credit this as being correct but those desirous of proving the fact for themselves will find ample evidence of the truth by a visit to the workshop.

"Of an eminently mechanical bent of mind and gifted with much constructive ability Mr T Trevethan [Thomas Jnr.] has made a study of motor-car building down south and is giving his ideas practical form in response to an order for a car from a local medico." [4]

In his writings Walter Trevethan tells of the early problems with the car: "At the first few trials, we could not get the machine to move. We found out eventually that the low gear was designed to do about 45 miles per hour."[5]

Back to the drawing board

Eventually they got the vehicle going and the first proving run, all the way from Toowoomba to Crows Nest—a bit over 40 kilometres—was half successful. That is to say, the car didn't break down until Walter was on his way back to Toowoomba. He managed to improvise, as early motorists became extremely adept at doing, and got back under the car's own steam.

But it was always going to be an adventure, as Walter related: "My next long trip was to Brisbane. I will never forget the time we had getting over Liverpool Range. We got stuck in some heavy sand, and I stepped out to start up the engine. My friend was to steer straight while I pushed. In leaning over to push and help with the steering, the pin in the crank shaft (used for steering purposes) became entangled in a certain portion of my clothes... fortunately they were not very strong, and though other trouble was averted I arrived in Grandchester minus half my apparel. We must have looked a 'tough' lot, as the publican insisted on £1 [one pound] deposit before he would lend me a pair to continue with. I could fill a book with experiences of the old 'Ly E. Moon' - but enough!"[6]

Peculiar name

Curiously the car was called the *Ly-E-Moon* (or *Ly-ee-Moon*), named after a ship involved in a terrible disaster off the town of Eden in southern NSW. In 1886 the vessel, caught in a ferocious gale, was driven onto rocks and smashed to pieces. There were tales of terrible tragedy from the shipwreck. One woman was dragged from the wreckage by a ship's officer and almost made it onto the nearby reef but was struck by parts of the *Ly-ee-Moon* and killed. When the bow of the ship was torn off 30 passengers were trapped below decks.

The only survivor of those imprisoned was a small boy who had the presence of mind to put his head out through a porthole and was able to breathe. One notable victim of the sinking was the mother of Australia's only saint, Mary McKillop. Seventy-one passengers and crew perished in the sea below the lighthouse at Green Cape. The remains of the 24 whose bodies were found are buried in a cemetery created for them at Green Cape, not far from where the tragedy occurred. This was done as it would have been impossible to take them back to Sydney for burial due to the remote nature of the place. [7] Just why the car was named for the *Ly-ee-Moon* is still a mystery.

Toowoomba comes to grips with this curiosity

In 1902 the Trevethan 'contraption' was still very much a novelty… and even treated with disdain and distrust by residents whose most common observation was that all the car was good for was scaring the horses. When the car made that proving run appearance in Crows Nest, Walter said he even had trouble convincing locals to just sit in the car as they were certain it would blow up.

At the factory, he had daily visits from horse owners asking what day he would be on certain roads so they would be sure to be absent from them on that occasion.[8]

And the roads themselves were nothing to speak of. They were the domain of the horse and buggy and until the arrival of the motor car, all that was needed was a surface good enough to allow a buggy or wagon to be towed across it by a horse or horses at extremely moderate speeds. With cars hurtling along at speeds of up to 45 miles an hour. (72kph) the appalling conditions led to discomfort and break-downs. Men wore goggles and caps, motoring jackets and heavy gloves while women covered their faces with multiple layers of scarves to filter out the dust.

The original Thomas Trevethan's Coach Works was established in 1863 in a building in Ruthven Street. The building was later established in Neil Street, Toowoomba. Source: John Oxley Library, State Library of Queensland.

The industry grows

However, with men like Walter Trevethan at the helm, the car business took off. He became involved with a vehicle and machinery company that sold 'Napier' cars and farm equipment and he became an early voice for the improvement of road conditions in Queensland. By 1907 he was advertising as 'The Trevethan Motor Agency, of Tank Street, Brisbane, and Neil-street, Toowoomba' with a wide range of new cars from 225 pounds and the best quality used cars. Their motto – *The best and the best only.*[9]

In those days, 225 pounds was a lot of money especially when you consider that the 'basic wage' which was introduced in 1907, was £2,2s (2 pounds, 2 shillings) per week... and many workers didn't get that much. But this was a nation with vast spaces and long distances to be conquered and the affordability matter was to be dramatically overcome with the arrival of the 'Tin Lizzie', Henry Ford's world-changer, the Model T Ford in 1908. By 1914 the price of a brand-new Model T was just 210 pounds for the Tourer and 190 for the Runabout as

Obey that urge ! Do it now ! Get a Ford ! It's the one "hunch" on which you can't go wrong. More than 325,000 owners will vouch for FORD merit—Ford simplicity—Ford serviceability—and Ford economy. Obey that urge ! Do it now !

Two hundred and ten pounds is the new price of the Ford touring car, and One hundred and ninety the Runabout. Get catalogue and particulars from—

Sole Importers :

DAVIES & FEHON MOTORS, LTD.,
112-114 Hunter-street, Sydney.
And at Keen-street, Lismore.

*Ford newspaper advertising.
Source: The Land, 1914.*

Napier tourer on its record breaking Brisbane - Toowoomba run, 1912. On board is Walter Trevethan and passengers Will Stevens, H. M. Russell and Frank Hooper. Source: John Oxley Library, State Library of Queensland.

advertisements extolled the virtues of the car that changed the world forever.[10] As Australian living conditions and wages rose, the price of the Model T dropped. By 1926 the price was down to 179 pounds and even more Australians took to the roads in their Model Ts.

Australia on the road

And the 'fathers' of the motoring industry were regarded as celebrities with their every move, especially if it was in a car reported in the press. The *Brisbane Courier* of 26 October 1917 kept its readers abreast of Walter's latest adventure: "On Monday next Mr Walter Trevethan (Chevrolet cars), accompanied by Mrs Trevethan, will leave by motor car for an extended trip through western and south-western Queensland. The route is to Charleville via Toowoomba, Dalby, Roma, and thence to Cunnamulla, Bollon, St. George, Dirranbandi, Inglewood, Texas, Leyburn, and back to Brisbane. Given fine weather, Mr and Mrs Trevethan expect to complete this long trip in three weeks".[11]

Not a bad effort for 1917! And you could almost be sure that following not far behind Walter and his wife would be the third brother now involved in the Trevethan automobile empire, E H Trevethan, who had previously taken to the highways in the north of the state, selling cars as he went.

Life had some tough breaks though for Walter. On 1 January 1942, after he and his wife had moved to the Gold Coast, he was told that his second son, Sergeant-pilot Verner Walter Trevethan had been killed. He was on active service with the RAAF in North Borneo when he died on 18 December 1941.[12]

Walter had a long, proud history in the motor trade in Queensland. He was a foundation member of the RACQ in 1905. He lived until the age of 94 and died at Southport in February 1968.

Thomas Trevethan, very much the engineer with a bent for invention, stayed in the coachbuilding business. Amongst his many creations was the rotary hoe, the patent for which he sold to Sunshine Harvesters in 1910. Thomas lived to 74 and died in June 1948. Both men are buried in the Drayton and Toowoomba Cemetery.

How to find the graves of Walter (BaptCong 1-005-0033) and Thomas (PRES 2-008-0013) in Drayton and Toowoomba Cemetery:

Walter: enter through the Anzac Avenue gate and turn left once inside the cemetery. Travel about 100 metres until you come to the first bitumen road to your right. Turn right and travel down until you reach a point where the road is divided by a palm tree. Walk from here to your right towards the military grave section and you will find the Trevethan grave slightly to your right when you near that section.

Thomas: enter through the Anzac Avenue gate and turn left once inside the cemetery. Travel down to Fifth Avenue and turn right. Continue down the road. Go past Pres 1 section on your right until you come to the Pres 2 sign also on your right. Go to the end of Pres 2 and count back eight rows of graves. The Trevethan grave is 13 in on the left-hand side.

References:

1 The Mayor's Opening Address. (28 Nov 1889). *The Sydney Morning Herald* (NSW: 1842 - 1954), p7. Retrieved 17 May 2019, from http://nla.gov.au/nla.news-article13751197

2 For the Motorist (4 Dec 1930). *Queensland Times* (Ipswich: 1909 - 1954), p4 Retrieved May 17, 2019, from http://nla.gov.au/nla.news-article115373059

3 *Daimler.* Company History Benz Patent Motor Car: The first automobile (1885–1886). Retrieved from URL: https://www.daimler.com/company/tradition/company-history/1885-1886.html

4 Motoring (21 Sept 1927). *Sydney Mail* (NSW: 1912 - 1938), p. 43. Retrieved May 24, 2019, from http://nla.gov.au/nla.news-article158297501

5 - 6 *The Steering Wheel* 1st May, 1916. pp. 39-40 My First Car by W. M. Trevethan (1874 - 1968). Retrieved from URL: https://www.ddvvmc.com.au/files/downloads/library/Trevethan.pdf

7 NSW Office of Environment and Heritage. *Ly-ee-Moon Disaster.* https://www.environment.nsw.gov.au/MaritimeHeritage/researchcentre/lyeemoon.htm

8 *The Steering Wheel*, April 1, 1926 pp. 115, 117, 119, 121, 123. Retrieved from: https://www.ddvvmc.com.au/files/downloads/library/Trevethan.pdf

9 Trevethan Motor Agency. (27 April 1907). *The Queenslander* (Bris, Qld: 1866 - 1939), p29. Retrieved 27 May 2019, from http://nla.gov.au/nla.news-article25977795

10 Advertising (1914, March 27). *The Land* (Sydney, NSW: 1911 - 1954), p. 16. Retrieved May 28, 2019, from http://nla.gov.au/nla.news-article102951501

11 Personal. (1917, October 26). *The Brisbane Courier* (Qld.: 1864 - 1933), p. 9. Retrieved May 28, 2019, from http://nla.gov.au/nla.news-article20194615

12 Two Queensland Airmen Killed (1942, Jan 1). *The Courier-Mail* (Bris, Qld: 1933 - 1954), p3. Retrieved May 28, 2019, from http://nla.gov.au/nla.news-article50151345

Images:

Paladin, Aldo, D.2013. 29620 Queensland Postcards 1900-1911 (Picture: Ruthven Street, Twmba 1900). *State Library of Queensland.*

Creator unidentified [photograph], 1902 Trevethan, the first car made in Queensland. Image ID: 185699, *State Library of Queensland.* Retrieved 4 June 2019 from URL: http://hdl.handle.net/10462/deriv/97216

Line of Motor Vehicles Parked in Front of T. Trevethan's Coachworks Building, Twmba, Ca. 1904: Accession No: 78-3-8. *State Library of Queensland.* Retrieved 4 June 2019 from URL: https://hdl.handle.net/10462/deriv/142747

Ford Advertising (1914, March 27). *The Land* (Sydney, NSW: 1911 - 1954), p. 16. Retrieved May 28, 2019, from http://nla.gov.au/nla.news-article102951501

Napier Tourer on Record Breaking Brisbane - Twmba Run, 1912 (2005). *State Library of Queensland.* Retrieved 4 June 2019 from: https://hdl.handle.net/10462/deriv/138177

The headstones of Emma Webb (left) and Helen Tolmie (right).

The medical history makers
Emma Webb and Helen Tolmie

Interred: **Emma Elizabeth Webb,** 19 December 1863 – 20 April 1949 (aged 85).
Location: Section CE1, Block 3, Allotment 45.

Interred: **Helen (Ella) Tolmie,** 1866 – 27 January 1945 (aged 79).
Location: Presbyterian, No. PRES1-004-0040.

Cemetery: Drayton and Toowoomba Cemetery, Anzac Avenue and South Street, Toowoomba, QLD 4350.

Emma Webb, around. 1900. Reproduced with kind permission from the Local History and Robinson Collections, Toowoomba City Library.

It was business as usual at the Webb bakery on Saturday morning, 11 March 1893. The bread loaves, bread rolls and cakes were in demand as always. Emma, 30, her husband Thomas, 36, and Thomas' brother Henry, 17, ran the bakery in Ruthven Street. Thomas might have been young but he had been apprenticed to the bakery trade since the age of 12,[1] which was quite normal in that era. Emma, like most women of her time, was a practical, hardworking woman. She was the mother of four, lived in a house at the rear of the bakery and worked in the shop.

But on this particular morning, Emma could no longer ignore the severe pain and vomiting she had been experiencing for several days. Emma's appendix was inflamed but in 1893, appendectomies had only been performed in the UK and the USA, and never in Australia. All that was about to change, and 27-year-old Dr Herbert Russell Nolan, a young Sydney University graduate,[2] was just the man to do it. He would be capably assisted by three doctors and a nurse from the Toowoomba Hospital, Miss Helen 'Ella' Tolmie, who would also make history.

Dr Nolan had spent his first years after graduation as a Resident Medical Officer at the Toowoomba Hospital, but the year before Emma's operation, he started his own practice in Russell Street. This was a time when most GPs were also surgeons.[3]

Emma didn't go to the hospital; maybe time did not permit it or home treatments were common, but when Dr Nolan arrived, he realised what needed to be done and the operation was performed on a kitchen table in the Webb family home at the back of the bakery.

The operation

We know what happened when Dr Nolan stepped in as, fortunately, four months after the surgery in July 1893, he gave an account of the incident to the *Australasian Medical Gazette*, that explained his first encounter with Emma and how she came to be the first person in Australia to have an appendectomy.

Summing it up, Dr Nolan said he had called around the afternoon prior and found Emma suffering from great abdominal pain and vomiting.

Above: an interesting photo of second-year medical students, University of Sydney,1886. Dr. Nolan is second from the right in the back row. The first woman medical student, Dagmar Berne, is in the front row. Inset: Dr. H. Russell Nolan. Source main shot: University of Sydney Archives. Inset: Local History and Robinson Collections, Toowoomba City Library.

For some days previously she had been suffering "but had continued to perform her household duties... Late that evening I found her in all the throes of acute peritonitis, with quick pulse, rising temperature, dry skin, and thoracic respiration. Her face wore a very anxious expression, with sunken eyes and pinched nose. After consultation with Dr. E. Roberts it was decided to operate early next morning.

"At 8.30 on the following morning… a tender bulging mass was felt high up. Her condition after this became very critical, and for a time she was in a state of collapse. Chloroform was administered by Dr. Falkiner and with the assistance of Drs. Roberts and Garde, I opened the abdomen… The cause of the trouble soon appeared in the shape of an appendix. This patient is alive today as the result of a prompt operation."[4]

Dr Nolan's only regret was that he had delayed by a few hours that morning to try something else before operating, which only caused additional pain and distress. And so it was, that in the back of a bakery in Toowoomba, 30-year-old Mrs Emma Webb became Australia's first ever person to have her appendix removed.

Miss Tolmie, on hand

While Dr Nolan and Emma were making history, so too was a young nurse who assisted at the historic operation, Miss Helen 'Ella' Tolmie.

Ella was a trailblazer on many levels. Heralding from Scotland as a child, she was the first nurse to commence training when it was introduced at the Toowoomba General Hospital in 1889. She spent most of her nursing career at the

Toowoomba General Hospital rising to the level of matron.⁵ But in 1893, it was 27-year-old Ella Tolmie on hand assisting with an appendectomy operation, with an equally young doctor, that made history.

Helen 'Ella' Tolmie, who assisted at the first ever appendectomy operation in Australia, and went on to have an amazing nursing career. Kindly supplied by the Toowoomba Historical Society.

What became of…

Emma Webb (nee Hooper): Emma outlived everyone who was present at her surgery, dying in 1949 aged 85. When asked in 1944, 51 years after the operation, what she remembered, Emma recalled: "A lot of boiling water, a lot of carbolic and a lot of fuss."[6] Today the Toowoomba Hospital remembers the significant part Emma played in national medical history – the main building of the Toowoomba Hospital is named the *Emma Webb Building* in her honour.

The Webb family's bakery: Thomas and his younger brother, Henry, dissolved their bakery partnership after a few years. Henry remained in retail but later became Mayor and one of Toowoomba's longest-serving alderman. He married, had three children and died aged 77 in 1936.[7] As a large landowner, Henry donated land to the city of Toowoomba for Webb Park in Dudley Street.[8] Thomas, Emma's husband, died 18 January 1928, aged 71. He is buried in the Anglican section of the Drayton & Toowoomba Cemetery.

Dr Herbert Nolan: Emma's surgeon and a progressive man, Dr Nolan left Toowoomba to fight in the Boer War.[9] He survived despite suffering from typhoid and returned home to specialise in ear, nose, eye and throat complaints, becoming an Honorary Nose and Throat Surgeon on the staff of the Royal Prince Alfred Hospital in Sydney in the early 1900s.[10] Dr Nolan, a husband and father of three sons, died in Sydney on 3 February 1915, aged 49.[11]

Nurse Ella Tolmie: Ella nursed in Toowoomba for most of her life. She was the matron of the Toowoomba General Hospital from 1897-1917 and was a founding member of the Mothers' Hospital Committee. Ella did leave Toowoomba for a while with a view to serving overseas during the war. She enlisted in October 1918 aged 53, but the need at home was much greater and she took up a post at the Military Hospital at Kangaroo Point, Brisbane. Toowoomba beckoned however and Ella eventually returned, acquiring St Andrew's Private Hospital on the corner of Clifford and Herries Street. Here she stayed until retiring in 1942, dying after a short illness three years later on 27 January 1945, aged 79.

How to find Emma Webb's grave in Section CE1, Block 3, Allotment 45, Drayton and Toowoomba Cemetery:

Enter through the Anzac Avenue gate and turn right once inside the cemetery. Travel about 150 metres until you come to the C of E 1 sign on your left and turn left. Continue down the path about 20 metres and the Webb grave is six in on the left-hand side.

How to find Helen (Ella) Tolmie's grave in Presbyterian, No. PRES1-004-0040, Drayton and Toowoomba Cemetery:

Enter through the Anzac Avenue gate and turn left once inside the cemetery. Travel down to Fifth Avenue and turn right. Continue down the road until you come to the start of Pres1 section on your right. The Tolmie grave is 11 rows down and just off the path to your right. It is partially covered by an overhanging tree. There are two Helen's in this grave plot, so scan down the headstone to find the Helen featured in this story.

References:

1 Toowoomba Regional Council, *Toowoomba City Council Mayors*, 16 April 2018. Retrieved 8 May 2019 from URL: http://www.tr.qld.gov.au/our-region/history/past-mayors/11431-toowoomba-city-mayors
2 Clarke, Drury, Dr., *The first appendicectomy in Australia was performed at Toowoomba in the colony Of Queensland*, 27 April 1978. Retrieved 8 May 2019 from URL: https://bit.ly/2LDwQrM
3 - 4 Ibid.
5 Toowoomba Regional Council, *Helen (Ella) Tolmie - medical pioneer*, 15 July 2015. Retrieved 8 May 2019 from URL: http://www.tr.qld.gov.au/our-region/history/notable-characters/125-helen-ella-tolmie-medical-pioneer
6 Clarke, Drury, Dr., 27 April 1978. Op.cit.
7 Toowoomba Regional Council, *Toowoomba City Council Mayors*, 16 April 2018. Op.cit.
8 Clements, John, Emma Webb, *Lives and Times of Downs Folk*, 2001. Retrieved 8 May 2019 from URL: http://downsfolk.wikidot.com/emma-webb
9 Australia's First Appendicectomy (1944, October 3). *Morning Bulletin (Rockhampton, Qld. : 1878 - 1954)*, p. 3. Retrieved May 8, 2019, from http://nla.gov.au/nla.news-article56318728
10 Clarke, Drury, Dr., 27 April 1978. Op.cit.
11 Ibid.

Images:

Emma Elizabeth Webb, Toowoomba, ca. 1900 [picture], BRN: 310291. Reproduced with kind permission from the Local History and Robinson Collections, Toowoomba City Library. Retrieved 8 May 2019 from URL: https://toowoomba.spydus.com/cgi-bin/spydus.exe/FULL/OPAC/BIBENQ/18697191/2966419,1?FMT=IMG

Second Year Medical Students 1886, published with the kind permission of the University of Sydney Archives, ID: G3_224_0007. Retrieved 8 May 2019 from URL: http://sydney.edu.au/arms/archives/media/me_objects/4

Dr H. Russell Nolan. Image kindly supplied from the Local History and Robinson Collections, Toowoomba City Library.

Helen 'Ella' Tolmie [image]. Kindly supplied by the Toowoomba Historical Society. http://www.toowoombahistory.org.au/

The March of the Dungarees
Private Victor Denton

Interred: **Private Victor Denton**, 14 August 1894 – 13 June 1915 (aged 20 years).

Location: Gravesite unknown (somewhere on the Gallipoli Peninsula, Turkey). Memorial at Nobby Cemetery.

Cemetery: Nobby Cemetery, 86 Mount Kent Boundary Road, Nobby, QLD 4360.

As Melbournians took the tram home from work on the evening of Friday 7 August 1914, had they opened their copy of the *Herald* and turned to page 14 they would have seen two pieces that summed up Australia's position when it came to involvement in what would be erroneously called 'the war to end all wars'. In the centre of the page was a story which announced: "Great North Sea Battle Won by British Fleet". In obvious excitement, the piece boldly reported 80 German sailors were captured with no British casualties.

Next to that story was a letter from the British Secretary of State for the Colonies accepting Australia's offer of military support with the words: "His Majesty's government gratefully accepts the offer of your Ministers (sic) to send a force of 20,000 men to this country."[1]

He added he would be glad if the force could be despatched as soon as possible. World War I had begun.

For many, this was excitement in the offing and with an invitation to get involved. The recruitment offices were overrun with young men desperate to enlist before the fighting was over. Preference was given to men who were good horsemen and handy with a rifle. They had to be unmarried, between 20 and 40 years old and at least five foot six inches tall (171cm). By the end of 1914, 52,561[2] young men had joined up but an amazing one-third[3] of all those who applied were rejected on medical grounds and for many of those it was a devastating blow.

The push is on

Pressure from their mates, expectation from their families and the constant barrage from politicians via the media put immense pressure on young men to comply, to do the right thing, to support 'Mother England' and sign up. If they were seen in the streets of towns and cities, while their peers were on ships on the way to war, assumptions were often made before questions were asked and they were branded as cowards or handed a white feather by women in the streets – a sign of cowardice.

As author Bill Gammage says in his book, *The Broken Years*: [One man] "was told that his eyesight was defective and was twice turned away before a £2 [two pounds] tip facilitated his passage into the Australian Infantry Force. Rejected men stumbled in tears from the tables, unable to answer sons or mates left to the fortunes of war. They formed an association and wore a large badge to cover their civilian shame. Those who sailed against Turkey were the fittest, strongest, and most ardent in the land."[4]

These badges were issued to medically unfit volunteers to prevent them from being handed white feathers, a sign of cowardice, by women in the streets. This badge was worn by Guy Marten Berry. He volunteered twice for active service and was rejected. Guy Berry was accepted for military service in late 1916, and sadly was killed in service in 1917. Source: State Library of Victoria.

Victor Denton, taken 4 October 1914 in Brisbane on the day Victor enlisted. Kindly provided by the Denton family and descendant, Trish Wearne, in memory of Victor and his niece, Alice Denton who never forgot him. Sourced by Stephanie Johnson, via ancestory.com

Among the throng that besieged recruiting offices around the nation was a young man by the name of Victor Denton. He was listed in some records as a 20-year-old stockman, in others as a blacksmith. He was six feet tall (183cm) and one of four Denton brothers who lived near the small Queensland town of Nobby. Victor signed up on 4 October 1914. He became part of the 2nd Light Horse Regiment, one of three regiments of the First Light Horse Brigade.

The regiment had been raised at Enoggera, Brisbane, in August 1914 and sailed for the Middle East in September. Victor, and presumably others who were listed as 'reinforcement for Light Horse Regiment', left Australia from Sydney on 20 December on board *HMAT A42 Boorara*. We know little of his movements until he turned up in Gallipoli in May 1915. And when he did turn up it was in one of the most dangerous places in the Dardanelles, Monash Gully.

The Valley of Death

The 2nd Light Horse Regiment was sent to Gallipoli after the initial ANZAC landings and arrived there without its horses on 12 May 1915. The unit largely served in a defensive capacity although it was involved in one disastrous charge on enemy lines in which the initial assault wave of troops was mown down. The men of the regiment were scattered below the sandy hillsides up which they had to battle to reach the Turkish defenders. The Turks, on the other hand, held safer positions on the ridges where they could pick off Australian soldiers using snipers and machine guns. They were deadly and ingenious, even developing a round grenade nicknamed 'cricket ball' by Aussie troops, that could be rolled down the steep valley sides to take out soldiers.[5]

And Monash Gully had no respect for rank. Major General Sir William Throsby Bridges, who was instrumental in establishing the Royal Military College Duntroon and was the commander of the Australian troops on Gallipoli, was shot and severely wounded as he attempted to make his way up Monash Gully. Despite warnings of the danger the General was hit in the right leg by a sniper's bullet. The round severed major arteries in his thigh and gangrene set in. He died three days later on a hospital ship on the way to Cairo.

This is where Victor ended up. We are not sure exactly where he was when a bullet—in all probability also from a sniper's rifle—smashed into his chest. The service record card amongst the military paperwork of 618 Private Victor Denton is a brief, cold and thankless record of the life of the boy from Nobby from when he set sail for the Great War. It simply says:

Embarked at Sydney per A42 "Forty Two" on 20/12/14.
31/5/15 Killed in action, Gallipoli Pen.
31/5/15 Wounded seriously, Monash Valley
13/6/15 Died of wounds
13/6/15 Buried by Chaplain G Green at Hilside Cem. Anzac.[6]

Victor's record, p60. Source: National Archives of Australia.

The cost of war

The Gallipoli campaign was brutal and the death toll was horrendous. It didn't take long for all involved to realise there would be no victory, no triumphant march into the Ottoman Empire capital, Constantinople. It was a staggering reversal of expectation. At first, there was enthusiasm, excitement, and bravado. Now the number of dead, wounded and crippled for life, even after just a few months, sent a chill through average Australians who had seen their boys go off to war.

In May 1915 there were scenes at Gallipoli that were the stuff of nightmares. The enemy troops of the Ottoman Empire launched a massive attack on the ANZAC lines employing 42,000 of their troops. They were beaten back – 10,000 of their soldiers died. On May 24 an armistice was declared from 7.30am to 4.30pm during which time Turkish and ANZAC dead were gathered from where they were killed, and buried.

It was the month when both General Bridges and Victor Denton died from their wounds and the nation lost 2298 dead. At that rate, it wouldn't be long before almost everybody in this country of just under five million people knew someone who suffered loss, be it a son, a husband, a brother, or uncle. The August 1915 death toll was 2666 and by January 1916, when the last Australian was out of the place, the Dardanelles Campaign had cost us 8709 dead and 17,260 wounded, gassed or suffering shell shock. There were also apparently 70 Australians captured at Gallipoli.[7]

In October 1915 Australian journalist Keith Murdoch had visited Gallipoli at the request of Prime Minister, Andrew

Fisher. He described the Gallipoli campaign as: "One of the most terrible chapters in our history" and added "What I want to say to you now very seriously is that the continuous and ghastly bungling over the Dardanelles enterprise was to be expected from such a general staff as the British Army possesses ... the conceit and self-complacency of the red feather men are equalled only by their incapacity." [8]

Had we had come a long way from the position Andrew Fisher held when he gave an election speech in July 1914 and said: "Australians will stand beside the mother country to help and defend her to our last man and our last shilling?"[9]

No doubt the sentiments of most Australians lay with the 'mother country', but patriotic rhetoric was wearing thin. Maybe the real feelings about the loss of life and management of our troops were reflected in the recruitment numbers after the Gallipoli death rates became known.

Route march recruitment

It was estimated that Australia needed to provide 5300 men every month to maintain its overseas forces at an operational level. However it became obvious that by 1916 there would not be enough volunteers turning up at recruitment stations to meet our commitment to the English war machine, despite height and fitness standards being reduced.

In mid-1915 state-based parliamentary recruitment committees had been formed anticipating the possibility of recruitment numbers falling and after some embarrassing monthly quota shortfalls the committees, which were now operational in towns and shires, tried something new.

They introduced the 'snowball' march which they thought would encourage eligible men in rural towns to follow the example of those marching and 'Fall-in' – that is enlist. The first of the marches started in Gilgandra in central NSW. The 'Gilgandra snowball' as it was dubbed was heading for Sydney and by the time it got there, its numbers had swelled from 20 to some 300. This march was later known by the somewhat more patriot name as the *Coo-ee March*.

Norman Lindsay's 1918 Fall-in! poster. Source: National Library of Australia.

The Dungarees recruitment march led by an army band, passing through Ipswich en route to Brisbane, 1915. Source: Australian War Memorial.

But not everyone agreed they were what was needed. The *Brisbane Courier* commented: "the slacker, who is equally fit in physique and unencumbered, but is not amenable to such promptings, remains unaffected by all the clamour for volunteers. Should he escape his responsibilities because he is too lethargic or too craven to shoulder the weight of them?"[10]

More than just a march

After Gilgandra began its quest to raise a 'snowball army', the *Singleton Argus* reported: "The proposal to march a company of recruits from Gilgandra to Sydney – 320 miles – has been taken up with much enthusiasm and the Premier is communicating with all the other recruiting associations in the state suggesting that they initiate similar route marches. The recruits commenced their march on Sunday."[11]

The marches also provided means by which other Australians could feel they were part of the war effort. Farmers put up their hands to plant, tend and harvest the crops the volunteers would normally have done on their own properties; to look after their cattle, their fences and dams. Along the routes, local communities fed and housed the men. The marches gained huge publicity drawing more attention to the issue in the cities which, after all, probably provided the bulk of volunteers. The total number of marchers was only about 1500[12] but the contribution they made to the recruitment issue was invaluable.

Even their names helped create patriotic fervour – 'The Currajongs', 'The Waratahs', 'The Boomerangs' and 'The Men from Snowy River.' And there was one march that snaked its way across the south west of Queensland – 'The March of the Dungarees' – that would also have a special moment in the little town of Nobby.

Nobby remembers

When the residents of Nobby and surrounds heard of the fate of Victor Denton of the 2nd Light Horse regiment there was stunned disbelief in the town. He was well-known and well-liked in the small community. Like most others who went to war, Victor would never have been able to imagine what lay ahead… just as those who stayed behind could not know either. Enthusiasm, patriotism, or maybe just getting a job, erased any thought that this war would be anything but a great adventure. Everyone in the town expected to see Victor return home with tales of his exploits and close calls, probably marry a local girl and get on with his life.

And even when danger was contemplated, the digger with his rifle and slouch hat was seen as a gallant hero risking his life for King and Country. If he was wounded or worse still, killed, it would be in the face of the enemy or saving his mates.

But the reality was that many good men died from disease: "Dysentery and paratyphoid broke out in an environment where water and sanitation were rudimentary at best. Swarms of flies carried infection from refuse, latrines, and rotting corpses to food being eaten in unwashed mess tins. Hardly the stuff of the recruiting posters. Disease was just as much a threat to the troops as the enemy."[13]

More than 665 Australian volunteers died of disease in the Dardanelles[14] but for Victor Denton it was a bullet to the chest – he lingered on for almost two weeks, finally dying of his wounds on 13 June 1915. His Father, Thomas Denton, was notified and the family left to grieve for their son and brother. There would be no body brought home for burial in the Nobby Cemetery as British military practice dictated soldiers who were killed should be buried where they fell.

But the community in which this family lived was not prepared to leave it at that – to leave Victor Denton, unrecognised. Money was raised by public subscription—donations—and the well-known Toowoomba Masons, Bruce Brothers, engaged to design and craft a memorial to Victor which would stand in the Nobby cemetery.

The memorial was a spontaneous and highly visible reaction by locals to the loss of one of their own. It is believed this was the first memorial in Queensland to an individual who died in the First World War. In time there would be many more substitute graves for young men buried in foreign soil. They were known in the day as 'cenotaphs', which translated literally means, "a monument to someone buried elsewhere, especially one commemorating people who died in a war."[15]

The ironies of war

There are some curious interactions between the people involved in this story. Private Victor Denton, shot and wounded in Monash Gully, would be the first World War I casualty with a cenotaph memorial in Queensland. Major General Sir William Throsby Bridges, the commander of Australian forces in Gallipoli, also shot and wounded in Monash Gully and who died later would be the only

Australian casualty brought home for burial from the hideous war. He is now buried on Mount Pleasant overlooking the Royal Military College, Duntroon.

And the third significant crossing of paths involved the Dungaree marchers who had set off from the Queensland town of Warwick in November 1915. On the third night of their recruitment trek and after 'collecting' 37 willing souls to volunteer, the men spent the night in the small town of Clifton about 50 kilometres south of Toowoomba. The next day's march would take them to Nobby where they had a task above and beyond the recruitment of soldiers. Nobby had already given Victor Denton; Victor Denton had given his life and now these men marching off to war would be asked to honour him as they passed through the town.

Dungarees passing along Ipswich Road, Moorooka, 1915. The Dungarees were marching from Warwick to Brisbane. Source: State Library of Queensland.

As the marchers approached Nobby, they were met on the road by people who lived in the town and together the two parties formed a procession which made its way to the Nobby Cemetery. There Reverend J Elliott unveiled the memorial to Victor. The *Last Post* was played and the assembled people sang *Nearer My God to Thee*.[16] It was a simple yet dignified recognition of one young Australian who died at war.

Lest we forget

The marchers moved on, making their way to Brisbane expecting to be sent to where Victor had died—Gallipoli—but all the Australians had been withdrawn from there by early January 1916. These volunteers would soon hear other foreign sounding names like 'The Somme', 'Verdun', 'Passchendaele' and 'Fromelles'. Places where one in every five of them would die.

Nearly 40 per cent of the Australian male population aged 18 to 44 enlisted during World War I. A total of 331,781 went to the front and of those 60,284 died, 155,133 were wounded, gassed or suffered shell-shock and 4044 were taken prisoner. To put it even more starkly, the Australian casualty rate was almost 65 per cent, some say the highest of all the combatants in the conflict. World War I lasted 1560 days and, on average, every day 38 Australian soldiers like Victor Denton died.[17]

How to find Victor Denton's memorial:

You will find Victor's memorial right in the centre back of the Nobby Cemetery, next to his family's plot. The cemetery is unmissable as you head towards the town of Nobby. It can be very muddy, so go prepared!

References:

1 Australia's Offer Accepted (1914, August 7). *The Herald (Melbourne, Vic.: 1861 - 1954)*, p. 14. Retrieved April 26, 2019, from http://nla.gov.au/nla.news-article242297753

2 A.G. Butler, *Special problems and services: the official history of the Australian Army Medical Services in the war of 1914–1918*, vol. III (Canberra: Australian War Memorial, 1943, p. 889).
https://www.awm.gov.au/articles/encyclopedia/enlistment/ww1#year

3. Enlistment standards, *Australian War Memorial*, Oct 2017. Retrieved 13 May 2019 from URL: https://www.awm.gov.au/articles/encyclopedia/enlistment

4 Gammage, B 2010, *The broken years: Australian soldiers in the Great War*, Melbourne University Publishing, Carlton, Vic. http://ergo.slv.vic.gov.au/explore-history/australia-wwi/home-wwi/rush-enlist

5 Turkish 'Cricket ball' grenade fragments: Lone Pine, Gallipoli, *Australian War Memorial*. Retrieved 13 May 2019 from URL: https://www.awm.gov.au/collection/C117699

6 Your story, Our history, NAA: B2455, DENTON V, c.1914-1920. *National Archives of Australia*. Retrieved 13 May 2019 from URL: https://recordsearch.naa.gov.au/SearchNRetrieve/Interface/ViewImage.aspx?B=3501886

7 Australian Fatalities at Gallipoli, *Australian War Memorial*, March 2017. Retrieved 13 May 2019 from URL: https://www.awm.gov.au/articles/encyclopedia/gallipoli/fatalities

8 National Archives of Australia. *Australia's Prime Ministers*. Andrew Fisher. In Office. Retrieved 18 June 2019 from URL: http://primeministers.naa.gov.au/primeministers/fisher/in-office.aspx

9 Fisher, Andrew. 'To the last man'—Australia's entry to war in 1914, Speech during election campaign, Colac, Victoria. *Parliament of Australia*, 31 July, 1914. Retrieved 13 May 2019 from URL:
https://www.aph.gov.au/About_Parliament/Parliamentary_Departments/Parliamentary_Library/pubs/rp/rp1415/AustToWar1914

10 The "Dungarees." (1915, December 1). *The Brisbane Courier (Qld.: 1864 - 1933)*, p. 6. Retrieved May 11, 2019, from URL: http://nla.gov.au/nla.news-article20072000

11 Recruiting Campaign. (1915, October 12). *Singleton Argus (NSW: 1880 - 1954)*, p. 2. Retrieved April 30, 2019, from URL: http://nla.gov.au/nla.news-article80173779

12 Recruiting Marches 1915-1916, *Australian War Memorial*, October 2017. Retrieved 13 May 2019 from URL: https://www.awm.gov.au/articles/encyclopedia/recruiting_march

13 Anzac voices. *Australian War Memorial*. Retrieved 13 May 2019 from

URL: https://www.awm.gov.au/visit/exhibitions/anzac-voices/life-gallipoli
14 Australian Fatalities at Gallipoli, *Australian War Memorial*. Retrieved 13 May 2019 from URL: https://www.awm.gov.au/articles/encyclopedia/gallipoli/fatalities
15 English Oxford Living Dictionaries. *Cenotaph*. Retrieved 13 May 2019 from URL: https://en.oxforddictionaries.com/definition/cenotaph
16 The "Dungarees." (1915, December 1). *The Brisbane Courier*. Op.cit.
17 Enlistment statistics, First World War, *Australian War Memorial*. Retrieved 13 May 2019 from URL: https://www.awm.gov.au/articles/encyclopedia/enlistment/ww1

Images:

Australia. Department of Defence. (1915). Volunteered for Active Service. Medically Unfit [realia]. *State Library of Victoria,* retrieved 13 May 2019 from URL: http://handle.slv.vic.gov.au/10381/165282

1914, Victor Denton portrait (4 October 1914), taken in Brisbane on the day he enlisted. Kindly provided by the Denton family and descendant, Trish Wearne, in memory of Victor and his niece, Alice Denton, who never forgot him, 2019. Sourced by Stephanie Johnson, via ancestory.com

NAA: B2455, DENTON V., c1914-1920, Your History, Our History, *National Archives of Australia*. p60, Series number B2455. Retrieved 13 May 2019 from URL: https://recordsearch.naa.gov.au/SearchNRetrieve/Interface/ViewImage.aspx?B=3501886

Lindsay, Norman (1918). *Fall-in!* Govt. of the Commonwealth of Australia, Sydney. *National Library of Australia*. Retrieved 13 May 2019 from URL: https://trove.nla.gov.au/version/10567365

Unknown [photograph], The Dungarees recruitment march, led by an army band, passing through Ipswich en route to Brisbane. The Dungarees march commenced in Warwick, Queensland on 16 November 1915... *Australian War Memorial Photograph Collection,* Retrieved 13 May 2019 from URL: https://trove.nla.gov.au/version/252028135

Dungarees Marching along Queen Street, Brisbane, 1915 (2008). Web. *State Library of Queensland*. Retrieved 13 may 2019 from URL: https://hdl.handle.net/10462/deriv/64714

Dungarees Passing along Ipswich Road, Moorooka, 1915 (2008): Accession Number: 79-10-4. Web. *State Library of Queensland*. Retrieved 13 may 2019 from URL: https://hdl.handle.net/10462/deriv/57240

Healing hands, fighting spirit
Sister Elizabeth Kenny

Interred: **Elizabeth Kenny**, 20 September 1880 – 30 November 1952 (aged 72).

Location: See directions at the end of this chapter.

Cemetery: Nobby Cemetery, 86 Mount Kent Boundary Road, Nobby, QLD 4360.

Nurse Elizabeth Kenny, photographed in 1915 as she went to nurse in England during World War I. Source: State Library of Queensland.

T his way is better! Imagine having nursing experience—no formal qualification[1]—and taking on Australia's doctors and medical fraternity with a view that your own methods of treatment for a certain illness was better than their existing methods... meet Sister Elizabeth Kenny. A formidable, practical and clever woman who would challenge the system and save many from a life of disability. Her own life was one of service – unmarried, self-trained and passionate in her belief in her treatments and the nursing profession.

A passion for nursing

Young Elizabeth Kenny, daughter of an immigrant Irish farmer, Michael, and his local wife, Mary, had a limited school education in New South Wales and Queensland. What she learnt about nursing—her chosen career—she learnt on the job. Elizabeth started with voluntary work at a small regional maternity hospital and then in about 1910, when she was 30, began to offer her nursing services for free, working from her family's home at Nobby on the Darling Downs in Queensland. Elizabeth would respond to any request, mount her horse or later, her motorbike,[2] and ride to her patient, tending the ill for no fee.[3]

It was 1911, Elizabeth was 31 when some strange new cases appeared in several infant patients – a form of infantile paralysis. Elizabeth had befriended a Toowoomba surgeon, Dr Aeneas McDonnell, who had once treated her for a broken wrist[4] after falling from a horse. He encouraged her interest in the profession and conferring by telegram, advised her: "Do your best. There is no cure."[5] Treating her patients, Elizabeth applied a hot cloth soaked in a strong infusion to the area.⁶ It did the trick, her patients recovered.

This infantile paralysis would come to be known as polio, one of the most feared and easily spread diseases at the start of the 1900s that affected children and adults.⁷ And this was the beginning of Elizabeth's lifelong passion to help those afflicted with this disease. She would evolve her methods to include physical therapy treatments involving bending and flexing of the joints.⁸ This was in stark contrast to the orthodox method of putting the joints in splints or callipers.

Next, Elizabeth decided she needed premises and opened a small hospital at Clifton, just 11 kilometres (seven miles) from Nobby and just short of 50 kilometres (31 miles) from Toowoomba. But the Great War was impending and Elizabeth wanted to enlist. She called on her friend and advocate, Dr Aeneas McDonnell, to provide a nursing reference and enlisted on 30 May 1915.⁹

Elizabeth found herself a long way from Nobby as a staff nurse in the Australian Army Nursing Service serving on the troopships that brought the wounded home to Australia. Very early on she was hit by shrapnel and sent back to England.¹⁰ On recovering,

Elizabeth's friend and supporter, Dr Aeneas McDonnell and his dog, 1937. Source: Toowoomba City Library.

she returned to duty and spent four years in the army. In 1917 she earned a promotion to Sister and used that title for the rest of her life.

It was a harsh life; on one ship influenza felled all the nursing staff except two, one of whom was Elizabeth. Between them, the two nurses cared for more than 500 wounded soldiers. After the journey, Elizabeth was found to have overtaxed her heart and was discharged as unfit. In March 1919 she returned home just in time to assist with an epidemic of influenza which caused her more heart trouble. She sought treatment overseas including a visit to Lourdes.[11] Eventually, Elizabeth returned to Nobby.

Like many families, the Kennys paid an enormous price in World War I. During her time overseas, Elizabeth lost eleven cousins fighting in the Dardanelles, another 20 were serving on the front and her brother was on General Birdwood's staff.[12]

Inventions and interventions

Back home, life changed for Elizabeth. When a struggling Pittsworth mother ran an advertisement in the *Toowoomba Chronicle* pleading for someone to adopt her daughter, Elizabeth became a mother for the first time. Sadly, advertisements such as this were not a rarity, rather a sign of the times and the struggle to stay afloat with scarce work and little government support.

Young Mary, born 31 October 1916, became Mary Stewart Kenny and came to live with Elizabeth and Elizabeth's mother, whom she would come to call 'Gran'. Mary went to Nobby State School and later received private tuition.[13] Like her adopted mother, she would involve herself in the care and treatment of patients for the rest of her life.

> **WANTED** kind person to adopt two little children—ages six and two. Apply "Mother," care "Chronicle" office 956a
>
> **WANTED** someone to adopt lovely baby girl, three weeks old. Apply 414. 414a

Adoption ads during these tough years were not uncommon and how Elizabeth came to adopt Mary. Source: Toowoomba Chronicle, 1919.

Sister Elizabeth Kenny now applied herself to community work, taking on the first role of president of the Nobby chapter of the Country Women's Association. Noticing a need for an ambulance stretcher that reduced shock for patients in transit, Elizabeth created and patented one in 1927, named the 'Sylvia' – the name of the first patient carried on the stretcher.[14] The newspaper reported that one of "Sydney's famous surgeons remarked that it was the best article of the kind he had ever encountered."[15]

However, throughout this period, the horror that was polio continued to spread. While many patients recovered from it, there were also many young patients who effectively lost the use of limbs and would spend their lives in braces or callipers. There was no cure for it but some drugs combatted the effects. It was spread by contact between people, by nasal and oral secretions – it could enter the mouth and progress through the body. In some cases, patients died if the paralysis affected their breathing.[16]

From her former success with treating polio (infantile paralysis) before the war, Elizabeth took up the challenge again and in 1932 opened a clinic in Townsville to treat patients of this disease and of cerebral palsy – another disease which affects body movement and muscles.[17] Her treatment was "hot baths, foments, passive movements, the discarding of braces and callipers and the encouragement of active movements."[18] She fell out of favour with doctors and masseurs who regarded her treatment as ridiculous and "considered her explanations of the lesions at the site of the paralysis… bizarre."[19]

But Elizabeth was no shrinking violet. A strong woman, now in her fifties, who had spent a lifetime nursing, she was said to have "an obsessional belief in her theory and methods,"[20] and she didn't hold back in her return criticism of her opposers who believed her "recommendation to discard immobilization to be criminal."[21] Elizabeth established another clinic in Brisbane, then in other cities around Australia.

On 8 March 1935, the Director General of Health in Queensland, Sir Raphael West Cilento, was quoted in the newspaper as saying that:[22] "The Queensland Government or myself do not approve or disapprove of Sister Kenny's method. The Queensland Government deputed me to investigate Sister Kenny's claim. Acting on my report, the Government, opened a clinic at Townsville in March, 1934, for the purpose of giving Sister Kenny every opportunity to demonstrate her method. The clinic was established for a two-year period from funds provided by the Home Department until the two-year period expires and a full and detailed report of the results is made. The Government or myself will not say whether the method is a success or not."

However, he went on to say that two reports had been prepared, one by himself and the other by Dr Guinane. His report "was to the effect that Sister Kenny's treatment had improved the health of patients, particularly in regard to their general activity, but not, in any case, had she restored the functions that had been lost by nerve destruction. Dr Guinane believed that all cases treated had improved, some slightly, some considerably" and Sir Raphael Cilento said that Sister Kenny "was doing splendid work and her method to date had shown that the usual thumb and stereotyped treatment of rest and splintering among neglected cases was slovenly and dangerous."[23]

Two days later, following an exhibition in Canberra of her 'moving-picture film' that illustrated the improvement her treatment made to sufferers, Elizabeth secured an audience with the acting Prime Minister, Earle Page. He was impressed with the results and agreed to discuss it with the Health Minister, Mr Hughes, with a view to having Elizabeth's treatment accepted and readily available.

At this time, she was forced to defend herself against a claim that the Director-General of Health in Queensland (Sir Raphael Cilento) was said to be investigating her methods on behalf of the Queensland Government. She corrected this, saying: "I am in possession of a letter written by him dated January 31, 1935, portion of which reads:— 'I was satisfied that you had special ability in the handling of paralysed cases and had done some extremely good work, especially with early cases.' A later paragraph of the letter states: 'I mentioned my agreement to write a text book description of your methods if the Commonwealth authorities approved.' Would Sir Raphael Cilento be foolish enough to write a text book expounding a method of which he did not approve?" she asked.[24]

The believers and condemners

A person with less fortitude might have caved under the pressure that came to bear from the medical community, but for all the disbelievers, she was encouraged and hailed by some medical experts and community members. Grateful parents of now-healthy patients paid Elizabeth's fare to England where she made an impact at Queen Mary's Hospital in Surrey and shocked the establishment with her continued recommendations to get rid of the splinting that was applied to prevent the deformities, and her rebellion against the standard treatment.

On her return home, the contradiction continued – doctors damned her methods, but nevertheless, she was set up in a ward at the Brisbane General Hospital to treat cases.

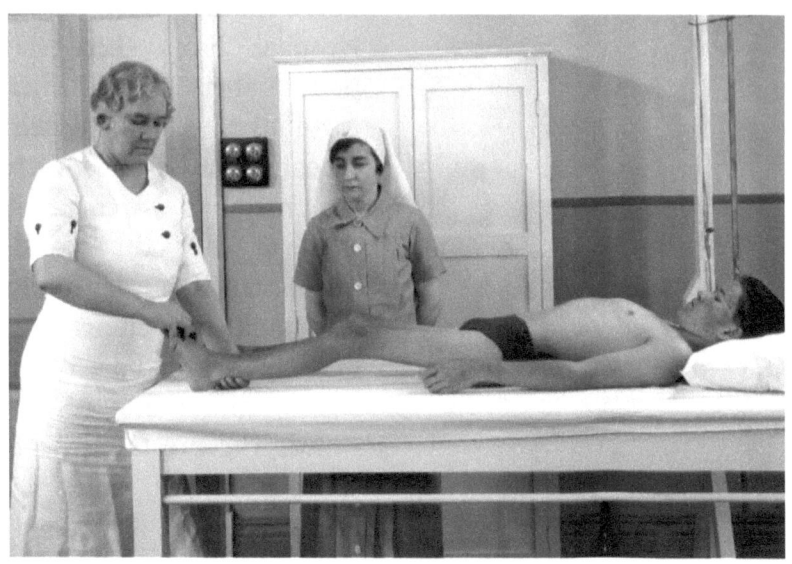

*Sister Elizabeth Kenny demonstrating her therapy, c1939.
Source: State Library of Queensland.*

There, Medical Superintendent, Aubrey Pye, said Elizabeth's patients "recovered more quickly and that their limbs were more supple than those treated by the orthodox method."[25]

In 1940, aged 60, Elizabeth headed to the Mayo Clinic in Minnesota, USA, bearing a letter of support signed by six Brisbane doctors.[26] The Queensland Government contributed 300 pounds to the fare for Elizabeth and her adopted daughter, Mary.[27] She experienced the same reaction from most doctors. In later years she would say that there was no place available to her: "They all said I meant well. They denied me without a trial."[28]

But three orthopaedists organised for Elizabeth to be given access to patients in the Minneapolis General Hospital. From there she proved herself and her methods became widely accepted. She began to teach her methods to medical staff all over the world. The Sister Kenny Institute was built in Minneapolis in 1942 followed by other Kenny clinics around the world. The greatest tribute came from the American President, Harry S. Truman, who conferred on Elizabeth the right to come and go

Sister Kenny encouraging a polio sufferer to stand at the Jersey City Medical Centre (USA). Source: Brisbane Telegraph.

to his country at her will. A public opinion poll "gave her second place to Mrs Eleanor Roosevelt as the most admired and respected woman in the United States."[29]

In these later years of her life, Elizabeth was widely lauded, and awarded with honorary degrees. She went on to write her autobiography, *And They Shall Walk*, published in New York in 1943, and she was portrayed in the film, *Sister Kenny* in 1946. Regardless, respect was still not forthcoming at home. Elizabeth returned to Australia in 1941, 1946, 1947 and 1949 and never to great acclaim. On her return in 1946, she told reporters: "Americans are much less conservative than B.M.A. [British Medical Association] doctors – which means they admit they don't know everything."[30] (Australia's BMA branches formally merged into the Australian Medical Association in 1962). She maintained, however, "I have no quarrel with the doctors but they do now want to understand me."[31]

During these years, Elizabeth's adopted daughter, Mary, now an adult, also travelled the world teaching the techniques pioneered by her mother. Mary was actively involved in managing the Kenny Clinic in Minneapolis and setting up a Kenny Clinic in Winnipeg, Canada. She visited Argentina and Costa Rica, practising in and establishing clinics funded by Reader's Digest. Providing a further treatment service for victims, in 1945 Mary set up rehabilitation centres for paralysed victims in Belgium.[32] It was in England where she met her husband, Stewart McCracken, a returned soldier. They would remain together for the rest of their days. Like her adopted mother, Mary too received numerous awards and honours including a Medal of the Order of Australia in 1997.[33]

Towards the end

Today, thousands of patients all over the world owe a debt of gratitude to Sister Elizabeth Kenny, including American actors Martin Sheen (*Apocalypse Now*, *The West Wing*) and Alan Alda, famed for his work as Hawkeye on the U.S. sitcom *M.A.S.H.* Sheen was struck down as a child and remained bedridden for a year while his doctor applied Sister Kenny's treatment; he retained full use of his legs.[34] Alda developed polio when he was seven. He recalls: "There really wasn't any treatment except Sister Elizabeth Kenny, a nurse from Australia had developed a treatment, which involved very hot wrappings of woollen blankets, almost scaldingly hot, and massage that involved sort of bending your thumb back down behind your back to stretch the muscles. Extremely painful… my parents had no money. They had to do it themselves… I remember being aware at the age of seven of getting ready to pound the bed in pain every two hours."[35]

Elizabeth retired to Toowoomba in 1951. She contracted Parkinson's Disease and the following year she lay critically ill with thrombosis, a blood clot in the cerebral region of the brain. Elizabeth's doctor telephoned Dr Innerfield in New York who had been working on a drug that appeared to dissolve blood clots. A package of the drug, Trypsin, was flown from the United States for her treatment but to no avail.[36] She died on 30 November 1952 and was buried in Nobby cemetery beside her mother. Her funeral procession was one of the largest that Toowoomba had ever seen and her coffin was draped with two flags – the Union Jack and the United States flag.[37] After the priest had concluded, red poppies were thrown into her grave and six soldiers each approached the grave, saluted and said, "Lest we forget."[38]

What became of…

Mary McCracken (nee Mary Stewart-Kenny): Elizabeth's daughter, Mary, died in Caloundra on 1 November 2011, aged 95. She lies with her adopted mother, Elizabeth and grandmother (also Mary) in the Nobby Cemetery. Mary's husband, Stewart died in 2004,[39] they are survived by their children and grandchildren.

Dr Aeneas McDonnell, Elizabeth's friend and supporter, died on 10 August 1939 aged 75. He had been connected to the Toowoomba General Hospital for over 50 years and was an honorary medical consultant at the time of his death.[40]

Polio: Today, a polio vaccine has almost eradicated the disease Sister Elizabeth Kenny spent her life combatting. According to the World Health Organisation, "Polio does still exist, although polio cases have decreased by over 99% since 1988, from an estimated more than 350,000 cases to 22 reported cases in 2017. Only 3 countries in the world have never stopped transmission of polio – Pakistan, Afghanistan and Nigeria."[41]

Fortunately, Sister Elizabeth Kenny lived long enough to receive the acclaim she so deserved.

How to find Sister Elizabeth's grave in Nobby Cemetery:

As you enter through the gate, walk straight towards the back fence of the cemetery. Turn left at the fence, and you will find Sister Kenny's grave in the rear left hand corner of the cemetery. Beside Sister Kenny is her mother and adopted daughter, Mary. It can get muddy if wet so be prepared.

References:

1 Patrick, Ross, 'Kenny, Elizabeth (1880–1952)', 1983, Australian Dictionary of Biography, National Centre of Biography, *Australian National University*. Retrieved 22 May 2019 from: http://adb.anu.edu.au/biography/kenny-elizabeth-6934/text12031
2 Rogers, Kara, Elizabeth Kenny, *Encyclopædia Britannica*, updated 23 April 2019. Retrieved 22 May 2019 from URL: https://www.britannica.com/biography/Elizabeth-Kenny
3 Patrick, Ross, 'Kenny, Elizabeth (1880–1952)'. Op.cit.
4 Rogers, Kara, Elizabeth Kenny, *Encyclopædia Britannica*. Op.cit.
5 The remarkable saga of Elizabeth Kenny (1952, December 1). *Brisbane Telegraph (Qld. : 1948 - 1954)*, p. 5 (STUMPS). Retrieved May 27, 2019, from http://nla.gov.au/nla.news-article217748162
6 Patrick, Ross, 'Kenny, Elizabeth (1880–1952)'. Op.cit.
7 The College of Physicians of Philidelphia, History of Polio (Poliomyeliti), *The History of Vaccines*, 2019. Retrieved 27 May 2019 from: https://www.historyofvaccines.org/content/articles/history-polio-poliomyelitis
8 Rogers, Kara, Elizabeth Kenny, *Encyclopædia Britannica*. Op.cit.
9 Patrick, Ross, 'Kenny, Elizabeth (1880–1952)'. Op.cit.
10 -11 Fighting Infantile (1944, Dec 16). *The Age (Melb, Vic.: 1854-1954)*, p9. Retrieved May 27, 2019, from http://nla.gov.au/nla.news-article205998469
12 (Caption cited) Unidentified (1915). Nurse Elizabeth Kenny photographed in 1915. Originally appeared in The Sydney Mail, 4 August 1915, p. 33 Retrieved 22 May 2019 from John Oxley Library, *State Library of Queensland*, via URL: https://trove.nla.gov.au/version/47943248
13 McVeigh, Hon. Tom, Obituary: Mary McCracken, *The Courier-Mail*, 21 February 2012. Retrieved 27 May 2019 from URL: https://www.couriermail.com.au/ipad/obituary-mary-mccracken/news-story/600f1379ee728b9da440f78c5e77ba79?sv=bce681ff568ebad0d8a9c8166e02722a
14 Rogers, Kara, Elizabeth Kenny, *Encyclopædia Britannica*. Op.cit.
15 "Sylvia" Stretcher (1927, Aug 8). *The Daily News (Perth, WA: 1882 - 1950)*, p1. Retrieved May 27, 2019, from http://nla.gov.au/nla.news-article78747569
16 The College of Physicians of Philidelphia, History of Polio (Poliomyelitis), *The History of Vaccines*, 2019. Retrieved 27 May 2019 from URL: https://www.historyofvaccines.org/content/articles/history-polio-poliomyelitis
17 - 21 Patrick, Ross, 'Kenny, Elizabeth (1880–1952)'. Op.cit.
22 - 23 Sir R.W. Cilento's Statement. (14 Mar 1935). *Western Mail (Perth, WA: 1885-1954)*, p13. Retrieved 27 May 2019 from http://nla.gov.au/nla.news-article38388129
24 Infantile Paralysis. (14 March 1935). *Western Mail (Perth, WA: 1885-1954)*, p13. Retrieved 27 May 2019 from http://nla.gov.au/nla.news-article38388130
25 - 26 Patrick, Ross, 'Kenny, Elizabeth (1880–1952)'. Op.cit.
27 - 31 The remarkable saga of Elizabeth Kenny (1952, December 1).

Brisbane Telegraph (Qld. : 1948 - 1954), p. 5 (STUMPS). Retrieved May 27, 2019, from http://nla.gov.au/nla.news-article217748162
32 - 33 McVeigh, Hon. Tom, OBITUARY: Mary McCracken. Op.cit.
34 Wikipedia contributors. (2019, May 26). Martin Sheen. In *Wikipedia, The Free Encyclopedia*. Retrieved 27 May 2019 from URL: https://en.wikipedia.org/w/index.php?title=Martin_Sheen&oldid=898936827
35 Public Broadcasting System (PBS), Alan Alda, 2 December 2004. *Tavis Smiley*. Retrieved 27 May 2019 from URL: http://www.pbs.org/kcet/tavissmiley/archive/200412/20041202_alda.html
36 New Drug Being Flown From. U.S. to Treat Sister Kenny (1952, November 28). *Queensland Times (Ipswich, Qld.: 1909 - 1954)*, p1. Retrieved May 27, 2019, from http://nla.gov.au/nla.news-article122028273
37 - 38 Sister Kenny Buried Near Mother At Nobby (1952, December 1). *Brisbane Telegraph (Qld. : 1948 - 1954)*, p. 2 (STUMPS). Retrieved May 27, 2019, from http://nla.gov.au/nla.news-article217748151
39 McVeigh, Hon. Tom, Obituary. Op.cit.
40 Dr. Aeneas McDonnell Dead (1939, August 11). *Maryborough Chronicle, Wide Bay and Burnett Advertiser (Qld.: 1860 - 1947)*, p. 6. Retrieved May 27, 2019, from http://nla.gov.au/nla.news-article151188504
41 Does polio still exist? Is it curable? *World Health Organisation*, March 2018, Retrieved 28 May 2019 from URL: https://www.who.int/features/qa/07/en/

Images:

Unidentified (1915). Nurse Elizabeth Kenny photographed in 1915. Originally appeared in *The Sydney Mail*, 4 August 1915, p. 33 Retrieved 22 May 2019 from John Oxley Library, *State Library of Queensland*, via URL: https://trove.nla.gov.au/version/47943248

(1937). Dr Aeneas John McDonnell and dog. Toowoomba, 1937. Image ID 53394835. Reproduced with kind permission from the Local History and Robinson Collections, Toowoomba City Library.

Adoption ads of the era from: "Advertising" *Toowoomba Chronicle (Qld.: 1917-1922)* 24 Dec 1919: 1. Web. Retrieved 27 May 2019 from: http://nla.gov.au/nla.news-article253042534 / Advertising (1919, June 24). *Toowoomba Chronicle (Qld. : 1917 - 1922)*, p. 1. Retrieved May 27, 2019, from http://nla.gov.au/nla.news-article252916399

Unidentified. Sister Elizabeth Kenny Demonstrating Her Therapy, c1939. Negative no.: 5400, John Oxley Library, *State Library of Queensland*. Retrieved 17 June 2019 from: http://hdl.handle.net/10462/deriv/74822

Encouraging a polio sufferer to stand from: Remarkable saga of Elizabeth Kenny (1952, Dec 1). *Brisbane Telegraph* (Qld.: 1948-1954), p5. Retrieved 27 May 2019, from http://nla.gov.au/nla.news-article217748162

Once upon a wonder horse
Gunsynd: The Goondiwindi Grey
Germain 'Winks' McMicking

Interred:	**Germain Nicholson McMicking**, 23 November 1911 – 9 July 1990 (aged 78 years).
Location:	Section F, Row 2, Plot 13.
Cemetery:	Goondiwindi Cemetery, Cemetery Road, Goondiwindi, QLD 4390.

Times were tough and poverty is no man's friend... but 'Winks' McMicking, a grazier from just out of town had a plan, an idea that might put a few shekels in the coffers. He had had his eye on a grey colt about to be auctioned in Brisbane. But he didn't have the wherewithal to do the deal himself so next trip to town, Goondiwindi, he dropped into the Victoria pub to see if he could round up any other starters in his scheme.

There he ran into two townies, Bill Bishop, who was the local newsagent and Jim Coorey, the town's draper, and also in on the conversation was the publican, George Pippos. Over a beer 'Winks' explained what he had in mind, telling the three others that he had tried to buy the sister of the grey the year before and she had won at her first start. They were all in, each chipped in one thousand dollars... and they were off to the 1969 Yearling sales in Brisbane.

The Victoria Hotel, Goondiwindi, where the syndicate was formed.

A stroke of luck

And what they came home with, having outlaid the bargain basement price of $1300, was ownership of that grey colt 'Winks' had in mind. But how did they get him so cheaply? It seems while the horse had promising but not outstanding breeding, one point that apparently stopped many potential buyers from getting into the bidding, was that he hurt his knee in the float on the way to the sales.[1] That put some buyers off and the Goondiwindi boys were able to pick him up at a fraction of what many thought he might bring.

How did he get his name? Bill Bishop recalls: "When the paperwork came through 'Winks' didn't want his name mentioned. So, he said 'put it in the name of the Goondiwindi Syndicate.' And as soon as he said that I said 'oh, that'll do him for a name, we'll abbreviate that and call it Gunsynd.'"[2] And it was a name that would become forever etched in Australian horse racing history.

Preparing to race

The next step was to get Gunsynd ready for the track and the syndicate gave the colt to trainer Bill Wehlow, a former station manager in the Goondiwindi area who was trying to break into horse training in Brisbane.

Under his guidance the colt, which would become the crowd favourite wherever he ran, won 12 out of 22 starts but, perhaps tellingly, only one major in 1969, the Hopeful Stakes and one in 1970, the Chelmsford Stakes. Punters soon dubbed him the 'Goondiwindi Grey', a nickname that stuck with him all his racing days, and most experts agree it wasn't until he was transferred to track legend Tommy

Smith at Randwick in Sydney that the mighty grey rose to be one of our great turf champions.

Off to the big smoke

That decision, which hit the newspapers in September 1971, was described as a "shock move" and articles carried reports of a possible dispute between Bill Wehlow and Gunsynd's regular jockey, Larry Olsen. Wehlow was quoted as saying he had heard rumours that he would lose the horse from his stable but had no instructions from the Goondiwindi owners.[3] But it was in the hands of Tommy Smith that the four-year-old flourished and what an end to 1971 he had. Looking back, Paul Daffy, writing for Melbourne's *The Age* in 2005, described it like this:

"Gunsynd's run in the 1971 Sandown Cup was the final run of a long campaign. After transferring to the Smith stable early in his four-year-old season, he had six races for wins in three premier mile races – the Epsom, Toorak and George Adams Handicaps – a second in a Rosehill flying and unplaced finishes in the Cox Plate and Caulfield Cup. The Sandown Cup was his seventh race in two months. [Jockey, Roy] Higgins said Sandown's spacious track and uphill straight suited the grey's swooping style. After starting 7-4 favourite, Gunsynd won comfortably. 'I've always said Light Fingers was my favourite horse, but Gunsynd was the most fun,' Higgins said."[4]

The punters' pet

And for that 'fun' and his determination to win, the punters loved him, and his 1972 performances would not have let one of them down – it was a remarkable period for the Goondiwindi Grey. He had five wins in succession including the Futurity Stakes and the Doncaster Handicap. He backed that up by winning the Cox Plate and a third place in the Melbourne Cup, carrying the punishing weight of 60.5 kilograms. Some race-goers reckon the roar as the third-place getter was posted was louder than the one for Piping Lane which won the race carrying 48 kilos. Gunsynd was named the Victoria Racing Club's horse of the year for 1972.

And he didn't ease up in 1973, taking home a consecutive Queen Elizabeth Stakes, a second Rawson Stakes, a Blamey Stakes and an Autumn Stakes. During his time in the hands of Tommy Smith he had 32 starts for 17 victories and only one unplaced finish. A remarkable effort.

He surely was a horse of a different kind. The Goondiwindi Grey was the only horse to win in all east coast capitals, Brisbane, Melbourne and Sydney – he would run anywhere in any conditions and never give up despite some horrendous weights he had to carry under the handicap system of the day.

And a show pony

The crowds at Australian racetracks were entertained by the mighty grey… and not only by his running. On its website the Goondiwindi Regional Council records some of the tricks he got up to: "Some of his lovable traits included, standing stock still at the gate before going out to race refusing to move until the applause reached the required crescendo. He would never give in during a race mostly under crushing weights. Often looking beaten, but when he heard the crowd roaring would raise another effort,

Above: Gunsynd appeared to love the crowd, and to play up to it, and the crowd reciprocated. This photo was taken at his win in the 1972 Cox Plate at Moonee Valley, ridden by Roy Higgins. Source: Fairfax Photographic Archive.

fight back and most times win. It is even said, that after a particularly good victory, Gunsynd would stop in front of the grandstand and bow to the applauding crowd."[5]

And like many Australian sporting heroes, there was even a song about him recorded by Tex Morton:

> "We've cheered him from the grand-stand and
> We've cheered him from the flat,
> We've cheered a little beauty,
> A real aris-to-crat;
> He's never thrown the towel in,
> Been a trier all the way,
> A horse we're really proud of —
> The "Goondiwindi Grey".[6]

It mightn't have been the deepest of ditties, but then how many of them do you hear on the radio? It got the punters' toes tapping and walked out the doors of record shops in such numbers that it became the Australia Performing Rights Association song of the year for 1974.

It's probably true to say that while the town had been in the headlines way back in 1922 when it became the place where scientists flocked to watch the total eclipse of the sun, Gunsynd put Goondiwindi on the map again.

And the mighty colt never lost the support of the town that gave him his name. Goondiwindi locals overloaded the special buses put on for the eight-hour-plus return trip to see him run in Brisbane. When he started interstate, they hired planes. And for those who couldn't make it to the tracks, the Goondiwindi TAB had a special window which only took bets on Gunsynd.[7]

At just about every track he raced at there was memorabilia which included T-shirts, flags, car stickers, posters and postcards, much of it sold for charity. But by early 1973 the racing days of the Goondiwindi Grey were almost over. His retirement was announced and inevitably there had to be that last race. Paul Daffy from *The Age* wrote: "Before his last race, the 1973 Queen Elizabeth Stakes at Randwick, he reportedly walked on to the track and bowed to the crowd in a final salute. The result was a gallant second to Apollo Eleven."[8]

The last race

Then followed a short 'good-bye' tour. At Randwick Racecourse in Sydney, more than 50,000 people turned out for his final appearance on Autumn Stakes day. Brisbane, where he first started racing didn't miss out... quite the contrary in fact. He put on an exhibition gallop at Eagle Farm and there was a Gunsynd Day at Doomben.

And then finally, the marvellous horse went to the town that had given him his name. He was still big news in women's magazines as well. *The Australian Women's Weekly* reported: "It was the Goondiwindi Grey's first real visit to the town which adopted him and which he put on the map. For hours he stood patiently as people flocked to see him – mums, dads, grandmas, teenagers, and swarms of excited children who reached up to pat him. Toward the end of the Hibernian Race Club's program, Gunsynd cantered a couple of furlongs along the dry, dusty track to be presented with a rug in his racing colors (sic) of purple and white 'from the people of Goondiwindi.'"[9]

A statue of the great horse was unveiled in Goondiwindi

in 1974. And the memories still live on. Author and veterinarian Bill Howey, who was a junior committeeman at the Scone Race Club, remembers the day the mighty grey, now out to stud, had his final racecourse appearance at the club's White Park Cup meeting in May 1973. Bill was on duty as a gate attendant: "I recall a young man leaving

Goondiwindi's Gunsynd statue. Source: Wikimedia Commons.

straight after 'Gunsynd' had paraded. 'Now I can die happy that I've seen him, I can go home' he said as he left through the gate. 'Where's home' I asked? 'Far North Queensland' he replied. He had driven 2000kms south and was turning around to do the same thing straight back! Such was the magnetic attraction and captivating appeal of 'Gunsynd'!"[10]

After Gunsynd was sold to stud, the partners in what had been a grand enterprise went their various ways. The man who started it all, the apparently camera-shy Mr McMicking, died in Moree, New South Wales aged 78 in 1990. He was taken home to Goondiwindi and is buried in the local cemetery. Gunsynd died from cancer aged 16 on April 29, 1983. He was inducted into the Australian Hall of Fame in 2005. In 2004 Gunsynd was one of the first 12 inductees on to the Queensland Heritage Icons list, as ratified by the National Trust of Queensland. His fellow icons included Goanna Oil, Bundaberg Rum, the backyard mango tree, and finishing sentences with the word 'hey'.[11]

Gunsynd – what a champion – hey?

How to find Germain 'Wink' McMicking's grave in Goondiwindi Cemetery:

Proceed through the entrance off Cemetery Road, travel about 50 metres and take the bitumen road to the left. Continue for a little over 100 metres and you will come to a parking area on your right. Go to the far end of the parking area, and on your right you will see section F. Walk past the end of section F until you see the section E sign and turn left along the grass path in front of the sign. Germain's grave is about 45 metres along on the left, adjacent to the path.

References:

1 Miller, Simon, Gunsynd: The Goondiwindi Grey, 13 November 2012, John Oxley Library, *State Library of Queensland*. Retrieved 4 June 2019 from URL: http://blogs.slq.qld.gov.au/jol/2012/11/19/gunsynd-the-goondiwindi-grey/

2 Gunders, Peter. Remembering the Goondiwindi Grey, 30 April 2013. *ABC Southern Queensland*. Retrieved 4 June 2019 https://www.abc.net.au/local/photos/2013/04/30/3748530.htm

3 Stable Switch For Gunsynd (1971, September 20). *Papua New Guinea Post-Courier* (Port Moresby: 1969 - 1981), p. 23. Retrieved June 4, 2019, from http://nla.gov.au/nla.news-article250202438

4 Daffey, Paul. Gunsynd's Sandown Cup, 1971, *The Age*, 12 November 2005. Retrieved 20 June 2019 faorm URL: https://www.theage.com.au/sport/racing/gunsynds-sandown-cup-1971-20051112-ge182h.html

5 Goondiwindi Regional Council. Gunsynd. Retrieved 22 June 2019 from URL: https://www.grc.qld.gov.au/visitors/heritage-history/gunsynd

6 *The Goondiwindi Grey*. words by Nev Hauritz, music by Brian Wallace, 1973. Retrieved from URL: https://www.alldownunder.com/australian-music-songs/goondiwindi-grey.htm

7 Daffey, Paul. Gunsynd's Sandown Cup, 1971, *The Age*. Op.cit.

8 Ibid.

9 Goondiwindi Farewells Gunsynd (1973, May 30). *The Australian Women's Weekly (1933 - 1982)*, p. 8. Retrieved June 22, 2019, from http://nla.gov.au/nla.news-article46077017

10 Howey, W.P., Scone Vet Dynasty. Gunsynd. 14 November, 2017. Retrieved 24 June 2019 from URL: http://sconevetdynasty.com.au/gunsynd/

11 Daffey, Paul. Gunsynd's Sandown Cup, 1971, *The Age*. Op.cit.

Images:

The Age Research Library [picture], The Age of Racing, *Fairfax Photographic Archive*, Image ID: FXJ210699. Retrieved 26 June 2019 from URL: https://consumer.fairfaxsyndication.com/archive/94---The-Age-of-2F3XC5U6OJRZ.html

Gunsynd statue (10 December 2017). *Wikimedia Commons*, the free media repository. Retrieved 26 June 2019 from URL: https://commons.wikimedia.org/w/index.php?title=File:Gunsynd_statue.JPG&oldid=271225850.

Edwin's headstone photo supplied by Ann Sainsbury. Source: Find A Grave.

When Goondiwindi helped Albert Einstein
Edwin Fletcher and Florence Monro

Interred: **Edwin Fletcher,** 1882 est. −10 October 1972 (aged 90).
Location: Section D, Row 1, Plot 43.

Interred: **Florence Doreen Fletcher Monro**, 6 June 1904 − 14 June 1992 (aged 88 years).
Location: Section D, Row 4, Plot 10.

Cemetery: Goondiwindi Cemetery, Cemetery Road, Goondiwindi, QLD 4390.

Light bends. That's the truth of it, but once upon a time, it was only a theory. A theory that the student, Albert Einstein came up with when he was 17, and he was keen to prove it. Albert worked on it for years until it became known in 1915 as his *Theory of Relativity*, and when it came time to test it, the town of Goondiwindi in 1922 would play a major part in proving his theory!

Even the unscientific amongst us have probably heard of the embellished story of young Isaac Newton sitting under a tree when an apple fell on his head and thus heralded the theory of gravity. This was about 350 years ago, in 1666. But in 1905, a young Einstein was working as a patent clerk and had a 'miracle year' with what was described as "four groundbreaking scientific papers"[1] including the renowned equation E=mc2 and a theory about that apple falling titled *'The Special Theory of Relativity'*.[2]

So, instead of gravity pulling the apple down, Albert believed it was 'pushed' and that Newton's gravitational pull didn't exist. Imagine having the courage and confidence to propose such a thing when for hundreds of years Newton's theory was unchallenged. And imagine Australia, Goondiwindi in particular, helping to prove this theory. Now Albert Einstein just had to find a way to measure the

Albert Einstein in 1905. Source: Wikimedia Commons

effects of gravity on the straight beams thrown from a light source. Hmm. Of course, he came up with an idea… he could prove this theory if he could show light from a star bending as it passed through the sun's gravitational field. And when might this be possible? Yes, you guessed it, during a solar eclipse because "when the sun's rays are blocked out by the moon during a solar eclipse we can see the stars around it… and these should appear to be slightly out of place from their actual positions as measured in the night sky because the light they emitted was bent as it went past the sun."[3] Just what you were thinking? Logical!

The first test

To Albert the wait must have seemed like an eternity but finally in 1919, there was an eclipse over South America and Africa. But the weather played havoc with the testing – cloudy one night and the next night the heat and humidity meant considerable corrections had to be done to get the results. But voila, it worked and "the Astronomer Royal announced that the measurements agreed with Einstein and not Newton. *The New York Times* announced, 'Stars all askew in the heavens,' and Einstein was famous overnight."[4]

But not everyone concurred. As there have always been with new discoveries—such as the world is not flat, diseases are spread by germs, black holes can shrink and so on—a healthy level of scepticism exists and so it did with Albert Einstein's *Theory of Relativity*. He hadn't convinced everyone. But here's the good news… the next eclipse where the theory could be tested again was going to be in the continent of Australia on 21 September 1922.

It was an Australian professor of physics from the University of Western Australia, Alexander Ross, who began a campaign for observatories to mount an expedition and test the theory again.[5] He persuaded William Campbell from Lick Observatory in California to take up the cause and our then Prime Minister, Billy Hughes, liked the idea and became actively involved. He delegated "the Trans-Australian Railway to transport scientists, and the Navy to provide a team of 10 officers to assist."[6]

From all over the world, scientists prepared to take part and for the equipment to be transported. In July that year, after much investigation, a number of locations were identified as best for testing. The key sites and the duration of the total eclipse as estimated were:[7] Goondiwindi, three minutes 33 seconds; Stanthorpe three minutes 28 seconds; Coongoola three minutes; and close to five minutes in Wallal in Western Australia – the longest 'stay' in Australia.

Path of the eclipse as it appeared in 'The Week', 1 September 1922.

The party prepares in Goondiwindi

In 1922, Goondiwindi was a town of about 1500 people, unbeknown to many Australians including the stargazers, doctors and professors from Australia's notable universities. But in September they arrived in force to undertake the testing to help save or sink Albert's theory. There were Professor Cooke and the Sydney Observatory party who set up at the west end of the main street;[8] Dr Baldwin, the Government Astronomer from Victoria who was managing a combined university group from Melbourne and Brisbane, and set up tents that looked "like a travelling circus"[9]; and a Sydney University party led by Professor Vonwiller that established themselves in a backyard secured from the tenant, a local bookmaker.[10]

An illustration of the camps of the NSW and Victorian astronomers at Goondiwindi as featured in the Sydney Mail, 27 September 1922.

The observatory at Goondiwindi. Source: State Library of Queensland.

Assisting Professor Vonwiller and his impressive team in the recording and photographing of results were two respected Goondiwindi locals, Edwin Fletcher and his daughter, 18-year-old Florence.[11] Edwin and Florence were requested to photograph, if possible, on a white sheet set up on the ground, the shadow bands as and if they appeared. Those 'in-the-know' say it is no easy feat to capture these wavy lines of dark and light that appear before and after an eclipse. There's also much speculation about what they actually are and what causes them. One theory is that they are "the last of the sun's rays being distorted by Earth's turbulent atmosphere… or as the sun's disk is reduced to a very narrow 'filament' of light, each point along the filament should appear to twinkle like a star. Thus, shadow bands might be the net result of light coming from each shimmering point."[12] At any rate, it was an exciting project for Edwin and Florence and most significant to the research.

Meanwhile… at the other stops

Heading to Western Australian was the team from the Lick Observatory of California with tons of telescopes. These overseas teams of experts were welcomed enthusiastically by our government. Their equipment, except for what could be built or purchased in Australia,[13] arrived in a two-masted schooner called the *Gwendolen*.

With a 'cast' of many including the scientists, their wives, naval officers, film crews and of course the budding astronomers,[14] Eighty Mile Beach (about half-way between the towns of Broome and Port Hedland) received a significant population boost.

The Lick Observatory party – Dr Adams, Mrs Adams, Dr Moore, Mrs Campbell, Dr Campbell, Dr Trumpler, Lt-Comr Quick, Dr Ross, Mr Hosking. Source: State Library of Western Australia.

Unfortunately, the low tide meant the *Gwendolen* had to moor over 6.5 kilometres (four miles) from the beach and all of the equipment had to be brought to shore on lifeboats, which took significant labour and many days, ably assisted by the local Aboriginal population, four-wheel carts and donkeys.

The excitement was palpable. It was like a pop-up village with a campsite, huts and a dark room, towers, telescopes and even regular postal deliveries courtesy of aviation pioneers Kingsford Smith and Norman Brearley.[15] To ensure that this time the testing was as accurate as it could be, rehearsal after rehearsal was held until the big day came.

Supplies and equipment carted up the beach by donkeys at Wallal during the 1922 Solar Eclipse Expedition, assisted by the local Aboriginal community. Courtesy of the State Library of Western Australia.

Back in Queensland, there was also considerable activity away from Goondiwindi. A group from the British Astronomical Association (NSW Branch) arrived in Stanthorpe; and in Coongoola—located between Cunnamulla and Wyandra—a magnetic observer from the Carnegie Institution[16] was set up ready for action.

In the guide that was prepared featuring towns from which to observe the eclipse, Coongoola was described as consisting of "a very small galvanized-iron railway station, and a small galvanized-iron hotel. Living accommodation of a homely character would be provided by Mrs Kruck, landlady of the hotel, if reasonable notice is given. Altogether, arrangements can be made for 20 to 30 guests."[17] Coongoola was on the map!

Excitement builds

The public and the media were hyped and excited as Australia became the scientific focus of the world. All eyes were upon us. The *Brisbane Courier* swept up in eclipse fever reported 19 days before the event that: "Goondiwindi owing to the climatic condition which prevail remains the 'Queen of observation stations'. Most of the chief scientists of the world, his Excellency the Governor of Queensland, and dozens of prominent persons will be visiting Goondiwindi, hundreds of others are coming, but there is room for thousands."[18]

As well as the regular service, special trains were scheduled for the day. Nobody wanted to miss out on being part of this phenomenal event.

Watching the eclipse from the roof of a building, Sydney, 27 September 1922. Source: Sydney Mail.

The moment arrives

In the backyard of the bookmaker's residence, James Nagle who was a member of the Sydney University team at Goondiwindi, shared the experience with the *Sydney Morning Herald* as it played out that day:[19]

"I shall never forget the spectacle of the total eclipse which I saw from a backyard... For some days we each rehearsed our tasks so that when the great moment arrived, scientific observation could proceed as rapidly as possible. When the day did arrive we were nervous, excited, and on edge. Just before the total eclipse, shadow bands, about three inches wide and three inches apart, raced across the earth like millions of snakes.

"Meanwhile, the moon was rapidly covering the face of the sun. The light became a bilious green.... Then, suddenly, day turned to night. We were able to look toward the sun with the naked eye. The scene for three minutes was indescribably lovely and eerie."

The *Brisbane Courier* wrote: "The eclipse of the sun here was a scene of incomparable and impressive grandeur. Glorious sunshine and a perfectly clear sky enabled the brilliant sight to be witnessed under the most favourable conditions. A finer day could not possibly have been ordered."[20]

An astronomer's record of the corona. Source: The Queenslander, 1922.

Edwin and Florence would have been delighted. The shadow bands that the father and daughter were assigned to capture were striking and noticeable, described as "visible distinctly in a series of waves… dark in colour and zig-zagged extraordinarily."[21] Some of the older astronomers declared "they have never seen anything so fascinating."[22]

The historic, life-changing results

But the results were not instant. Albert Einstein, now 42 years old, well known and respected, had to wait for this theory to be proven 'again'. William Campbell from Lick Observatory in California who was based in Western Australia for the experiment was unflappable and described as "meticulous".[23] He took his time gathering the results while everyone held their breath, and seven months later, in April 1923, the results were announced to Albert and to the world.

He was right! "Einstein was right, Newton's theory of gravitation was refuted,"[24] our understanding of science was changed forever, and the town of Goondiwindi joined in the celebrations. Albert Einstein had proven the *Theory of Relativity*.

What became of…

Edwin Fletcher – after contributing to the testing of Einstein's theory as part of the Goondiwindi team, Edwin, a keen amateur astronomer and solicitor, resumed his work representing the town in legal matters, including representing on one occasion 'Winks' McMicking whose story is also in this book. At one time, Edwin also served as the Mayor of Goondiwindi. On his retirement, Edwin's son, Donald, took over the law firm, and Edwin moved to Brisbane with his wife, Edith, who incidentally was the founding President of the Goondiwindi Country Women's Association.[25] A most civic family. Edith passed away in 1956 aged 79. Edwin outlived his wife, dying in 1962 aged 90. His son, Donald died four years later in 1966. They are all buried in Goondiwindi Cemetery.

Edwin Fletcher 1916 (standing far right), with the Town Committee 1911. Kindly provided by the Goondiwindi and District Family History Group and sourced by Goondiwindi Regional Council.

Florence Fletcher, Edwin's daughter, worked as a personal assistant and married, aged 26, in 1930 to Erle Monro. They were married for 28 years before Earl passed away in 1958. Florence remained in Goondiwindi and died in 1992 aged 88. She rests in the Goondiwindi Cemetery, her name forever recorded with the capturing of Albert Einstein's eclipse shadow bands.

How to find Edwin and Florence's grave in Goondiwindi Cemetery:

Progress through the entrance off Cemetery Road, travel about 50 metres and take the bitumen road to the left. Continue a little over 100 metres and you will come to a parking area on your right. Go to the far end of the parking area and on your right you will see sections F, E and D. Walk past the end of sections F and E and you will see the section D sign. Both Edwin and Doreen are in this section, row 1 and 4 respectively.

References:

1 Barker, Geoff, Einstein's Theory of Relativity Proven in Australia, 1922, Inside the Collection, 22 August 2012, *Museum of Applied Arts and Sciences*. Retrieved 3 July 2019 from: https://maas.museum/inside-the-collection/2012/08/22/einsteins-theory-of-relativity-proven-in-australia-1922/
2 - 3 Ibid.
4 - 6 Blair, David, 1922 Aussie outback expedition helped prove Einstein's theory, *ABC Radio National*, 22 August 2015. Retrieved 3 July 2019 from URL: https://www.abc.net.au/radionational/programs/scienceshow/1922-aussie-outback-expedition-helped-prove-einsteine28099s-/6714806#transcript
7 Solar Eclipse Base at Goondiwindi. (1922, July 7). *Warwick Daily News (Qld. : 1919 -1954)*, p. 2. Retrieved July 3, 2019, from http://nla.gov.au/nla.news-article177260835
8 - 11 Goondiwindi. (1922, September 27). *The Sydney Morning Herald (NSW: 1842 - 1954)*, p. 10. Retrieved 3 July 2019 from http://nla.gov.au/nla.news-article16028467
12 Rao, Joe, Shadow Bands Are a Solar Eclipse Mystery (and Not Everyone Sees Them), *Space.com*, 12 Aug 2017. Retrieved 3 July 2019 from: https://www.space.com/37776-shadow-bands-are-a-solar-eclipse-mystery.html
13 - 15 Blair, David, 1922. Op.cit.
16 -17 Miller, Simon, Total eclipse of the sun 1922 & 2012, State Library Blog, 8 Nov 2012. John Oxley Library, *State Library of Queensland*. Retrieved 3 July 2019 from: http://blogs.slq.qld.gov.au/jol/2012/11/08/total-eclipse-of-the-sun-1922-and-2012/
18 Advertising (1922, September 2). *The Brisbane Courier (Qld.: 1864 - 1933)*, p4. Retrieved July 3, 2019, from http://nla.gov.au/nla.news-article20568908
19 Eclipse of Sun (20 May 1937). *The Sydney Morning Herald (NSW: 1842-1954)*, p9. Retrieved 3 July 2019 from http://nla.gov.au/nla.news-article17369511

20 - 22 Impressive Grandeur. (22 Sept 1922). *The Brisbane Courier (Qld.: 1864-1933)*, p5. Retrieved 3 July 2019 from http://nla.gov.au/nla.news-article20573026

23 - 24 Blair, David, 1922. Op.cit.

25 Knitted bedspread (1951, September 25). *Brisbane Telegraph (Qld. : 1948 - 1954)*, p. 19 (CITY FINAL). Retrieved July 4, 2019, from http://nla.gov.au/nla.news-article211947719

Images:

Edwin Fletcher's grave by Ann Sainsbury from memorial page for Edwin Fletcher (unknown–10 Oct 1962), *Find A Grave* Memorial no. 202123012, Goondiwindi Cemetery, Goondiwindi. Reproduced with Ann's kind permission.

Albert Einstein in 1905. Einstein patentoffice.jpg. (2018, March 6). *Wikimedia Commons*. Retrieved 3 July 2019 from: https://commons.wikimedia.org/w/index.php?title=File:Einstein_patentoffice.jpg&oldid=291056818

Path of the Total Eclipse (1 Sept 1922). *The Week* (Bris, Qld.: 1876 - 1934), p20. Retrieved 3 July 2019 from http://nla.gov.au/nla.news-article192983167

Carlton [Illustrator], Camp of the NSW and Victorian astronomers at Goondiwindi. The Eclipse: Scenes at Goondiwindi and Sydney (1922, September 27). *Sydney Mail* (NSW: 1912 - 1938), p17. Retrieved 3 July 2019 from http://nla.gov.au/nla.news-article159023505

Sydney Mail [photo source] Observatory erected at Goondiwindi to view the eclipse in September 1922. *State Library of Queensland*. Retrieved 3 July 2019 from URL: http://hdl.handle.net/10462/deriv/115453

(1922). Lick Observatory party, 1922 Wallal Solar Eclipse Expedition. Image ID: 4131B/3/25. Photo courtesy of the *State Library of Western Australia*. Retrieved 4 July 2019 from URL: http://purl.slwa.wa.gov.au/slwa_b4847714_1

Supplies and equipment carted up the beach by donkeys at Wallal during the 1922 Solar Eclipse Expedition, assisted by the local Aboriginal community. Image ID: 4131B/1/30. Photo courtesy of the *State Library of Western Australia*. Retrieved 20 July 2019 from URL: http://purl.slwa.wa.gov.au/slwa_b4792886_1

On the Roof of Warwick - Building, Sydney. The Eclipse: Scenes at Goondiwindi and Sydney (1922, September 27). *Sydney Mail* (NSW: 1912 - 1938), p. 17. Retrieved July 3, 2019, from http://nla.gov.au/nla.news-article159023505

Unidentified [photographer], NSW Government Astronomer's record of the corona, from The Queenslander, 2 December 1922, p.25. *State Library of Queensland*. Retrieved 4 July 2019 from: http://hdl.handle.net/10462/comp/1665

Edwin Fletcher 1916, and in the Town Committee 1911. Kindly provided by the *Goondiwindi and District Family History Group* and sourced by *Goondiwindi Regional Council*.

'Black Magic'
Len Waters

Interred: **Leonard Victor Waters**, 20 June 1924 – 24 August 1993 (aged 69 years).

Location: Section D, Grave 402.

Cemetery: St George Cemetery, 12069 Carnarvon Highway, St George, QLD 4487.

Please note that this story includes images of deceased Aboriginal and Torres Strait Islander people.

The boy who dreamed big and fulfilled his ambition... Len Waters, c1944-45, when Len was 20 approximately. Source: Wikipedia.

The small Aboriginal boy who shaded his eyes against the glare of the summer's day made a curious sight as he shuffled around in small circles, arm stretched out skyward to block the sun as he tried to find the source of the engine noise that came from somewhere in the very blue Australian firmament above him. Young Len Waters knew a lot about planes, he'd read all the *Biggles* books, all about Bert Hinkler, Charles Kingsford Smith and Amy Johnson... yet his chance to see a real plane flying was something extremely rare in the semi-outback where he lived. But this lad would have his day. Against the odds, he would become one of those who would fly high to defend King and Country in a World War II Kittyhawk fighter named *Black Magic*.

What surprised many about the level of Aboriginal military enlistment in World War II was not that there were some who took up arms, but that they were willing to defend a country that only grudgingly recognised their existence. Reasons for joining up were varied: maybe war service would highlight the Indigenous fight for citizenship and equality; maybe the chance for equal pay – unheard of in 'civvy street'; or because the Army, Navy and Air Force were really discrimination-free places and their mates signed up. For Len Waters it was simple, he had always wanted to fly.

The Depression bites

There's not much at the tiny Queensland settlement of Boomi these days, let alone when Len Waters arrived into the world at the nearby local Aboriginal mission at Euraba in 1924. He was the fourth of 11 children of Don and Grace

Waters and as the family moved around a fair bit, he was educated at the Toomelah Aboriginal settlement just across the McIntyre River from Goondiwindi and the State School at Nindigully, just south of St George.

At the height of the 1930s Depression, Len left school to help support his family and worked with his father's ring-barking team. He wasn't yet 14 but, in those days, leaving school at such an early age wasn't frowned upon because the government believed Aboriginal people would not aspire to an occupation that required higher education.[1]

This lack of formal education would both deeply concern and motivate Len later in life. After a spell at ring-barking trees Len took to shearing until August 1942, when in the midst of World War II, and just after he turned 18, he decided to join up. His grandfather, George Bennett, served in the AIF during World War I, and also inspired by his fascination with flying he enlisted in the Royal Australian Air Force. After his rookie training at Maryborough in Queensland, he was taught aircraft mechanics in Sydney.

While Len wanted to fly there was considerable division in the Aboriginal community over the issue of Military Service during World War II. A man by the name of William Cooper, the Founder of the Australian Aborigines' League, probably typifies those who argued against enlisting. He lost his son in World War I and argued that Aboriginal sacrifice had not brought any improvements in rights and conditions, as some had argued it would. Cooper demanded improvements at home before taking up "the privilege of defending the land which was taken from him by the white race without compensation or even kindness."[2]

While at least 3000 Aborigines served their country

during World War II[3] it seems from their experiences that Cooper may have been at least partially right, as many Indigenous veterans reported when they got back from overseas that little had changed. Many who had served were banned from RSLs, except on ANZAC Day and most were not given the right to vote for another 17 years. Len Waters would experience this sort of treatment later in life, but all that was a long way from his mind when he applied for an aircrew position and pilot training… and got it.

Dangers for learners

For his initial training, Len was sent to No 1 Elementary Flying School at Narrandera in New South Wales. The flying school had been set up as part of the Empire Training Scheme and taught over 3000 pilots the elementary stages of flying during its four years of operation. It was a dangerous time for those learning and those teaching.

To give an idea of the casualty numbers, in just a little over six months in 1943, four pilots were killed in a mid-air collision between two Tiger Moths at 180 metres (600 feet) … both planes were destroyed. A pilot from the school was killed near Junee, about 100 kilometres from Narrandera, when his Tiger Moth crashed, and another pilot was killed and his crewman badly injured on 17 August after their Tiger Moth failed to recover from a spin. The names of 26 who died in training are listed on the Narrandera War Cemetery memorial and another two are buried in the Narrandera General Cemetery.

If you drive the Newell Highway you will pass through Narrandera and inside the visitors' centre, right on the

Leading Aircraftman Len Waters receiving his 'wings' during the graduation parade of No. 44 Course at No. 5 Service Flying Training School. Source: Australian War Memorial Photograph Collection.

highway, there is a Tiger Moth painted in its training yellow livery which is the centrepiece of the memorial to those who died while training or teaching at Narrandera. But Len survived and he survived well. He had put in hundreds of hours of study, inspired by his prior lack of education. He had not only mastered the Tiger Moth but went on to complete his training on Wirraways and receive his 'wings' as a Sergeant pilot.

The 'elite' in the Pacific

Of his time learning to fly, Len later said: "I was terribly keen to prove myself in the elite, which it is. There is no doubt about that. The flying part of the air force was the elite. Well, I was the coloured boy in it and I might add that there was 169 of us I think there was, started, on the course, and there were 44 or 46 finished up as pilots that graduated and got our wings ... they cut us down a bit. The end result when we got our wings ... there were only three blokes in front of me on my average. So, from my humble beginning I was pretty proud of what I am ... accomplished like." [4]

Not bad for a bloke who was so unsure of himself and his abilities that he took three five-pound bets that he wouldn't make the grade and get his wings. That cost him 15 pounds or more than he would earn in months.

But the big thrill for Len was when he was posted to Mildura, in northern Victoria, for operational training and stepped into a US-made Kittyhawk fighter. After the Tiger Moth with its top speed of 80 knots (148kph) the Kittyhawk was a beast of a different kind where things happened

Sgt Len Waters, 78 Squadron, RAAF, sitting in the cockpit of a P40M Kittyhawk, possibly 'Black Magic'. Source: Australian War Memorial.

much more quickly. It could manage more than 310 knots (574kph) and according to Len had a landing speed of almost 90 knots (166kph).

By the time Len had finished his training and been posted to a squadron, the war in the Pacific was on the turn. In New Guinea, where Len ended up, the Japanese invaders were being forced back and when the 'new boy' arrived at 78 Squadron at Noemfoor, Dutch New Guinea, the Americans were in the process of wiping out the last Japanese stronghold on the western-most point of New Guinea, a joint army and naval base.

Four pilots from No. 78 Squadron RAAF in Noemfoor Island, Dutch New Guinea, 1945. Left to right: Jack Eagle, Spike Jackson, Len Waters and Geoff Cutler. Source: Australian War Memorial Photograph Collection.

Daily dangers

In interviews with author Robert Hall, Len takes up the story: "And the Yanks – this is how brave they are – they wanted it knocked out, so they detailed 78th Wing to do the job – 36 Kittyhawks! At any rate, we went over and all hell opened up when we got over there. We went over at 16,000 feet and dived down to tree-top height and just cleared out. The next day we had to go again and it was tenfold the next day. It seemed to be... because there was flak! I got turned over twice in the bomb... in the blasts of the ack-ack [anti-aircraft artillery fire]... and bloody hell! Flicked it... the plane... twice!" [5]

Len didn't specify, but that plane was probably the Kittyhawk assigned to him when he arrived at the squadron. It was traditional for pilots to 'name' their aircraft by painting the chosen title on the plane, usually on the engine cowling. It's hard to imagine what Len must felt when he saw the name the aircraft had been given by its previous pilot, John Blackmore – *Black Magic*. Len didn't talk about it much but he did say he found the name amusing and chose to keep it.[6] Maybe it was a good luck omen as events were to prove.

The closest call of them all

One raid of Len's 95 operational sorties with 78 Squadron was to provide the closest call he had while flying with the RAAF. As the allies were pushing the Japanese progressively back to their homeland it was necessary to clear out pockets of resistance from Japanese forces left behind. This mission was to destroy a motor torpedo base in the Dutch

East Indies… now part of Indonesia. Len was leading the flight and the task was to dive-bomb the vessels and then go around for a strafing run. Len didn't get that far. As he released his cargo on the bombing run, he felt a 'clunk' under the aircraft. Len later said: "By this time we knew what sort of ack-ack fire… anti-aircraft fire that they had and it was a 37 millimetre – and I knew it had hit pretty close to where I was sitting because I felt the jar. And I thought now this is it… pretty close to me and I was just hoping, praying that it wasn't a high explosive one."[7]

The shell had the capability of detonating with the slightest jolt, leaving Len with a two-hour flight back to his base with what amounted to having a loaded gun at his head: "I told the others to land and clear the strip because I didn't like what had happened to me. I came in on my own and I just taxied to the end of the strip and the armourers came over, and I said to them, 'There is something underneath here.' Luckily, underneath the belly of a Kittyhawk is fabric, between the armour plating and the 75-gallon fuel tank. Now, if it had landed six or eight inches one way or the other, I wouldn't be here talking about it today. The armourers looked up inside, ripped it open and it was there – it was a live 37-mm shell. Incidentally, it was a high-explosive shell. I tell you, it's the smoothest landing I've ever made. I guarantee I could land it on eggs because I didn't want to jar out what was there."[8]

When the armourers examined *Black Magic* more closely they discovered the aircraft had been hit seven times. In his modest fashion whenever he related that story Len always added… "but not seriously".[9]

Len Waters was Australia's only World War II Aboriginal fighter pilot. By the end of the war, he was commanding operations which included commissioned officers. A colleague described him as a "gaunt, genial figure, humble despite his daring feats."[10] Apart from all that he also won the all-services boxing title while on Morotai Island.[11]

"Just another blackfella"

When the fighting was over Len returned home to Australia and to St George where he married waitress, Gladys May Saunders, two years his junior, who he had met briefly before he went to war. And he had a dream… to start an aerial taxi service for western Queensland. The roads were so bad that he reckoned it would be a sure-fire winner. But he could not secure the finance for such a project and was reportedly denied a civilian pilot's licence despite having the experience of flying fighter aircraft.[12] He had not experienced any discrimination in the RAAF and the post-war treatment prompted him to say that once he took off the uniform he was "just another blackfella".[13]

Len went back to what he knew. He worked briefly as a mechanic and road worker then travelled widely, shearing from Queensland down to Victoria. As a result of the 1956 shearers' strike, Len took his family to live in the Brisbane suburb of Inala where he worked as a truck driver and meat worker before going back to shearing.

In 1972 Len was involved in a car accident which left him an epileptic and restricted in the work he could do. According to his daughter, Kim Orchard, he was drawn back to the land and became the caretaker of a property in Goroke, Victoria, for a short time. Kim says that even in retirement he would go out to the sheds on country properties to cook for the shearers.[14]

Never forgotten

Despite his post-war disappointments, Len has never been forgotten by the RAAF community. In 1993 he was honoured at a number of special events organised by the Air Force in Marble Bar, Western Australia; Townsville in Queensland; and the reunion of 78 Squadron. He was also able to take a flight in an F18 Hornet – the RAAF's twin-engine, supersonic, all-weather, carrier-capable, multi-role combat jet. It must have been a remarkable experience for Len who once made the heady comparison between a Tiger Moth and a Kittyhawk – 80 knots maximum speed compared with 310 knots. The Hornet's top speed is 1034 knots… and Len reportedly took the controls.

Two months after those celebrations, on 24 August 1993, Len Waters was found on a footpath in Louisa Street, Cunnamulla. His daughter, Kim, says it's believed he had an epileptic seizure and was unconscious when his head hit the footpath.[15] He was 69 years old. The RAAF flew a Hercules transport aircraft carrying veterans from 78 squadron and media to Len's funeral.

Inside St George Anglican Church was standing room only, and it overflowed with mourners. Present were Len's widow, Gladys, and his children and family members.[16] The community of western Queensland remembered him as well. The funeral procession through the town extended the entire distance between the church and the cemetery – the complete length of the main street. As he was laid to rest nine Hornets roared over the small St George Cemetery. And the name, Len Waters, is still heard often in St George and Cunnamulla.

In 1995–96, Len was commemorated by Australia Post. Celebrating his heroism, his portrait with the wording 'Fighter Pilot, Len Waters' were depicted on a stamp along with that of his P-40 Kittyhawk fighter, *Black Magic* on an aerogramme.

Len's legacy also lives on in place names and locations around Australia. You will find Len Waters Place, a park in Inala, Brisbane; Moree Plains Shire

The 1995-96 stamp and aerogramme created to commemorate Len. Courtesy of Australia Post.

Council dedicated Leonard Waters Park in Boggabilla, New South Wales; and Len Waters Street in Ngunnawal, Canberra, was named after him. In 2003, Balonne Shire Council erected a monument to Len and local RAAF identity, Squadron Leader John Jackson, in St George *(pictured below)*. The suburb of Len Waters Estate was established in the City of Liverpool, New South Wales, in 2009. In 2011, the Sutherland Shire Council recognised Len Waters' memory and achievements by dedicating Len Waters Park, with a memorial plinth and plaque at Timbrey Circuit, Barden Ridge, New South Wales.

Black magic, indeed.

How to find Len's grave in Section D, Grave 402, St George Cemetery:

Enter the cemetery through the front entrance off the Carnarvon Highway. As you walk down the central path Len's grave is on your right-hand-side. Alongside the path, also on the right-hand-side, you will see small posts, about 30 centimetres high, with letters that denote the cemetery sections. Walk until you come to the letter 'D' and the graves immediately after it are section 'D'. Look to your right and you will see a grave with a white statue of an angel. Len's grave is just in front of the angel.

References:

1 Leonard Victor Waters - 20 June 1924 - 24 August 1993 – PILOT, Life on the job, *Australian Catholic University*. Retrieved 27 July 2019 from URL: https://webapps.acu.edu.au/onthejob/life_job/famous_people/Len_Waters.htm
2 *Australian War Museum*. Indigenous Defence Service, 24 October 2017. Retrieved 29 July 2019 from URL: https://www.awm.gov.au/articles/encyclopedia/Indigenous
3 *ABC News*. Anzac Day: Indigenous soldiers thought 'when we got back we'd be treated differently' 25 April 2017. Brennan, Bridget. https://www.abc.net.au/news/2017-04-25/anzac-day-Indigenous-soldiers-shunned-by-so ciety/8468364
4 - 5 Hall, Robert, A., Black Magic: Leonard Waters - Second World War Fighter Pilot, *Australian National University*, 1989 Retrieved 22 July 2019 from URL: http://press-files.anu.edu.au/downloads/press/p72311/pdf/article0310.pdf
6 Wikipedia contributors. (2019, June 14). Len Waters. In *Wikipedia, The Free Encyclopedia*. Retrieved 23 July 2019 from URL: from https://en.wikipedia.org/w/index.php?title=Len_Waters&oldid=901783239
7 Hall, Robert, A., Op.cit.
8 *National Indigenous Times*. Len Waters and his WWII Black Magic. 26 June 2018. Retrieved 23 July 2019 from URL: https://nit.com.au/len-waters-and-his-ww11-black-magic/
9 Hall, Robert, A., Op.cit.

10 Wikipedia contributors. (2019, June 14). Len Waters. Op.cit.
11 Furphy, Samuel, 'Waters, Leonard Victor (Len) (1924–1993)', Australian Dictionary of Biography, National Centre of Biography, *Australian National University*. Retrieved 29 July 2019 from URL: http://ia.anu.edu.au/biography/waters-leonard-victor-len-24662/text33318
12 *Australian War Museum*. Indigenous Defence Service. Op.cit.
13 Furphy, Samuel, Op.cit.
14 - 15 Orchard, Kim (nee Waters), Leonard Waters Aboriginal Fighter Pilot. Extract from *"My Father the Flyer – Was it Black Magic?"* 20 October 2008. Retrieved 29 July 2019 from URL:http://leonardwatersAboriginalfighterpilot.blogspot.com/2008/10/leonard-waters-Aboriginal-fighter-pilot.html
16. Rees, Peter, *The Missing Man: From the outback to Tarakan, the powerful story of Len Waters, Australia's first Aboriginal fighter pilot*. Allen & Unwin, 27 June 2018.

Images:

Len Waters, c1944-1945. In *Wikipedia, The Free Encyclopedia*. Retrieved 27 July 2019 from URL: https://en.wikipedia.org/w/index.php?title=Len_Waters&oldid=901783239

Uranquinty, NSW, 1944-07-01. Leading Aircraftman L. V. (Len) Waters receiving his 'wings'. *Australian War Memorial Photograph Collection*, Retrieved 27 July 2019 from URL: https://trove.nla.gov.au/version/252005367

Unknown photographer, 8144 Sergeant (Sgt) Leonard Victor Waters, 78 Squadron, RAAF, sitting in the cockpit of a P40N, c1944-45. *Australian War Memorial*, Accession Number: P01659.001. Retrieved 29 July 2019 from URL: https://www.awm.gov.au/collection/C251810

Unknown A P40M Kittyhawk (A29-310) aircraft of 2 Operational Training Unit (2OTU) in flight, believed to be piloted by 78144 Sergeant (Sgt) Leonard Victor (Len) Waters. *Australian War Memorial Photograph Collection*, Retrieved 27 July 2019 from URL: https://www.awm.gov.au/collection/C268693

Noemfoor Island, Dutch New Guinea, 1945. Four pilots from No. 78 Squadron RAAF. (Donor G. Waters), *Australian War Memorial Photograph Collection*, Retrieved 27 July 2019 from URL: https://trove.nla.gov.au/version/252005373

Australia Post Leonard Waters commemorate stamp and aerogramme, 1995-1996. Stamp designer: Sue Passmore; aerogramme designer: Janet Boschen; ©*Australian Postal Corporation*. Reprinted courtesy of Australia Post.

Henrietta does not have a headstone and we have marked the location for the purposes of this photo. The grave did have a metal marker bearing the number 629 lying on its location.

The utopian experiment
Roma's communes

Interred: Henrietta Tosi, 1888 – 15 March 1894 (aged six years old).

Location: Catholic section, Row 4, North Plot 629.

Cemetery: Roma Monumental Cemetery, Lewis Street, Roma QLD.

It was an interesting experiment – sending a small group of people to a new location to start a village, to work the land, to support each other and create a new Utopia… a socialist model of survival. Could it work in the south west of Queensland? This very experiment took place in the 1890s when 13 socialist communes were established, all with some government support. One of the 13 communes lasted 16 years; the remaining 12 lasted about two years and three of those communes were based in Roma.

New hope for a new life

It was a time of depression in Australia but it must have been an exciting time for the members of each commune as they packed up their former lives and headed to Roma by train. The communes had unusual but aspirational names – 'Excel Pioneer', 'Nil Desperandum' (meaning never despair), and 'Obertown Model'. The concept is not that different from the discussion that still goes on today – finding ways to move workers out of the city into the bush and supporting farming and agricultural communities. And thus, three groups came to start a new life in a new town.

A representative from each group had travelled by train to Roma earlier, on 21 November 1893 and inspected the land that was on offer to them. Fortunately, a good rainfall meant the area looked lush, the soil promising and the creeks were flowing. The land they accepted had been Mandandanji country and was resumed for agricultural purposes.[1]

The *Barrier Miner* reported on Wednesday 17 January 1894 that "two hundred and twenty men, women, and children belonging to the Excel Pioneer, Obertown Model, and Nil Desperandum co-operative communities have departed for the settlements."[2] Their new lives were about to begin.

Meet the communes

Nil Desperandum was led by a 25-year-old Canadian migrant, George Strickland, formerly a clerk. The commune had 35 members and families and was given 2266 hectares of land about 40 kilometres south of Roma. They had a mix of skilled people including "farmers, farm labourers, blacksmiths, carpenters, fruit-growers, gardeners, stockmen and dairymen."[3] And they had their own set of rules which said everyone had equal rights and responsibilities, and equal rights to profit. Five members were elected to manage labour, supplies, income and expenses. A general store was to be set up, medical needs were supported by the group and strong drink was not allowed.

Members of Nil Desperandum commune assemble for a photograph, 1894. Reproduced with the kind permission of Dr Bill Metcalf, Queensland Historical Atlas.

The Obertown Model commune had 45 members and their families, some up to 10 in size. This group was given 2914 hectares on the north side of Yalebone Creek, adjoining the Nil Desperandum commune and was led by 60-year-old, Joseph Oberthur. Initially, it was believed that Oberthur had a lot of experience for this type of experiment, but later it came out that he "had been a plumber, publican, armed bank-robber and prisoner – but never a farmer. He had also been described as 'the most polished scoundrel.'"[4] The Obertown Model members could choose their own politics and faith, and alcohol was allowed, but members could be expelled if they "interfere with the morality, peace, and order of the settlement."[5] What could possibly go wrong?

Excel Pioneers had a mixture of rules from both of the other communes. They had 45 members and their families, with the average age around 36.

Members of Excel Pioneers commune on Yalebone Creek, south of Roma, relax in front of their communal dining-room, 1894. Reproduced with the kind permission of Dr Bill Metcalf, Queensland Historical Atlas.

Most members were married and they had a good mix of trades under their belt for the challenges ahead. Their leader was 36-year-old George Legg, a carpenter. Their rules were clear cut. For nine hours a day they worked the land as a group, with everything going to the general fund. They also had their own small gardens and houses which the group built, and an established medical fund like Nil Desperandum. They allowed alcohol but it wasn't to be sold.[6]

Tensions and deaths

The establishment months were hard work with hard labour and no creature comforts. There were fallouts and personality issues. Nil Desperandum expelled a member; another complained that the appointed Secretary was submitting false invoices; Excel Pioneer's Secretary supposedly did not appear on the land (a no-show for work) until two months after the others; and Obertown Model's leader was accused of fraud.

The successes were slow in coming too. A letter from an Obertown Model member at the end of March in their first year explained there was little or no seed, and they had managed to plough 60 hectares at the mercy of the weather with a limited number of horses. "Our money is all out, therefore we cannot get any more goods or horses, and all the provisions will last only about three weeks more, and unless there is more at once, I do not know what will become of the great number of families here."[7]

Another member, John Brown, spoke of the dramas of transport with Roma being a great distance away and the tracks being poor. He "wished they had left the women and children in Brisbane so that the men could concentrate on farming rather than having to build houses."[8] Nevertheless, he was still "hopeful and determined to make this place their home."[9]

Add to this, in the first few months of the communes' establishment, the Jolly family of Nil Desperandum suffered the loss of their 14-month-old daughter, Alice. This was followed by the accidental death from scalding of six-year-old Henrietta Tosi[10] from the Obertown Model commune – a death that would fill her family with grief and no doubt leave them regretting their choice of a new life. In the interim, the Government came up with another 200 pounds for each commune to use for rations.[11]

Support for the communes

There were many Australians who believed that the communes and socialist model would be the saviour of Australia. New arrival, William Lane, a British-born printer and journalist, came to Australia from the USA where he had been working for the Detroit Free Press in 1881. He brought with him his Scottish-born wife, Anne,

Journalists, William and Anne Lane, 1893. Source: Wikipedia.

who was also a journalist working in 1882 in a Chicago newspaper office. With their infant daughter, Nellie, they arrived in Brisbane on board the immigrant ship, *Quetta*, on 29 June 1885.[12]

In May 1890, William became editor of the community-funded Brisbane weekly, *The Worker*, described as "radical, anti-employer, the government and anti-British."[13] Within a few months of its first edition, it had 12,000 subscribers.

William believed wholeheartedly in the establishment of the communes and that "there would be no real social change without a complete restructure of society along socialist lines. *The Worker* became increasingly devoted to a 'New Australia' utopia."[14] Prior to the establishment of the Roma communes, William had visited the first communal group in Queensland at Alice River, established near Barcaldine in 1891 by 72 rural labourers disaffected through the Shearers' Strike. At the time William visited, it was a resounding success and became an inspiration for the thirteen new communes including Roma's three. (Alice River thrived for over a decade until membership declined and it was sold out in 1907).[15]

You can imagine William's disappointment and that of the readers of *The Worker*, when in April 1894, just short of four months after the establishment of the Roma communes, the newspaper received a letter from Joseph Oberthur, secretary of the Obertown Model Group, saying:

"We have lived in the greatest of hardships. We have neither had butter nor milk, and the work is simply too hard for the ration the men are getting. We have since built a store, blacksmith's shop, seven houses, stockyard,

Staff at 'The Worker', Brisbane, 1892. Editor William Lane is second from the left in the second row. 'The Worker' became increasingly devoted to a 'New Australia' utopia. Source: State Library of Queensland.

and just finished fencing 150 acres, and cleared 20 acres. We put in a crop in the beginning of February, but it got burnt up for the want of rain. We have only rations enough for four weeks longer... I really don't know what we will do. We are fully determined to do our best."[16]

Nevertheless, William Lane did not lose faith. Today, he is regarded as one of Australia's most important socialists, who is said to have had "a profound impact on the development of trade unionism and the Labor Party in Australia."[17] William left Australia for Paraguay to form *New Australia*, a utopian commune. The story behind this would fill a book in its own right, but suffice to say that eventually the project fell apart and William left, demoralised. He moved to New Zealand in 1900 and continued life as a journalist. He became a patriot and support of our involvement in World War I[18] and lost a son at Gallipoli.[19] He died on 26 August 1917 in Auckland, aged 56.

The rot sets in

Back at the communes... it was now five months after commencement, August 1894, five members were expelled from Obertown Model, and there were complaints that not everyone was living and working for the betterment of the group. Excel Pioneer's Secretary, George Legg, complained about the loafers or as he called them 'sundowners' who did little between meals. George Strickland, of Nil Desperandum, appealed for more funds as the last 200 pounds provided was used and their commune was "almost destitute of clothing".[20]

At this time Land Commissioner, Lewis Jackson, decided a visit was in order and he reported after visiting all three communes that there was "a good deal of discontent" and that the chances of them being self-sufficient was not only "very shadowy"[21] but he was concerned that without the government's support they would be destitute, with Obertown Model commune not showing any real sign that it could survive. This was reinforced by the visit of a parliamentary delegation who confirmed that "Excel Pioneer, although they had received over £900, had little to show for it, not even houses. Obertown Model, which had received over £1000, was 'perhaps in a more hopeless condition'... one woman despaired 'we have plenty of nothing but children.' Excel Pioneer was also struggling with one member, Charles Warner, writing that "none of the members are working, and have not done so since last Christmas. If I remain here much longer I will be driven into a conviction or a lunatic asylum."[22]

The three communes bravely carried on for another six months with little to show for it. Mary Gilbert, mother of five children and a Nil Desperandum commune member died, and two-week-old Frank Newman of the Obertown Model commune also passed away. There was more loss to come – Nil Desperandum experienced three deaths in one family – Emily Hackles died after childbirth along with her baby and then her husband, William, drowned. Their two orphaned children were left in the care of Emily's two brothers fortunately group members – Ernest and Frederick Holloway. The Obertown Model commune lost 17-month-old Bertha Lederhose.[23]

By now, Nil Desperandum (never despair) was indeed despairing. Of the 35 original members, 22 remained with no shared cooperation and "their crops and gardens had failed and they were totally dependent on rations."[24] Obertown Model commune fared no better. Of their 45 members, 14 members and families had nothing and were living off government rations. Land Commissioner, Lewis Jackson, recommended the groups be disbanded.

An end to a vision

It was a vision that was embraced enthusiastically but in less than two years it was over for the Roma experiment along Yalebone Creek. But it was not only the three Roma communes that failed. Eventually, all thirteen communes were shut down, although the Protestant Unity commune south of Gympie was continued by many of the members after it was shut down, and formed the town we now know as Pomona.[25]

Protestant Unity commune, near Pomona, with road (the old Bruce Highway) running through centre. Reproduced with the kind permission of Dr Bill Metcalf, Queensland Historical Atlas.

Co-operative Groups.
Communities Dissolved.
Intention of the Settlers.

The whole of the 12 groups of persons who originally took up areas under the Co-operative Communities Land Settlement Act of 1893 have now been dissolved under the Amendment Act of 1895. This proclamation was made at the request of the settlers themselves, it being the intention of existing members — that is members at present resident on the areas—to apply under the provisions of the lastmentioned Act for individual allotments on the respective areas lately occupied by the groups. Instructions will be issued shortly to the land commissioners for the districts in which these areas are situated to proceed to the lands, and arrange an equitable division of both the land and the assets of the groups amongst existing members. The present strength of the various groups is as follows :—

Mizpah	14
Nil Desperandum	1
Obertown Model	0
Excel Pioneers	5
Reliance	7
Monmouth	18
Woolloongabba Exemplars	5
Resolute	16
Bon Accord	8
Byrnestown	15
Industrial	8
Protestant Unity	23
Total	120

Of these 120 existing members, it is more than likely that only three-fourths will apply for individual selections when the commissioners visit the land to divide it At present, however, nothing can be said definitely as to the number of applicants. In the case of the Protestant Unity and the Woolloongabba Exemplars, instructions have already been issued, but owing to the wet weather the commissioners have not been able to proceed to the areas.

Communities dissolved notice, 25 February 1896. The Telegraph.

In Roma, the official end came on 26 November 1895 and the families began to make their way to their original home towns. Eleven of the 12 families at the Nil Desperandum departed; only one of the 11 Obertown Model families stayed in Roma, and eight of the 13 families in the Excel Pioneers model departed. The *Brisbane Courier* reported that the families "are at present quartered in the Immigration Depot, Kangaroo Point."[26] A woman from the Obertown Model Group spoke of their last six weeks' living on "wallaby and kangaroo rat. They had no butcher's meat, and to see the women and children sitting down eating dry bread and sugar, with a bite of wallaby was very pitiful."[27]

Failure and speculation

There was a great deal of hard work, hope and money thrown into the project but to no avail and there was much review and speculation as to why the communes failed. A member of Nil Desperandum interviewed on his return to Brisbane told the reporter the failure was due to climatic influence (no rain), distance to market, and that: "the classing of a number of men together perfectly unknown to each other, with different opinions, etc, made it impossible to carry on… the executive were [sic] chosen from among ourselves, and that executive had to work upon laws which they had no power to enforce."[28]

One can only imagine the hope that each family had when the vision was first realised, only to return home with nothing to show for their efforts, no new home or community, and in some cases, with the loss of their loved ones.

Today Roma's residents may boast some familiar names – descendants from those commune members who chose to stay and build their life in and around Roma including Obertown Model's Joseph Bootle and John Thwaite; Excel Pioneer's Manuel and Sarah Baldo, Joshua and Susannah Gorton; and George and Mary Legg.[29]

When discussed in The Legislative Assembly on Monday 2 December 1895, Parliamentarian Mr McDonald "admitted it had been proved that co-operation in farming was a failure." Mr Murray added it "was not in the nature of things to suppose that a number of men taken from the streets of a town and put down on land which they knew nothing about, could make a living for themselves. Individual effort was required to make a successful farmer. The lesson to be derived… a man to succeed must rely upon his individual endeavour."[30]

Today nothing remains at the site where once more than two hundred people lived, over 20,000 acres[31] were tilled, great hopes were held and Utopia failed.

How to find Henrietta's grave in the Catholic section Row 4, North Plot 629, Roma Monumental Cemetery:

Little Henrietta died during the early months of the commune experiment after a domestic scalding accident. To find her grave, enter the cemetery off Tiffin Street and go straight ahead until the road turns to the right and becomes the central road through the cemetery. On your right-hand-side, you will see row numbers on white stakes. Henrietta's grave is in row 4. Walk away from the road until you come to a headstone marked 'Ramsay'. Henrietta's grave is halfway between that and the 'Smith' headstone. When we were there the grave was locatable by a metal marker bearing the number 629 lying on its location. As Henrietta does not have a headstone nor do the two people resting either side of her, John O'Malley and Kate Short, you will be able to find her by locating the graves of Aphra Ramsey or Louisa Smith. Positions as follow:*

Marking	Location	Family name	First name
Headstone	1552	RAMSEY	APHRA GERTRUDE
No headstone	2137	O'MALLEY	JOHN
No headstone	629	TOSIE	HENRIETTTA
No headstone	528	SHORT	KATE
Headstone	1845	SMITH	LOUISA

Source: kindly supplied by the Maranoa Regional Council.

References:

1 Metcalf, Bill, Dawson, Veronica, *Three Doomed Communes: A Roma Romance?* 2016, Queensland History Journal. Retrieved 26 June 2019 from URL: http://hdl.handle.net/10072/339269
2 Queensland. (1894, January 17). *Barrier Miner* (Broken Hill, NSW: 1888-1954), p3. Retrieved 21 June 2019 from http://nla.gov.au/nla.news-article44109891
3 - 9 Metcalf, Bill, Dawson, Veronica, *Three Doomed Communes: A Roma Romance?* Op.cit.
10 Queensland News. (1894, March 20). *The Telegraph* (Bris, Qld.: 1872-1947), p5. Retrieved 21 June 2019 from http://nla.gov.au/nla.news-article172551595

11 Co-operative Groups. (1894, June 6). *The Telegraph (Bris, Qld.: 1872-1947)*, p4. Retrieved June 21, 2019, from http://nla.gov.au/nla.news-article173161644
12 - 14 Thompson, Stephen, Objects Through Time: 1893 The New Australia Colony Collection, Feb 2013, *Migration Heritage Centre NSW*. Retrieved 22 June 2019 from URL: http://www.migrationheritage.nsw.gov.au/exhibition/objectsthroughtime/1893-the-new-australia-colony-collection/index.html
15 Metcalf, Bill, Dawson, Veronica, *Three Doomed Communes: A Roma Romance?* Op.cit.
16 Obertown Model Group. (1894, April 14). Worker (Bris, Qld.: 1890 - 1955), p. 3. Retrieved June 21, 2019, from http://nla.gov.au/nla.news-article70863384
17 - 18 Flyn, Conor, The life and times of William Lane, *The Socialist*, 21 June 2016. Retrieved 22 June 2019 from URL: https://thesocialist.org.au/the-life-and-times-of-william-lane/
19 Souter, Gavin, 'Lane, William (1861–1917)', Australian Dictionary of Biography, National Centre of Biography, *Australian National University*, 1983. Retrieved 22 June 2019 from URL: http://adb.anu.edu.au/biography/lane-william-7024/text12217
20 - 25 Metcalf, Bill, Dawson, Veronica, *Three Doomed Communes: A Roma Romance?* Op.cit.
26 Co-operative Village Settlement. (1895, Nov 28). *The Brisbane Courier (Qld. : 1864-1933)*, p5. Retrieved 21 June 2019 from http://nla.gov.au/nla.news-article3613839
27 OTHER'S OPINIONS. (1895, Nov 30). *Queensland Times, Ipswich Herald and General Advertiser (Qld. : 1861 - 1908)*, p. 6. Retrieved June 21, 2019, from http://nla.gov.au/nla.news-article130384808
28 Co-operative Village Settlement. (1895, November 28). Op.cit.
29 Metcalf, Bill, Dawson, Veronica, *Three Doomed Communes: A Roma Romance?* Op.cit.
30 PARLIAMENT. (1895, December 3). *The Brisbane Courier (Qld. : 1864 - 1933)*, p. 7. Retrieved June 21, 2019, from http://nla.gov.au/nla.news-article3614061
31 A Dream Shattered (1930, May 2). *Morning Bulletin (Rockhampton, Qld. : 1878 - 1954)*, p. 11. Retrieved June 21, 2019, from http://nla.gov.au/nla.news-article55363602

Images:

Members of Nil Desperandum commune, 1894. Collection of Lionel Coxen, Toowoomba, 25 August 2010. Reproduced with the kind permission of Dr Bill Metcalf, *Queensland Historical Atlas*. Retrieved 25 June 2019 from URL: https://www.qhatlas.com.au/photograph/nil-desperandum-commune-1894

Members of Excel Pioneers commune on Yalebone Creek, south of Roma, 1894. Collection of Lionel Coxen, Toowoomba, 25 August 2010. Reproduced with the kind permission of Dr Bill Metcalf, *Queensland Historical Atlas*.

William Lane, Sydney Worker 1893 and Anne Lane c1893. Courtesy *Wikipedia*. Originally sourced from S. Thompson, Objects Through Time: 1893 The New Australia Colony Collection, Feb 2013, *Migration Heritage Centre NSW*. Retrieved 22 June 2019 from: http://www.migrationheritage.nsw.gov.au/exhibition/objectsthroughtime/1893-the-new-australia-colony-collection/index.html

Unidentified, and *Worker*. Worker Staff, Brisbane, 1892, *State Library of Queensland*. Retrieved 22 June 2019 from: http://hdl.handle.net/10462/deriv/107703

Protestant Unity commune, near Pomona, with road (old Bruce Hwy) running through. Reproduced with the kind permission of Dr Bill Metcalf, *Queensland Historical Atlas*.

Communities dissolved notice: Co-operative Groups. (25 Feb1896). *The Telegraph* (Bris, Qld.: 1872-1947), p2. Retrieved 21 June 2019 from http://nla.gov.au/nla.news-article172425636

Lawrence does not have a headstone and we have marked the location for the purposes of this photo. The grave beside Lawrence had a metal marker bearing the number 1734 lying on its location.

The man who breathed in three centuries
Lawrence Tobin

Interred: **Lawrence Tobin**, 6 November 1799 – 10 May 1908 (aged 109).

Location: Catholic, Row 8, Grave 1354, no headstone.

Cemetery: Rom a Monumental Cemetery, Lewis Street, Roma QLD.

There are not many people who can lay claim to having lived in three centuries... who have seen massive changes in society, in lifestyle, in technology and medicine, but Lawrence Tobin can, and he did it with great spirit!

Born in the eighteenth century in Kilkenny, Ireland, Lawrence moved to Australia in the nineteenth century and died in Roma in the twentieth century,109 years later. Bear in mind it was only eleven years before Lawrence was born that the first fleet arrived in Australia to find our Indigenous people inhabiting the land; by the time Lawrence died, he would be one of many new Australians establishing a life for himself and his descendants.

A wife and sea life

Lawrence bucked the trend to wed young. Some stories say he was 40 when he betrothed Irish lass, Margaret Remilton in 1848 and that Margaret was considerably younger, around 18 at the time of their marriage.[1] Her sister and brother-in-law lived in New South Wales,[2] which might have inspired their move to Australia. But immigration ship records list different ages for them both, and it may be that Lawrence altered his age to assist with entry into Australia.

It appears that Lawrence and Margaret sailed to Australia on 19 March 1850 on the *Reliance*, with the records showing the married couple as Lawrence, 30, a labourer from Kilkenny who could read and write, and Margaret, 23, a wife, who could read.[3] Margaret gave Lawrence two sons—Martin and James—but passed away twelve years after their marriage.[4] Despite his long life, Lawrence would never remarry – amongst other things, he may well have broken a record for the number of years lived as a widower.[5]

After a long sea journey, they arrived as gold rush fever prevailed, and Lawrence took up the pan and joined the miners at Ballarat. Here, every man was focussed on getting gold, and the heat, lack of water, licence fees and hard toil made it a hot bed of tension.

At this time the Australian states were forming; England stopped sending convicts to our shores, although Tasmania still received their share;[6] wool and minerals were a strong currency; and life was simple – no cars, no electricity, no frills.

Etching of the Ballarat diggings, showing tents, and miners at work in the 1850s, when Lawrence was there. Source: State Library of South Australia.

Football, hard work and progress

The 1850s were a time of enormous growth. Australia-wide, the population was booming – out from 400,000 in 1850 to one million by the end of the decade.[7] In the same decade, Lawrence would marvel at the advent of the first steam railway and the first stagecoach service, along with the first telephone and telegraph line established in 1858. What sights to be seen and written home about!

It was also in that same year the first recorded game of Australian Rules football was played.[8] Lawrence was a keen footballer and played well into his eighties. In an interview in later years, he said: "My favourite recreation? Football! I kicked many a goal when I was well over 80, I suspect they wouldn't select me now. Think I'm too old over 100! Well, I suppose a man must retire from the field, sooner or later."[9]

In the 1860s Lawrence continued to toil as Burke and Wills headed off to explore and map the land between western New

Above: Cobb & Co. coach service, 1853, carrying 98 passengers. Source: National Library of Australia.

Burke, Wills and King on the way back from the Gulf of Carpentaria. Source: Wikimedia Commons.

South Wales and the northern Gulf of Carpentaria (dying in 1861 near Cooper Creek after successfully crossing the continent from south to north).[10]

It was the decade in which Queensland's first rail line opened between Ipswich and Grandchester (1865) and Cobb & Co. began its coach route between Brisbane and Ipswich (1866).[11] The town of Roma was surveyed (1862) and declared a municipality in 1867.[12] Now in his sixties, Lawrence wouldn't have imagined that he would live another fifty years and spend his last years in Roma.

In the 1870s, when land first went on sale in Victoria, Lawrence bought up[13] and began farming his land in Wycheproof, 136 km from Bendigo. Then, settlers selected 820-acre blocks close to the township, and the town grew with a police station, hotel, post office, school and eventually a railway station (opened 1883).[14]

Above: Lawrence's new hometown; locals at the Wycheproof Post Office, 1897. Source: State Library of Victoria.

The 1870s came and went and Lawrence and his sons continued to work the farm while the construction of the Ghan railway line in South Australia began, and the first Brisbane rail terminal station was built at Roma Street. One can only imagine the changes Lawrence saw unfolding.

In the 1880s, when workers went on strike for better wages and conditions, and women began to enter the workforce, Lawrence worked the land still. In that same decade, for the first time, the Sydney GPO and Circular Quay were lit using generators and Edison incandescent light bulbs![15] Let there be (artificial) light. But it would be Tamworth, a small town in NSW that would be the first place in Australia to enjoy an electricity supply to the public, in November 1888, followed by the Victorian town of Nhill in 1891.[16] Other country towns soon followed and Lawrence would have packed away the candles and turned on a bulb!

Room to breathe

Still on the farm, the outback areas became overstocked in the late 1880s and early in the 1890s drought arrived. Lawrence, 99 (and not out), desired more land. So he and his sons sold up and moved to Coobang, eight miles from Parkes in New South Wales.[17] The tale goes that arriving in Parkes by train after one of his sons' arrival, there was some confusion and he wasn't expected. He asked a stranger for directions to Coobang, the property taken up by the Tobins. "He was informed it was eight miles off. 'Well,' said the 99-year-older, 'I'll have a hearty breakfast, and walk there by lunchtime. I'll surprise my sons.' 'What!' cried the stranger, 'are you the father of those old fellows?' 'They're my youngsters,' intimated the veteran, with a twinkle in his bright eyes.'" As it turns out, he was speaking to a nephew, who got to meet his 99-year-old uncle for the first time and gave him a lift to the family home.[18]

Lawrence's obituary told of how then, he still worked as hard as any young man, doing the fencing, clearing, burning off, and walking to church in Parkes every Sunday… about eight miles. He was an amazing sight to behold at 99. He walked with a straight back and didn't need the aid of glasses to read from the church book.[19] He had thick white hair and often wore "white collar, white tie and white waistcoat, and with his brushed clothes and brushed boots, he was as clean-looking as a snowscape."[20]

A new century

And so the new year welcomed in a new century – 1900, and Lawrence, 101 years of age, lived on to see the design

Above: Lawrence arrived in Roma, where an artesian bore in 1900 yielded Australia's first natural gas. In 1906, this apparatus separated natural gas from artesian water at the Roma Gas Works.
Below: Roma from a distance, 1899. Lawrence made Roma his final resting place. Source: State Library of Queensland.

of the Australian flag, women having the right to vote (1905 in Queensland), the bubonic plague or dengue fever – diseases that felled many fellow Australians, the Boer War campaign (the first Queensland contingent left for South Africa in 1899)[21] and Roma's artesian bore in 1900 that yielded Australia's first natural gas.

In 1907 Lawrence, 108, moved with his son James and family to Roma where again they took up the land. In this, his last decade on earth and the first decade of the new century, Lawrence lived to see or hear of some cities lit by electric street lighting; the first successful Australian petrol-driven car being manufactured; and observatories tracing Halley's Comet, returning for the first time since 1844. Did Lawrence see it in 1844? In the year of Lawrence's death, 1908, men reached the south magnetic pole.[22] It was also the year that Rugby League was established as a separate sport from Rugby Union.[23] Lawrence might have liked that.

Words to live by

In the last few years of his life when Lawrence was asked about his vitality and longevity, he answered in the straight-shooter manner in which he lived his life: "Plain living and good batching… the food was simple, sound and wholesome; none of the tasty stuff sold to-day to tickle the appetite, with all the good ground out, boiled out, or steamed out of it. Beef and bread, milk and vegetables, plenty of fresh air, plenty of work, plenty of rest, and plenty of pleasure!

"Well, perhaps my wife's death was the only real trouble I had, I am happy, and I'm happy to see others happy… I take an interest in everything, but I never attempt to set the world right, nor do I interfere with the ideas of my neighbours on any question. Am I a teetotaller? I always have a drop in the house… because I like it. But I never took too much. The pipe has been a great comfort to me, There's no plain living and good batching without a pipe."[24]

And so, on 10 May 1908, aged 109, Lawrence Tobin drew his last breath, after breathing in three consecutive centuries. A rare feat, an extraordinary man.

How to find Lawrence's grave in Roma Cemetery, Catholic, Row 8, Grave 1354, no headstone:

Enter the cemetery off Tiffin Street and go straight ahead until the road turns to the right and becomes the central road through the cemetery. On your right-hand-side, you will see row numbers on white stakes. Lawrence's grave is in row 8. Walk away from the road until you come to a headstone marked 'Britton'. Lawrence's grave is halfway between that and the 'Enright' headstone. When we were there the unmarked grave beside Lawrence (that of Francis Nuss) was locatable by a metal marker bearing the number 1734 lying on its location.

References:

1 Margaret (Remilton) Tobin (1830 - aft. 1859), *WikiTree*, 18 June 2018. Retrieved 13 June 2019 from URL: https://www.wikitree.com/wiki/Remilton-5

2 109—OUT! (1908, July 11). *National Advocate (Bathurst, NSW: 1889-1954)*, p.2. Retrieved 13 June 2019 from http://nla.gov.au/nla.news-article157186674

3 Assisted Immigrants (Digital) Shipping Lists, NSW State Archives and Records, retrieved 12 July 2019 from: http://indexes.records.nsw.gov.au/ebook/list.aspx?Page=NRS5316/4_4817/Reliance_19%20Mar%201850/4_481700091.jpg&No=7

4 From Ancestry, https://www.ancestry.com.au/ Researched by Stephanie Johnson, 20 August 2019.

5 109—OUT! (1908, July 11). *National Advocate (Bathurst, NSW: 1889-1954)*, p.2. Retrieved 13 June 2019 from http://nla.gov.au/nla.news-article157186674

6 Rickard, John David, Veevers, John J. & Others, Australia, *Encyclopædia Britannica*. Retrieved 12 June 2019 from: https://www.britannica.com/place/Australia/History
7 - 8 Decade Timeline, My Place for Teachers, *Australian Children's Television Foundation and Education Services Australia Ltd*. Retrieved 13 June 2019 from URL: https://myplace.edu.au/decades_timeline/decade_timeline_landing.html
9 109—OUT! (1908, July 11). *National Advocate*. Op cit.
10 - 11 Queensland Government, *Queensland's history—1800s*, the State of Queensland 1995-2019. Retrieved 15 June 2019 from URL: https://www.qld.gov.au/about/about-queensland/history/timeline/1800s
12 The Editors of Encyclopaedia Britannica, Roma, *Encyclopædia Britannica*, 6 June 2018. Retrieved 14 June 2019 from: https://www.britannica.com/place/Roma-Queensland
13 Death of a Centenarian at Roma. (10 June 1908). *Western Star & Roma Advertiser*. Op.cit.
14 *Wycheproof Historical Society*. Retrieved 30 July 2019 from URL: https://wychehistory.webs.com/firstsetlers.htm
15 Decade Timeline, *My Place for Teachers*, Op.cit.
16 GloBird Energy, 14 fascinating facts about the history of electricity in Australia, 2019. Retrieved 13 June 2019 from URL: https://www.globirdenergy.com.au/14-fascinating-facts-about-the-history-of-electricity-in-australia/
17 - 20 109—OUT! (1908, July 11). *National Advocate*. Op.cit.
21 Queensland Government, *Queensland's history—1800s*. Op.cit.
22 Decade Timeline, My Place for Teachers. Op.cit.
23 Queensland Government, *Queensland's history—1900s.* , the State of Queensland 1995-2019. Retrieved 15 June 2019 from URL: https://www.qld.gov.au/about/about-queensland/history/timeline/1900s
24 109—OUT! (1908, July 11). *National Advocate*. Op.cit.

Images:

(1852). *The Bullarat Diggings* [photograph], A.C. Kelly Collection. Image No. B 29496, *State Library of South Australia*. Retrieved 13 June 2019 form URL: https://trove.nla.gov.au/version/228737744
Deutsch, H. (1853). *Cobb & Cos. Leviathan coach, carrying 98 passengers.* Retrieved 13 June 2019 from http://nla.gov.au/nla.obj-135867709
Burke, Wills and King. Nicholas Chevalier-2.jpg. image c1868. *Wikimedia Commons*. Retrieved 1 July 2019 from: https://commons.wikimedia.org/w/index.php?title=File:Burke_and_wills_nicholas_chevalier-2.jpg&oldid=323712127
(1897). *Wycheproof* [post office], Sands & McDougall, Melbourne, ID: H27288/4g. Retrieved 13 June 2019 from: http://handle.slv.vic.gov.au/10381/273304
Unidentified (1906). Apparatus for separating natural gas from artesian water at the Roma Gas Works, Queensland, ca. 1906. *John Oxley Library, State Library of Queensland,* Negative number: 39114. Retrieved 13 June 2019 from URL: https://trove.nla.gov.au/version/167830555
Unidentified (1899). *Distant view of Roma, 1899*. John Oxley Library, State Library of Queensland, Negative number: 191024. Retrieved 13 June 2019 from URL: https://trove.nla.gov.au/version/167826414

Switzer sisters' grave kindly supplied by Melissa Everitt, Find A Grave.

The drowning of the Misses Switzer
Ethel, Ada and Elsie Switzer

Interred: **Ethel Avina Switzer**, 1902 – 5 January 1921*
(aged 19 years old).
Ada Viola Switzer, 1910 – 5 January 1921*
(aged 11 years old).
Elsic Dora Switzer, 1911 – 5 January 1921*
(aged 10 years old).

Cemetery: Charleville Cemetery, off Francis Street, Charleville, QLD 4470.

Please note the deaths of the young ladies happened on 5 January 1921, despite the headstone listing the date of death as 15 January 1921.

It was an exciting time, a holiday for the Switzer family – father Alfred, mother Alice, and their five daughters and one son, aged from four to 19, were heading to the 'big smoke', Sydney. They were travelling from their home over 54 kilometres (33 miles) from Charleville in their wagonette with plans to catch the Western Mail[1] train from the Charleville station to Toowoomba en route to Sydney. It was a grand adventure, especially for the children.

Alfred, a grazier,[2] hailed from Alberta, Canada[3] and four years prior, in 1917, had bought Gum Creek grazing farm[4] with a view to starting a new life in Queensland with his family. The locals were advised by a notice that ran in *The Queenslander* (10 November 1917). These same locals would later describe Alfred as "a fine settler in the western districts."[5]

SALE OF GRAZING FARMS.

CHARLEVILLE, October 31.
The sale is reported, on account of Mr. Thomas Wade, of his Gum Creek grazing farm, situated on the Lanlo River, Adavale-road, to Mr. Switzer, a Canadian, recently arrived in Queensland. The farm is unstocked, but improved.

That fateful day

It was the first week of a new year, the Christmas and New Year holiday season, summer and the season of cricket. Just the day prior we had won the second test against the Poms by an innings and 91 runs at the MCG. Australia would eventually win all five tests to claim the Ashes.

Perhaps the Switzer family had plans to go to the fifth test in Sydney in February, or perhaps they were visiting friends, or they just wanted to visit Australia's largest city with nearly one million inhabitants.[6]

But on this day, they chose the wrong crossing. They were only six kilometres (four miles) from their home when they reached Middle Creek, which was about 48 kilometres (30 miles) from Charleville on the Charleville to Langlo Crossing and Adavale Road[7] (and up to six hours travelling time to the Charleville railway station where they were headed for their connection). But, Middle Creek was not fit for crossing.

The Charleville Railway Station, where the Switzer family were headed for their train connection. Source: State Library of Queensland, 1928.

The Western Mail train, 1927 which the Switzers planned to catch. Photo kindly supplied by the Queensland Railways Historical Collection.

The family succumb to the water

Camped at Middle Creek were two men who saw the danger that the swollen creek with its rushing water presented. They warned Alfred Switzer, saying "not to go into the crossing as it was a swim."[8] As Alfred had been in Australia for less than four years,[9] he may not have truly understood the danger of Queensland floodwaters, and thus the wagonette with its precious load entered the creek, which the newspaper later reported "was running a flood of water as a result of the recent storms"[10] and water had flooded in from the higher districts.

Some reports say that Alfred was riding in front of the wagonette, in which his wife, Alice, and the children were contained. A rope was attached to his horse and to the horse leading the wagonette, to steer them on the culvert. Meanwhile the eldest daughter, Ethel, was driving the wagonette.[11] Other reports at the time place Alfred in the driving seat of the wagonette with Ethel following behind on a black pony.[12]

Regardless, it must have been a terrifying moment as the wagonette slipped into the deeper and rushing waters, pulling the family and horses with it. By this time, the family was about halfway across the creek.[13] Their horses were swept away[14] and they were sent flailing into the torrent. Ethel, 19, Ada, 11, and Elsie, 10, were in immediate trouble.

The two men camped at the creek bravely, and with no thought to their own safety, raced to help the family as they attempted to scramble to the bank. Alice (Mrs Switzer) was in desperate trouble but with her husband, Alfred, and three of the children—Albert, 4 [15] and his sisters Bernice, 5, and Hannah, 7[16], was saved; young Albert had clung to the wagonette until he could be rescued. The horses drowned.[17]

Of the three eldest girls, Ethel, who until recently had attended the Presbyterian College at the Range, Toowoomba,[18] and was said to be an excellent swimmer, struggled to remain afloat. Her sister, Elsie, clung on to her for life before they both disappeared below the water, out of sight.[19] Ethel, Ada and Elsie could not be found.

The missing girls

As the waters continued to rise, the chances of finding the girls alive diminished and it became impossible to find their bodies. Police arrived at the scene by motor car and with grappling irons to drag the creek[20] but escalating waters deterred their efforts. They struggled on with the search finding the wagonette and the horses, but not the girls. Eventually the search for the girls had to be called off as evening fell.[21]

The remaining Switzer family members were taken to a neighbour's residence, about six miles from the scene of the tragedy, to wait until morning when the search would resume.[22]

The next day the bodies of Ethel and Elsie were recovered. A mounted constable reported that the body of Ethel "was recovered about 300 yards [274 metres] downstream with her arm half-round the trunk of a tree and the body of Elsie about 200 yards [182 metres] farther down, washed up against a butt of a tree – about 400 yards [365 metres] from where the accident happened."[23]

Police and locals continued to search for the third young girl, Ada. Early on Saturday morning, 8 January 1921, three days after the terrible accident, the funeral for Ethel and Elsie took place with many community members present. That evening the family received word that Ada's body had been found, and she was buried shortly after.[24]

Described by locals as a "fine family",[25] had Alfred known the area as well as the locals did or had he heeded the warning of the creek's treachery and not to cross it when flooded, disaster may have been averted.

An end to an adventure

The tragedy caused "shock and gloom over the town and district."[26] It was said if not for the bravery of the travellers camping at the creek, the whole family may have perished.[27]

Within nine days of the accident, on 14 January 1921, a

magisterial inquiry was conducted at the police court. The rescuers gave testimony at the inquiry and were identified as David Bryant, a drover, and George Henry Lane.[28]

In closing, the Police Magistrate, Marcus Gallagher,[29] declared: "the Switzer family is very fortunate indeed that Bryant and Lane were present... I hope the authorities will take the matter up and show that their action is appreciated."[30]

Less than a week later on 20 January, the matter of recognition for the heroes was addressed at a public meeting in Charleville and the Mayor, Alderman H. J. Carter *(pictured)*, led the discussion on the best recognition to be given to Mr Bryant and Mr Lane. A number of people spoke and the Mayor told of their heroics. The party unanimously agreed to write to the Royal Humane Society asking for the men to be recognised.[31] They were not.*

Mayor Carter, 1925. The Brisbane Courier.

After the terrible tragedy it was not surprising that Alfred and Alice Switzer and their remaining three children left Queensland, passing on a message to the group at the meeting that "notwithstanding the kindness of the people of Western Queensland, they could not stop."[32]

Ethel, Ada, and Elsie remained behind, buried in Charleville Cemetery after the terrible accident which would come to be known as the Middle Creek Tragedy.

*The Royal Humane Society of Australasia Inc confirmed the men were never award recipients.

References:

1 Three Sisters Drowned (1921, January 6). *Toowoomba Chronicle (Qld. : 1917 - 1922)*, p. 5. Retrieved June 28, 2019, from http://nla.gov.au/nla.news-article253167179
2 Appalling Drowning Accident (1921, Jan 11). *The Armidale Express and New England General Advertiser (NSW : 1856 - 1861; 1863 - 1889; 1891 - 1954)*, p. 6. Retrieved June 28, 2019, from http://nla.gov.au/nla.news-article192013423
3 Drowning Tragedy. (1921, January 6). *The Telegraph (Brisbane, Qld.: 1872 - 1947)*, p. 5 (SECOND EDITION). Retrieved June 28, 2019, from http://nla.gov.au/nla.news-article180537410
4 Three Sisters Drowned (1921, Jan 6). *Evening News (Sydney, NSW: 1869-1931)*, p.4. Retrieved 28 June 2019 from http://nla.gov.au/nla.news-article117299319
5 Drowning Tragedy. (1921, Jan 6). *The Telegraph (Brisbane, Qld.: 1872-1947)*, p.5 (2nd ed.). Retrieved 28 June 2019, from http://nla.gov.au/nla.news-article180537410
6 Census of the Commonwealth of Australia, 1921
7 Appalling Drowning Accident (1921, January 11). *The Armidale Express and New England General Advertiser (NSW: 1856 - 1861; 1863 - 1889; 1891 - 1954)*, p. 6. Retrieved June 28, 2019, from http://nla.gov.au/nla.news-article192013423
8 Appalling Drowning Accident (1921, January 11). *The Armidale Express and New England General Advertiser.* Op cit.
9 Middle Creek Tragedy. (1921, January 7). *Toowoomba Chronicle (Qld.: 1917-1922)*, p. 5. Retrieved June 28, 2019, from http://nla.gov.au/nla.news-article253167960
10 Appalling Drowning Accident (1921, January 11). *The Armidale Express and New England General Advertiser (NSW : 1856 - 1861; 1863 - 1889; 1891 - 1954)*, p. 6. Retrieved June 28, 2019, from http://nla.gov.au/nla.news-article192013423
11 Charleville Tragedy. (1921, January 7). *Warwick Daily News (Qld. : 1919 -1954)*, p. 2. Retrieved June 28, 2019, from http://nla.gov.au/nla.news-article177265737
12 Middle Creek Tragedy. (1921, Jan 7). *Toowoomba Chronicle.* Op.cit.
13 Three Sisters Drowned. (1921, January 6). *The Argus (Melbourne, Vic. : 1848 - 1957)*, p. 4. Retrieved June 28, 2019, from http://nla.gov.au/nla.news-article1731668
14 Appalling Drowning Accident (1921, January 11). *The Armidale Express and New England General Advertiser (NSW: 1856 - 1861; 1863 - 1889; 1891 - 1954)*, p. 6. Retrieved June 28, 2019, from http://nla.gov.au/nla.news-article192013423
15 Triple Drowning Case. (1921, January 8). *Darling Downs Gazette (Qld. : 1881 - 1922)*, p. 5. Retrieved June 28, 2019, from http://nla.gov.au/nla.news-article183224167
16 Charleville Notes. (1921, January 18). *Townsville Daily Bulletin (Qld.: 1907 - 1954)*, p. 6. Retrieved June 29, 2019, from http://nla.gov.au/nla.news-article63515693
17 Three Sisters Drowned (1921, January 6). *Evening News.* Op.cit.
18 Triple Drowning Case. (1921, Jan 8). *Darling Downs Gazette,* Op.cit.
19 Middle Creek Tragedy. (1921, Jan 7). *Toowoomba Chronicle.* Op.cit.
20 Three Girls Drowned. (1921, Jan 6). *The Daily Mail (Brisbane, Qld.: 1903 - 1926)*, p. 7. Retrieved June 28, 2019, from http://nla.gov.au/nla.news-article213057818
21 Drowning Tragedy. (1921, January 6). *The Telegraph.* Op.cit.
22 - 23 Middle Creek Tragedy. (1921, Jan 7). *Toowoomba Chronicle.* Op.cit.
24 Triple Drowning Case. (1921, Jan 8). *Darling Downs Gazette* Op.cit.
25 - 26 Appalling Drowning Accident (1921, January 11). *The Armidale Express*

and New England General Advertiser (NSW: 1856 - 1861; 1863 - 1889; 1891 - 1954), p. 6. Retrieved June 28, 2019, from http://nla.gov.au/nla.news-article192013423
27 Three Sisters Drowned (1921, Jan 6). *Toowoomba Chronicle (Qld.: 1917 - 1922)*, p. 5. Retrieved June 28, 2019, from http://nla.gov.au/nla.news-article253167179
28 Western Drowning. (1921, January 14). *Darling Downs Gazette (Qld. : 1881 - 1922)*, p. 5. Retrieved June 28, 2019, from http://nla.gov.au/nla.news-article183214844
29 Middle Creek Tragedy (1921, January 14). *Toowoomba Chronicle (Qld.: 1917 - 1922)*, p. 4. Retrieved June 28, 2019, from http://nla.gov.au/nla.news-article253172038
30 WESTERN DROWNING. (1921, Jan 14). *Darling Downs Gazette.* Op.cit.
31 - 32 For Bravery (1921, January 20). *Toowoomba Chronicle (Qld. : 1917 - 1922)*, p. 5. Retrieved June 28, 2019, from http://nla.gov.au/nla.news-article253175618

Images:

The Switzer sisters' grave [photograph] by Melissa Everitt from memorial page for Ada Viola Switzer, *Find A Grave* Memorial no. 48997138, Charleville Cemetery, Charleville. Reproduced with Melissa's kind permission.

Sale of Grazing Farms. (1917, Nov 10). *The Queenslander (Brisbane, Qld. : 1866 - 1939)*, p. 36. Retrieved June 29, 2019, from http://nla.gov.au/nla.news-article22344240

Charleville Railway Station, 1928 (2007): Acc No. 82-2-4. *State Library of Queensland*. Retrieved 29 June 2019 from: https://hdl.handle.net/10462/deriv/86432

The Western Mail train, 1927. Photo kindly supplied by the *Queensland Railways Historical Collection*.

The Mayor: How A City Was Created in the Great South-West. (1925, March 6). *The Brisbane Courier* (Qld.: 1864 - 1933), p. 11. Retrieved July 30, 2019, from http://nla.gov.au/nla.news-article20911253

(Below) How the news was reported: THREE SISTERS DROWNED (1921, January 6). *Toowoomba Chronicle (Qld. : 1917 - 1922)*, p. 5. Retrieved June 29, 2019, from http://nla.gov.au/nla.news-article253167179

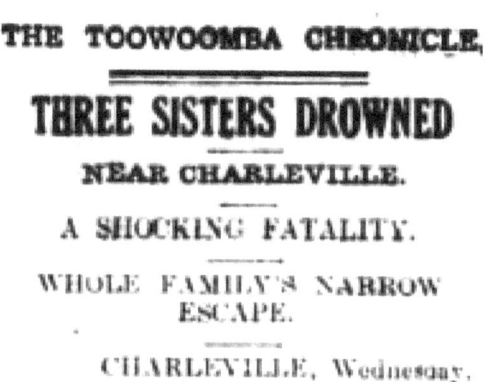

Harry Corones' grave in Charleville Cemetery. Photograph by Melissa Everitt. Supplied and reproduced with Melissa's kind permission.

The best in the West
Harry Corones

Interred: Haralambos (Harry) Coroneos, 1883– 22 March 1972 (aged 90 years).

Location: Allotment 3, Section 74/13B Grave number 30740.

Cemetery: Charleville Cemetery, off May Street, Charleville, QLD 4470.

The story goes that when the 'bush' was booming because wool was selling at a 'pound for a pound', Corones Hotel in Charleville, Queensland, had the same silver service dining room menu as Lennons Hotel in Brisbane, the epitome of fine dining in the state.

In October 1952 *The West Australian* newspaper reported that 248 pence per pound was paid for five bales of superfine wool from Mayvale Station in north western NSW.[1] While that may not have been the everyday price everywhere, the article indicates that it had been reached previously. In the early 1950s the 'bush' was wealthy and demanded attention.

Made possible by this wealth, and therefore the power that pastoral businesses generated, regional centres looked after themselves. Decisions were made in provincial centres rather than miles away in capital cities. The emphasis was on looking after the locals. For example, QANTAS, the outback airline which had its first scheduled flight out of Charleville, operated in the north and west of the state for nine years before flights were extended to Brisbane.[2]

And one of the towns where western wealth was on show was Charleville, and deeply involved in much of what happened there over 60 or so years was a man called Harry Corones… the man who built the hotel of the same name that rivalled its capital city counterparts some 750 kilometres away.

Haralambos Coroneos, to give him his birth name, was born in 1883 on the Greek island of Kythira in the Mediterranean Sea. His father, Panayiotis Coroneos, was a fisherman and his mother, Stamatea, was part of the Freeleagus family which would play a vital role in the rise of Harry's empire.

Not much is known about Harry's early life but it was probably fairly carefree on the island until he turned 21 and commenced two years of compulsory military service as a first-aid orderly attached to a military hospital. But what next? There was little prospect for Harry on Kythira. He could join his father as a fisherman or tend the family's small piece of land. The family decided that given the limited opportunities, Harry would have to emigrate and take his young nephew Demetrios (Jim) with him. The family had spoken. Harry's first choice of a new place of residence was the United States. He applied to emigrate but for medical reasons he was rejected. Australia was next on the list… and why not, his mother had relatives living in Brisbane.

Harry Corones and his nephew, Jim Corones, 1914.
Source: State Library of Queensland.

The adventure begins

Harry and young Jim stepped down onto Circular Quay in Sydney on 10 August 1907 and after a short stay moved to Brisbane, where Harry got a job in the Freeleagus Brothers' Oyster-saloon in George Street. The connection with his mother's relatives was to be the beginning of a most agreeable business venture for Harry Corones.

However, working for someone else shucking oysters and filleting fish was not what the new arrival had in mind as his future. He wanted his own business and he began to think where that should be. The word was that the west of Queensland was the land of opportunity and Harry came across a café for sale in Charleville. He negotiated a loan from the Freeleagus brothers and in 1909 headed west.

The café needed lots of work, but Harry wasn't afraid of a bit of toil. He built the business by offering good service, good food and warm hospitality. Just a year or so later he went into partnership with another Greek and they opened a second, bigger café in town. It was called the Paris and not only provided the fine standards of Harry's first café but from the rear of the premises, Harry operated a silent-picture cinema and staged vaudeville shows with performers brought from Brisbane and Sydney. Charleville had never seen anything like it.

New horizons

The Paris was also the place where Harry would meet the person who took him on the next step of his journey, Paddy Cryan, a travelling salesman from Perkins Brewery in

Brisbane who suggested that Harry should move into the hotel business as the Hotel Charleville, just down the road from his café, had become vacant. Harry was sceptical, he didn't know anything about hotels. But Cryan persisted so Harry talked it over with Jim and they decided – publicans they would become and signed the lease on the Hotel Charleville for five years at a rent of six pounds per week. [3]

Things were moving quickly. In 1912 Harry decided to commit himself to his new homeland. He was naturalised and became a proud citizen of Australia.

Harry Corones and Paddy Cryan. Source: State Library of Queensland.

*Harry and Eftyhia (Effie) Corones at the Hotel Charleville, 1915.
Source: Library, State Library of Queensland.*

Two years later he took a trip to Sydney where in April 1914 he married Eftyhia Phocas who was the daughter of a Greek Orthodox priest. Effie, as she was to become known, became Harry's life-long partner and together they raised five children. Influenced by Effie's own education, the couple sent their children to schools as far away as Athens.

But Harry and Effie's biggest challenge was still in front of them. While Harry had been in Sydney getting married, the Hotel Charleville was destroyed by fire. It was a disappointment, but Harry and Effie rebuilt the hotel bigger and better. It was probably at this point they had the idea of building even a larger, more luxurious hotel in the town. But that was a few years off yet.

Flying high

While he was running the Hotel Charleville in 1919, a chance encounter with one of aviation's best-known names gave Harry an interest in flying as a means of counteracting the vagaries of travelling in the outback, where there were few roads and even fewer bridges across flooded rivers. On a flight from Darwin to Sydney to collect their prize money for being the first to fly from England to Australia in less than 30 days, Sirs Keith and Ross Smith landed at Charleville. They needed fuel and urgent repairs and Harry entertained them and their crew for the three months it took to procure the parts to get their Vickers Vimy flying again. It just came naturally to Harry and Effie that that's what you do when visitors drop in.

So, when Sir Hudson Fysh, Paul McGinness and Fergus McMaster came up with the idea of an airline to serve exactly what its name suggested, Queensland and Northern

Territory Aerial Service, Harry was in like a shot and was one of the first investors, purchasing 100 one-pound shares. But it didn't stop there. Early meetings of the airline directors were held at Harry's hotel and the coming and goings of aircraft at Charleville's early airport gave Harry an idea. The town was becoming an important port for the airline... many passengers passed through the airport but what did they do for food and drink? Before long Harry and Effie became the airline's first caterers, providing picnic hampers for Qantas aircraft. The story goes that the influence of Harry was so great that after he suggested the idea, five of the airline's first seven aircraft were named after Greek mythological characters – Perseus, Pegasus, Atalanta, Hermes and Heppomenes.[4]

Boom or Bust

As is the case today, the fortunes of those who live and work in regional areas of the country are largely dictated by the weather. In the early 1920s Charleville and the west of Queensland were about to be devastated by what the Charleville Chamber of Commerce called the "worst season known by black or white man with losses of sheep to the enormous extent of eleven million."[5] For many rural towns it was the beginning of the slide into the Great Depression of the 1930s.

It was against this backdrop that Harry Corones was considering taking his biggest gamble yet, to risk his entire empire which now consisted of the Charleville cafes, the Hotel Charleville, a hotel in Quilpie and two cinemas – one in Charleville and the other in Quilpie. July 1924 was crunch time. That month the lease on the Hotel Charleville ran out and just a few days after it expired Harry launched his plan to not only have the best hotel in Queensland outside Brisbane, but to rival anything the city could offer as well. And such was the mindset of the west at that time that no-one thought this Greek businessman was totally mad when he planned to invest more than 50,000 pounds, a small fortune in those days, in his latest grand passion.

He bought a dilapidated hotel in Charleville called the Norman Hotel as well as the whole block along one side of the street on which it stood and engaged architect William Hodgen Jnr, son of pioneer Toowoomba building contractor William Hodgen, to design his dream. It is regarded as Hodgen's major single work and the highlight of his career.[6]

And the new hotel, built in stages over the following five years, lived up to expectations… both in price and quality. "Built at a cost of, £50,000, it contained a lounge and writing room, a dining-room for a hundred and fifty people, a private and a public bar, a barber's shop and, attached to the hotel, a magnificent ballroom capable of seating three hundred and twenty people at a banquet, while upstairs were bathrooms, about forty single and double bedrooms each with French doors opening to a veranda (the double rooms also had private bathrooms) and an upstairs lounge."[7]

The new hotel was truly the most excellent in Queensland outside the capital city. It was an attraction for local and international luminaries: "celebrities such as Amy Johnson, Gracie Fields, and the Duke and Duchess of Gloucester were guests at the hotel. In 1936 there were on average 133 guests per week and during World War II when American servicemen occupied the local aerodrome and hospital, 'Poppa' [as the GIs nicknamed Harry] did a roaring trade with dances held every night in Corones Hall."[8]

Above: Interior view of Hotel Corones, ca. 1930. Source: State Library of Queensland. Below: the Hotel Corones today, 2019.

But amidst the success of the new hotel and the visitation of the rich and famous, tragedy struck the Corones family in May 1931 with the cruel and unusual death of Alick Corones, the second child of Harry and Effie, while he was away at school in Ipswich. The *Brisbane Courier* reported: "The lad, who was 15 years of age, was a student at the Ipswich Grammar School. He was resident at the school, and on Thursday while playing football he knocked his toe. Blood poisoning quickly developed, causing the boy's death."[9]

A place for everyone

No doubt Harry Corones' success was brought about by hard work but also because he cared about people. Locals who knew Harry will tell you that everyone was welcome at the Hotel Corones, no matter who they were. When drovers, black or white, were out of town on long trips Harry would make sure their families had enough food and help with any other problems they may encounter. Out of respect for what they did, doctors and nurses at the Charleville hospital were banned from paying at Corones Hotel. Being there in any capacity other than as Harry's guest was out of the question.[10] In 1965 he was awarded an M.B.E.

There are plenty of stories about Harry's tenuous grip on the English language that are still related around the town and elsewhere by those who knew him. One is told by George Karanarkis in his stories of Greek Settlers in Australia: "On one occasion, one of Harry's guests had been a circuit judge from Brisbane who used to stay at the hotel, and who, every year, would go duck shooting with Harry. His visit to Charleville over, the judge had taken the train back to Brisbane when Harry discovered that he had left his gun behind, so Harry telephoned him to let him know. But the line between Charleville and Brisbane was very poor, compounded by Harry's heavy accent, and the judge could not understand what Harry was talking about. "Spell it" the judge said, becoming rather exasperated. So, Harry spelt "G for Jesus, U for onion, N for pneumonia"! [11]

In July 1966 his nephew Jim, with whom he had travelled from Kythira to the other side of the world, passed away. It was a shattering blow for Harry to lose his closest friend and partner after all those years and his own health began to deteriorate. He progressively lost his hearing and eyesight and on 22 March 1972 Harry Corones passed away. There were unparalleled scenes in Charleville on the day of Harry's funeral. Most of the town turned out and friends and former hotel guests came from all over the country to be there. Two years later on 8 March 1974, Effie died and was buried next to Harry in the Charleville cemetery.

In the Hotel Corones there was a custom of ringing the dinner bell to call diners each evening. The bell had been fashioned by Harry from the lining of a bore-water shaft and bronzed. The day after Harry's funeral it was not rung and as a mark of respect it has been silent ever since.

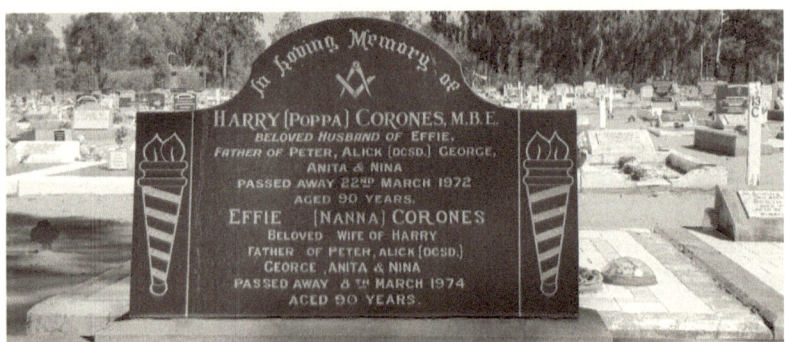

References:

1 Pound for A Pound at Wool Sales (1952, October 22). *The West Australian (Perth, WA: 1879 - 1954)*, p. 1. Retrieved July 30, 2019, from http://nla.gov.au/nla.news-article49059509
2 Qantas through the years. https://www.qantas.com/travel/airlines/history-through-the-years/global/en
3 Karanarkis, George, *In the Wake of Odysseus. Portraits of Greek Settlers in Australia*. RMIT University 1997. Greek-Australian Archives Publications. https://www.kythera-family.net/en/people/notable-kytherians/harry-haralambos-corones
4 Dianne Byrne, 'Corones, Haralambos (Harry) (1883–1972)', Australian Dictionary of Biography, National Centre of Biography, *Australian National University*, http://adb.anu.edu.au/biography/corones-haralambos-harry-9828/text17381 Retrieved 2 August 2019.
5 "Hotel Corones, Charleville (entry 601282)". Queensland Heritage Register, *Queensland Heritage Council*. Retrieved 1 August 2014. https://apps.des.qld.gov.au/heritage-register/detail/?id=601282
6 Ibid.
7 Karanarkis, George. Op.cit.
8 "Hotel Corones, Charleville (entry 601282)". *Qld Heritage Register,* Op.cit.
9 Schoolboy's Death. (1931, May 16). *The Brisbane Courier (Qld.: 1864 - 1933)*, p.7. Retrieved 3 Aug 2019 from http://nla.gov.au/nla.news-article21693311
10 - 11 Karanarkis, George. *Op.cit.*

Images:

Harry Corones' grave [photograph] in Charleville Cemetery, Charleville, by Melissa Everitt for Grave Tales. Initial contact via Find A Grave – https://www.findagrave.com/ Supplied and reproduced with Melissa's kind permission.

Harry Corones and Jim Corones, Charleville, Ca. 1914 (2004): Accession Number: 85-7-7. Brisbane John Oxley Library, *State Library of Queensland,* Negative number: 49961. Retrieved 8 August 2019 from URL: https://hdl.handle.net/10462/deriv/145043

Harry Corones and Paddy Cryan (2004): Accession Number: 85-7-7. Brisbane John Oxley Library, *State Library of Queensland,* Negative number: 49958. Retrieved 8 August 2019 from URL: https://hdl.handle.net/10462/deriv/142163

Harry and Effie Corones at the Hotel Charleville, Ca. 1915 (2007): Accession Number: 85-2-1. *State Library of Queensland*. Retrieved 19 August 2019 from URL: https://hdl.handle.net/10462/deriv/141229

Unidentified, and Hotel Corones. Interior View of the Foyer in Hotel Corones, Charleville, Ca. 1930. Negative number: 34462, John Oxley Library, *State Library of Queensland*. Retrieved 8 August 2019 from URL: http://hdl.handle.net/10462/deriv/1144

Edwin Helton's grave in Augathella Cemetery. Photograph by Melissa Everitt. Supplied and reproduced with Melissa's kind permission.

The poisoning of Mrs Roche
Edwin Helton

Interred: **Edwin Helton**, 22 June 1901 – 17 October, 1973 (aged 72 years).

Location: Row I, Grave 490.

Cemetery: Augathella Cemetery, off Jane Street, Augathella, QLD 4477.

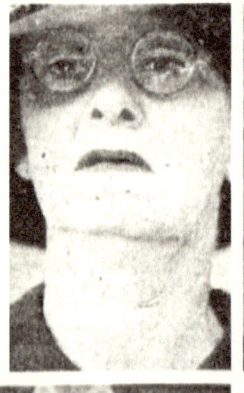

The people involved in the mystery of the death of Mrs Margaret Roche. Above: Edwin Helton and his love, Margaret Roche. Right: Bridget Russoc and Dr McIntosh. Below from left: Aubrey Carter, Detective Frank Bischof and Detective Senior-sergeant Dan Mahoney, and Sub-inspector Thomas Smith. (Source: Truth 1938).

Sweetheart, I am lonely for you. I do wish you were here. I love you dearly, and will never be happy without you. Truthfully speaking, I love you too much,[1] wrote Edwin Helton to the woman he loved, Margaret Roche. He left his wife to live with Margaret and sent her "oceans of love"[2], and then Edwin murdered her with poison. Or did he?

The good people of Augathella no doubt knew that widow Mrs Margaret Roche, 50, a very wealthy woman and owner of the Claren Hotel, lived with 36-year-old Mr Edwin Helton.[3] Edwin was a married man whose wife, Agnes Frances Crow,[4] lived across the road from the hotel; she was clearly very much alive. Margaret's husband had passed away in 1935.

Edwin, a storekeeper and baker by trade, was married in 1923 but had been a boarder at the Claren Hotel since 1933.[5] As Edwin explained: "Mrs Roche and myself have had most unhappy married lives, and we found that we understood each other. That is how I came to be living here.... We would have been man and wife only for one obstacle, the law."[6]

Margaret not only enjoyed the company of Edwin, living as a man and wife would, but she relied on him to manage a big part of her business affairs, which also included the Telegraph Hotel in Charleville. But it was while reading the newspaper on the verandah on Friday 10 September 1937, that Margaret felt ill. Toppling from her chair, she called for help; about forty minutes later she died in Augathella Hospital. Dr McIntosh had his suspicions and performed a post-mortem to find that Margaret was poisoned with strychnine, but how it was administered was a mystery.[7]

The lover in the spotlight

Immediately, the police spotlight shone on lover, Edwin Helton, who sobbed loudly in the company of Sub-inspector Thomas Smith before allegedly asking him to ensure Margaret's will was read aloud at the burial in front of the relatives to confirm it was legal.[8]

Brisbane's Detective Frank Bischof also interviewed Edwin and pointed out that he was to benefit from nearly all of Margaret's estate valued at around 7000 pounds, including the two hotels. Edwin's alleged reply was, "Yes, she was a dear friend of mine. She adored the ground I walked on."[9]

It was not the first time Edwin had been involved with the police. His own grocery store that had some insurance, was totally destroyed by fire in August 1934[10] and the year prior to Margaret's death, in 1936, a fire had occurred at the Claren Hotel on 29 September – at the time Edwin was a boarder. Edwin was questioned, along with a number of other guests and boarders at the time.[11] The hotel was insured. In March the next year, 1937, plans for its rebuilding were approved and the newspaper listed Margaret as the licensee and Edwin Claude Helton as the owner.[12] An interesting occurrence given Edwin later had to fight to claim the hotel from Margaret's will. Since the fire, the Claren had been functioning with a temporary bar in part of the building not destroyed by the flames.[13]

Despite Edwin's protestations of love, the police were not convinced that Edwin had good intentions and he was charged with wilful murder, to appear in the police court the very next day. He proclaimed: "Why, I would not hurt one hair of her head. Why do it this way? Can't you hold an inquest? I am as innocent as you are."[14] Edwin was allowed out on bail of 500 pounds but had to report daily to the police station.[15]

The police court proceedings

It was as sordid as a soap opera. The police subpoenaed 26 witnesses, and Edwin was defended by Mr N. J. Moynihan of Brisbane.

Aubrey William Carter, whose wife was Margaret's stepsister,[16] was painting Margaret's hotel the afternoon of her collapse. He told how he heard her cry for help and that she seemed fine just prior to the attack. Aubrey ran to her side and she insisted she would be alright, but after he fetched her some water, she deteriorated. He saw Edwin across the road standing on the footpath; on hearing Margaret was ill, Edwin went to her.[17] She was transferred to the hospital complaining of pain in the stomach and died shortly after.

Edwin did not want a post-mortem examination conducted and exclaimed: "I will not allow it. The body is mine. I am sole executor and I can do what I like with it."[18] Aubrey replied it was in the hands of the police.[19]

Margaret's bank passbook was tendered and it indicated regular large sums had been transferred to Edwin, totalling over 1400 pounds.[20] Edwin advised that they were loans. Margaret's popularity in the town was raised as a means of suggesting someone else may have been involved in foul play. Edwin responded that, "She was not unpopular, but she was hardly popular either."[21]

The salmon eaten for lunch and brandy consumed by Margaret was tested for the poison but none was found.[22]

When asked, Edwin said Margaret had not been well for some time, suffering from nerves and he was satisfied that she had just collapsed.[23] During this time, Edwin fronted at the Charleville Police Station asking for a copy of Margaret's will which the police had previously confiscated from the property. The will was drawn up in Brisbane and Margaret had gone to the Charleville bank to get it witnessed. Edwin could not recall if he accompanied her on that occasion but he was very insistent that the police lock it up in a safe.[24]

At the conclusion of the three and a half days and accounts of 20 witnesses, Edwin was committed for trial at the criminal sittings of the Circuit Court to be held at Charleville.

The trial

Seven months later, the trial began on 25 May 1938. The Crown Prosecutor, J. A. Sheehy, described Edwin's motive for the murder as "greed, gain, and avarice." Evidence of the loans, his control over her will and estate were presented. Mrs Bridget Russoc who had worked for Margaret as a servant said she had overhead Edwin reminding Margaret that he was the boss, and asking would she leave him money in her will, at which Margaret told him to stop worrying her about money.[25]

The jury was also shown letters between Margaret and Edwin celebrating the fact that Edwin's wife—referred to as the 'dame'—appeared to have a partner, and if he could catch her out, Edwin may be able to divorce her on the grounds of adultery: "I would dearly love to catch them so as I could divorce her."[26] And there were letters where he expressed his love to Margaret while she was in Brisbane: "I will now close with as much love as there is water in the sea, from your sweetheart, Ted."[27]

Aged pensioner, William Harrex, whose residence was behind the Claren Hotel, told of hearing Edwin and Margaret having a fight about 12.30pm on the day of Margaret's death, and that Edwin had once offered Mr Harrex some strychnine to get rid of the birds eating his vegetable garden.[28]

The State Analyst, Leone Alexander Meston, presented her findings of "one-tenth, of a grain of strychnine in the stomach and one-fourteenth of a grain in the bowel of the dead woman."[29]

Mr Sheehy, the Crown Prosecutor, told the jury that Edwin "was the only person at the Claren Hotel at the times when a dose of strychnine could have been administered… death from strychnine was usually two hours after administration."[30]

Edwin's Counsel, Mr Moynihan, said the Crown's case against his client was "childishly weak."[31] He suggested Margaret might have chosen to take her own life, upset by the situation of being with a married man or she had met with an accident.[32] He also asked the jury why his client would walk across the road after administering it.[33]

The judge, Justice Macrossan, appeared to find it ridiculous that Edwin, a man of 36, would be interested in a woman aged 50. He noted: "Here is a man battening on a woman 14 years his senior. Yet he spoke of them as man and wife – perfectly ridiculous."[34] Yet Edwin's first wife was also 14 years his senior… they married when Edwin was 22 and his wife 36. They had a 15-year-old daughter.[35] Given this, his love of Margaret does not seem so unusual. He said of her that "he loved her very much. She was a beautiful woman, and a wonderful housekeeper and cook."[36]

In his summation, Mr Justice Macrossan said: "The whole of this case naturally turns on circumstantial evidence. Two persons sat down to a meal at the Claren Hotel on September 10. One is dead, the other is the prisoner. His conduct was that of a man who lives on a woman and takes advantage of her fascination of him and infatuation for him. Do not consider horror or sentiment, just deal with it as a matter of cold fact, and see where you get."[37]

The verdict and appeals

Once all the evidence was presented, Edwin's Counsel, Mr Moynihan, asked for the case to be taken from the jury on the grounds that "the evidence of means and opportunity of administering strychnine to the deceased were insufficient."[38] Justice Macrossan refused, advising that evidence indicated Margaret died from strychnine poisoning, and the jury might reasonably conclude that she did not suicide, but was murdered.[39] And that's exactly what the jury found, returning their verdict with confidence – guilty. Edwin received a sentence of life imprisonment.[40]

Edwin applied to appeal his conviction on the grounds that "the jury's verdict was wrong in law, that there was no evidence or insufficient evidence to support it, that evidence was wrongly admitted and wrongly rejected, that the examination of witnesses by the judge was such as to result in a mis-trial, and that the judge misdirected the jury.... Mr Moynihan [Counsel for Edwin] said that the Crown relied on circumstantial evidence."[41]

A hearing was held in August of that same year, 1938, almost one year since Margaret's death. Three months later, in November 1938, the court granted Edwin a new trial.[42]

The new trial

In February 1939, Edwin began his new trial in the Supreme Court, Brisbane. Here he took the stand again protesting his love, and the evidence was reintroduced along with attempts to consider suicide and other means of death.

Three weeks later in March, Mr Justice Henchman delivered the longest summing-up in a criminal case for 20 years, and possibly the longest in Queensland history – a reading of the evidence for 12.5 hours.[43]

The jury returned and announced their verdict to dramatic screams and cheers: not guilty of murder, not guilty of manslaughter. The trial was over, Edwin, with his mother, left the court a free man 17 months after he was arrested and having spent six months in jail.[44]

With no hard evidence against Edwin, but ample circumstantial evidence, we'll never know if Edwin really did murder Margaret. We can only trust that the jury got it right, hopefully. As Edwin's Counsel concluded, the question of how Margaret took the strychnine "was a matter of conjecture."[45]

HELTON FOUND NOT GUILTY

Dramatic End To Augathella Case

Cheers And Screams

BRISBANE, March 6.

"NOT guilty of murder, not guilty of manslaughter," was the verdict given by the jury tonight in the case in which Edwin Claude Helton, 36, storekeeper, was charged with having murdered Margaret Jane Roche at Augathella on September 10, 1937.

Men cheered and women screamed when the verdict was announced. "Silence," cried Mr Justice Henchman, who presided in the Criminal Court, which was packed with a perspiring crowd.

Helton stood up in the dock and seemed bewildered.

Above: dramatic news!
Source: Morning Bulletin, 1939.

The fight for the will benefits

But it was still not over. Edwin was not content to be a free man, he now wanted the fortune left to him by Margaret. So, Edwin was back in the Charleville Circuit Court contesting Margaret's will against Mrs Isabella Allen, Margaret's mother and next of kin who was seeking administration rights for the estate. Edwin claimed that Margaret's will was legal and she was of sane mind when she made it.[46]

The verdict shocked everyone present in the crowded gallery on that day of 21 June 1938. It took six hours to reach and the jury found that Edwin did not influence the inclusions in Margaret's will, but he did unlawfully kill her.[47] His Honour deferred the matter to Brisbane. There Mr Justice Philp said he could find no similar case and ruled that the will was valid, but Edwin could not benefit from it. However as he had been acquitted by a criminal court jury, he was not able to be found guilty by the civil jury.[48]

But there's more… Edwin fought on, appealing to the State Full Court, where he also lost, but he won through the High Court and was ordered a retrial.[49] Edwin was now representing himself, most likely for financial reasons, and he lost in this High Court retrial. But it didn't end there. Margaret's mother issued a writ against Edwin to reclaim money lent to him by Margaret. Remember, he did say in court that the cash advances were loans. Edwin contested this in the Full Court… and lost with costs.[50] Margaret's mother, Isabella, never got that money back – Edwin was declared bankrupt in the Bankruptcy Court on 7 January 1942.[51] He had run his course. If Edwin had murdered for money, he was a free man but had not gained a cent.

And no-one truly knows how or why Margaret Jane Roche died that warm September afternoon.

What became of...

Edwin Helton died on the 17 October 1973, aged 72 years, and 36 years after Margaret. He is buried in Augathella Cemetery, off Jane Street, Augathella. His estranged wife, Agnes, died before him, in 1961. Isabella Allen, Margaret's mother and Edwin's rival, died in 1951 aged in her nineties.[52]

Margaret's grave is in Charleville Cemetery, Lot/Section 2E, Grave No. 1894. If you wish to pay your respects, enter through the front gate, and turn left. Section 2E is the closest to the front fence, and the grave is five rows from there.

Margaret Roche's grave in Charleville Cemetery. Photograph by Melissa Everitt. Supplied and reproduced with Melissa's kind permission.

References:

1 - 3 Helton's Love-Letters to Woman He Cruelly Murdered with Poison (1938, May 29). *Truth (Brisbane, Qld.: 1900 - 1954)*, p. 21. Retrieved August 2, 2019, from http://nla.gov.au/nla.news-article206135204
4 Conolly, Pauline, A Will to Find Justice, 2017. Retrieved 7 Aug 2019 from: https://paulineconolly.com/2019/a-mother-pursues-justice-via-her-dead-daughters-will/
5 Augathella Fire (4 Dec 1936). *The Charleville Times (Bris, Qld.: 1896-1954)*, p 7. Retrieved 7 Aug 2019, from http://nla.gov.au/nla.news-article76556861
6 - 9 Helton's Love-Letters to Woman... *Truth.* Op.cit.
10 Augathella Shop Burnt (20 April 1934). *The Courier-Mail (Bris, Qld.: 1933-1954)*, p13. Retrieved 7 Aug 2019 from http://nla.gov.au/nla.news-article119142
11 Augathella Fire (4 Dec 1936). *The Charleville Times (Bris, Qld.: 1896-1954)*, p7. Retrieved 7 Aug 2019 from http://nla.gov.au/nla.news-article76556861
12 Hotel Applications Granted (1937, March 23). *The Courier-Mail (Bris, Qld.: 1933-1954)*, p15. Retrieved 7 Aug 2019, from http://nla.gov.au/nla.news-article36883781
13 AUGATHELLA STOREKEEPER FOR TRIAL (1937, October 22). *The Charleville Times (Brisbane, Qld. : 1896 - 1954)*, p. 7. Retrieved August 7, 2019, from http://nla.gov.au/nla.news-article76695358
14 Helton's Love-Letters to Woman... *Truth.* Op.cit.
15 FIRST ACT IN WESTERN MURDER CHARGE (1937, October 17). *Sunday Mail (Brisbane, Qld. : 1926 - 1954)*, p. 6. Retrieved August 7, 2019, from http://nla.gov.au/nla.news-article97901545
16 AUGATHELLA STOREKEEPER FOR TRIAL (1937, October 22). *The Charleville Times (Brisbane, Qld. : 1896 - 1954)*, p. 7. Retrieved August 7, 2019, from http://nla.gov.au/nla.news-article76695358
17 AUGATHELLA STOREKEEPER FOR TRIAL (1937, October 22). Op.cit.
18 - 19 Helton's Love-Letters to Woman... *Truth.* Op.cit.
20 - 23 AUGATHELLA TRAGEDY (1937, October 19). *Tweed Daily (Murwillumbah, NSW : 1914 - 1949)*, p. 5. Retrieved August 6, 2019, from http://nla.gov.au/nla.news-article193709583
24 AUGATHELLA STOREKEEPER FOR TRIAL (1937, October 22). Op.cit.
25 AUGATHELLA MURDER TRIAL (1938, May 26). *The Telegraph (Brisbane, Qld. : 1872 - 1947)*, p. 15 (CITY FINAL). Retrieved August 7, 2019, from http://nla.gov.au/nla.news-article184128813
26 - 27 Helton's Love-Letters to Woman... *Truth.* Op.cit.
28 AUGATHELLA MURDER TRIAL (1938, May 26). *The Telegraph.* Op.cit.
29 Case to Go to Jury (27 May 1938). *The Courier-Mail (Bris, Qld.: 1933- 1954)*, p3. Retrieved Aug 7, 2019 from http://nla.gov.au/nla.news-article40995626
30 Augathella Murder Trial (27 May 1938). *The Telegraph (Bris, Qld : 1872-1947)*, p.13 (2nd ed). Retrieved Aug 7, 2019 from http://nla.gov.au/nla.news-article184129638
31 - 32 Helton's Love-Letters to Woman... *Truth.* Op.cit.
33 Augathella Murder Trial (1938, May 27). *The Telegraph.* Op.cit.
34 Helton's Love-Letters to Woman... *Truth.* Op.cit.
35 - 36 Helton Testifies (1 Mar 1939). *The Northern Miner (Charters Towers, Qld.: 1874-1954)*, p2. Retrieved 7 Aug 2019 from http://nla.gov.au/nla.news-article85431673
37 Helton's Love-Letters to Woman... *Truth.* Op.cit.

38 - 39 DEATH OF WOMAN AT AUGATHELLA (1938, May 27). *Morning Bulletin (Rockhampton, Qld. : 1878 - 1954)*, p. 9. Retrieved August 7, 2019, from http://nla.gov.au/nla.news-article55975072
40 Helton's Love-Letters to Woman... *Truth*. Op.cit.
41 Edwin Helton's Appeal Against Conviction (1938, Aug 4). *Maryborough Chronicle, Wide Bay and Burnett Advertiser (Qld: 1860 - 1947)*, p9. Retrieved August 7, 2019, from http://nla.gov.au/nla.news-article152159623
42 Augathella Case (1938, Nov 15). *The Dalby Herald (Qld.: 1910-1954)*, p. 3. Retrieved August 7, 2019, from http://nla.gov.au/nla.news-article217537437
43 Jury Retires in Helton Case After Record Summing Up (1939, March 6). *The Telegraph (Brisbane, Qld. : 1872 - 1947)*, p. 1 (2nd ed). Retrieved August 7, 2019, from http://nla.gov.au/nla.news-article185996925
44 Helton Found Not Guilty Dramatic End To Augathella Case (1939, March 7). *Morning Bulletin (Rockhampton, Qld. : 1878 - 1954)*, p. 7. Retrieved August 7, 2019, from http://nla.gov.au/nla.news-article56017667
45 Decision Reserved. (10 Aug 1938). *The Northern Herald (Cairns, Qld.: 1913-1939)*, p19. Retrieved 7 Aug 2019 from http://nla.gov.au/nla.news-article150833712
46 MRS. ROCHES WILL (1939, June 9). *Cairns Post (Qld. : 1909 - 1954)*, p. 8. Retrieved August 7, 2019, from http://nla.gov.au/nla.news-article4218443
47 FINDING IN ROCHE (1939, June 22). *The Courier-Mail (Brisbane, Qld. : 1933 - 1954)*, p. 3. Retrieved Aug 7, 2019, from http://nla.gov.au/nla.news-article40852194
48 No Similar Case (1939, July 4). *The Telegraph (Bris, Qld.: 1872-1947)*, p. 1. Retrieved August 7, 2019, from http://nla.gov.au/nla.news-article188594544
49 Helton's Appeal. (1941, June 20). *Cairns Post (Qld.: 1909 -1954)*, p. 4. Retrieved August 7, 2019, from http://nla.gov.au/nla.news-article42296142
50 Helton's Appeal Dismissed (1941, Dec 13). *Warwick Daily News (Qld.: 1919-1954)*, p 4. Retrieved 7 Aug 2019 from http://nla.gov.au/nla.news-article186820066
51 HELTON ADJUDGED A BANKRUPT (1942, January 8). *Maryborough Chronicle, Wide Bay and Burnett Advertiser (Qld. : 1860 - 1947)*, p. 4. Retrieved August 7, 2019, from http://nla.gov.au/nla.news-article152793526
52 Conolly, Pauline, *A Will to Find Justice*, 2017. Retrieved 7 August 2019 from: https://paulineconolly.com/2019/a-mother-pursues-justice-via-her-dead-daughters-will/

Images:

Margaret Roche and Edwin Helton grave photographs by Melissa Everitt for *Grave Tales*. Initial contact via Find A Grave – https://www.findagrave.com/ Supplied and reproduced with Melissa's kind permission.

Edwin Helton, Margaret Roche, Bridget Russoc, Dr McIntosh, Aubrey Carter, Detective Frank Bischof and Detective Senior-sergeant Dan Mahoney, and Sub-inspector Thomas Smith. Source: Helton's Love-Letters to Woman He Cruelly Murdered with Poison (29 May 1938). *Truth* (Brisbane, Qld.: 1900 - 1954), p. 21. Retrieved 2 Aug 2019, from http://nla.gov.au/nla.news-article206135204

Press announcement: Helton Found Not Guilty Dramatic End To Augathella Case (1939, March 7). *Morning Bulletin* (Rockhampton, Qld.: 1878 - 1954), p. 7. Retrieved August 7, 2019, from http://nla.gov.au/nla.news-article56017667

Acknowledgements:

We are grateful to everyone who shared their time, wisdom, photographs and enthusiasm to help us with this volume:

- Sarah Little, Goondiwindi Regional Council
- Goondiwindi and District Family History Group
- Sue Cutler, The Royal Humane Society of Australasia Inc
- Katie Woodhead, Goondiwindi Regional Council
- Jayne Royal, Special Collections Librarian at Toowoomba Regional Council (and former school classmate of Helen!)
- Melanie, Picture Ipswich, Ipswich Library
- Dr Bill Metcalf for his generosity sharing his work and images in our Roma communes story
- Ilona, Royal Historical Society of Queensland
- Peter Cullen and the Toowoomba Historical Society - http://www.toowoombahistory.org.au/
- Susan Kotzur, Special Collections Library Assistant, Toowoomba Regional Council
- Michelle Richmond, Library Local Studies Historian, Northern Beaches Council
- John and the team at the Australasian Mine Safety Journal
- Michelle Scott, Maranoa Regional Council - so patient, thanks Michelle!
- Maree Worland – President, Roma & District Family History Society Inc
- Roma History Lodge: Family and local Maranoa history
- Gina Garza, Ipswich Cemeteries
- Rebecca and the team at Lockyer Valley Regional Council
- Laura Conroy, Toowoomba Hospital Foundation
- Toowoomba Hospital Museum Committee
- Sandi Jones, Ipswich Historical Society Inc

- Susanne Ruijs for the Rosewood Scrub Historical Society
- Karin Brennan, University of Sydney Archives
- Sigourney Jacks and Anne-Marie Deboni, National Gallery of Victoria
- Tara Fernandez, Media Adviser, Queensland Rail
- Melissa Everitt, Find A Grave member, for her kind assistance with the Charleville and Augathella grave photos of Harry Corones, Margaret Roche, the Switzers and Edwin Helton. Truly appreciated, Melissa!
- Mike Fitzpatrick for kindly allowing us to use the beautiful image of Norah Murphy
- Ann Sainsbury, Find A Grave member for kindly providing the headstone photo for Edwin Fletcher
- Trish Wearne, descendant of Victor Denton for kindly supplying his beautiful portrait for inclusion
- Stephanie Johnson for her hours of voluntary research work and her passion for the subject
- And Joanne James, our editor, who finds our errors no matter how smart we think we are each time!

Donation: We are proud to donate $1 from the sale of every *Grave Tales* paperback to providing gravestones or restoring damaged gravestones for the people we feature in our *Grave Tales* series. Please refer to our website for our current projects.

About the Grave Tales team:

Helen Goltz, Author: Helen is a journalist and producer with a 30-year history of working for newspapers, magazines, in marketing, and producing television and radio programs for clients including News Ltd, the Seven Network and Macquarie Media. She is the author of 12 books and is published by Atlas Productions and Clan Destine Press. Helen is postgraduate degree qualified with majors in Literature and Communications.

Chris Adams, Author: Two-time Logie Award winner, Chris started his journalism career in radio before spending over thirty years in broadcast current affairs including working as a journalist and producer for Channel Nine's *Today Tonight* and Executive Producer of Channel Seven's *State Affair*. In 1991 he was a War Correspondent for the Persian Gulf War and in 1993 for the Civil War of Somalia. He is credited with over forty television documentaries before returning to radio as News and Program Director of 4BC. He is now engaged full-time in writing projects, and speaking engagements.

Hastings Goltz-Adams: can sniff out a good bone (uh, story) from a mile away. He accompanies the authors where possible.

Joanne James, Editor: Joanne's editing experience extends from proof-reading university handbooks and course guides to editing annual reports and publicity brochures for local government. With a background in primary school teaching, noticing spelling errors is second nature to her – she has been known to correct take-away menus and return them!

Stephanie Johnson, Family History Researcher: Steph's family history research experience and passion span over a decade. Self-described 'genealogy enthusiast' and 'cemetery creeper' she likes to say she loves dead people! Her strong attention to detail, administrative skills and project management experience complement her dedication to family history research perfectly. Steph is shaking the family trees for us.

We would love to connect with you.

Website: www.gravetales.com.au

Podcast: https://www.gravetales.com.au/tune-into-the-podcast/

Facebook: www.facebook.com/gravetalesAUS/

Instagram: https://www.instagram.com/gravetales/

Email: enquiries@gravetales.com.au

www.ingramcontent.com/pod-product-compliance
Lightning Source LLC
Chambersburg PA
CBHW020417010526
44118CB00010B/296